THE VOLVO TOUR

•PGA EUROPEAN TOUR OFFICIAL REVIEW•

1996

Lennard
Queen Anne Press

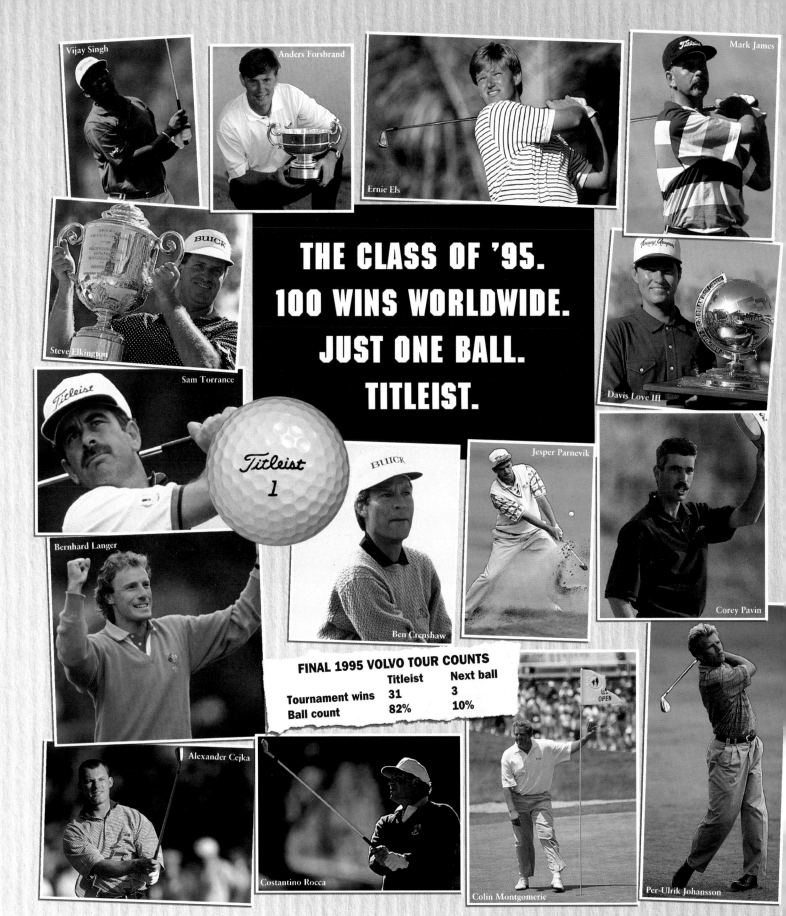

THE CLASS OF '95.
100 WINS WORLDWIDE.
JUST ONE BALL.
TITLEIST.

Vijay Singh

Anders Forsbrand

Ernie Els

Mark James

Steve Elkington

Sam Torrance

Davis Love III

Bernhard Langer

Ben Crenshaw

Jesper Parnevik

Corey Pavin

Alexander Cejka

Costantino Rocca

Colin Montgomerie

Per-Ulrik Johansson

FINAL 1995 VOLVO TOUR COUNTS		
	Titleist	Next ball
Tournament wins	31	3
Ball count	82%	10%

1995 has been a remarkable year for Titleist golf balls - even by Titleist's standards. Top players all over the world have chosen to play Titleist in increasingly large numbers. The reason for this is simple.

No other ball can deliver the superb feel, control and consistency that a Titleist ball can.

That's not just an empty claim. It's something Tour Pro's everywhere have been proving*. For instance, it's no coincidence that the Masters, the US Open and the US PGA Championship were all won with a Titleist.

Nor is it just luck that every single player in the top 20 of the European Order of Merit plays Titleist. And what about the Pro's playing a Titleist who won 31 of the 36 events on the Volvo Tour? And the fact that 19 of the 24 Ryder Cup contestants and all the winning Dunhill Cup team play Titleist?

So the message from 1995 is clear. Without a doubt, Titleist players are, like the golf balls they use, in a class of their own.

Titleist
Nº1 ball in golf.

Titleist, St. Ives, Cambs PE17 4LS.

Introduction
from the PGA European Tour

Editor
Chris Plumridge

Consultant Editor
Mark Wilson

Photographic Editor
David Cannon

Art Director
Rob Kelland

Production Co-ordinator
Denise Thurling

The Volvo Tour Yearbook 1996 is published by
PGA European Tour Enterprises Ltd,
Wentworth Drive, Virginia Water,
Surrey GU25 4LX.

Distributed through Lennard Queen Anne Press.

Colour reproduction and printing by
The Manson Group.

© PGA European Tour Enterprises Ltd.

ISBN 1 85291 556 0

A very warm welcome to the 25th Anniversary season of the PGA European Tour.

The Tour – which has indeed developed to the highest standards exemplified by international sports since given its inspired initial direction by first Tournament Director General, John Jacobs, in August 1971 – has much to look forward to in the year of 1996. Volvo, the Tour's first and only overall corporate sponsor, becomes the Tour's principal sponsor in a continuing powerful partnership which additionally sees the Tour regain its operating identity in this important Anniversary season.

With the increasing co-operation between the five major Tours, the world of tournament golf continues to offer more opportunity to players and more exposure through international television to sponsors and armchair followers. On the field of play Tour players again distinguished themselves during the 1995 season.

Pride of place goes to Bernard Gallacher's Ryder Cup squad which regained the prized trophy in a magnificent encounter with the United States at an equally magnificent Oak Hill venue in Rochester. Both Costantino Rocca and Colin Montgomerie tied major championships before going down in play-offs for the Open and US PGA Championships respectively. Colin also hung on superbly to the Volvo Order of Merit title for a third successive year but only after a titanic battle with evergreen Sam Torrance and Volvo PGA champion Bernhard Langer. Sam, who won three times and entered the final Volvo Masters in pole position, finished third at Valderrama behind the brilliant young German winner Alexander Cejka and – yes – Colin Montgomerie, by one final stroke. It was a wonderful climax to a contest which is likely to be continued in future seasons.

Please enjoy the Tour competition at all our superb locations.

Kenneth D Schofield

KENNETH D SCHOFIELD
Executive Director • PGA European Tour

Contents

Volvo Masters champion Alexander Cejka (opposite).

Proof of a priceless ability

Victory in the Ryder Cup demonstrated the PGA European Tour's enduring ability to nurture and sustain future talent

*I*n retrospect the 1995 season will stand as a crucial chapter in the modern development of European golf because it delivered conclusive evidence of the professional sport's longevity at the highest level.

It is an unavoidable penalty of any famous achievement that it must be repeated, if only to confirm that the first conquest was not just a one-off, but rather reliable proof of a rare and priceless ability. It is a judgement placed on individuals and can also be imposed on a collective basis.

Thus the PGA European Tour found itself faced with a curious paradox at the beginning of the 1995 season when its world-class standards were recognised with three of the top five places in the Sony Ranking. Its financial structure was secure. Its appeal still attracted aspiring and established players from all over the world to 17 countries on a route that stretched to the Far East (and even beyond in future). Yet there was need for a more public declaration of this healthy

Happy homecoming for the Ryder Cup.

state of affairs because of the frantic pace and expectation that had been set by previous success when that exciting crop of then young stars – Seve Ballesteros, Nick Faldo, Bernhard Langer, Ian Woosnam and Sandy Lyle – swept all before them as they captured the major titles and, more importantly, established a global reputation for the PGA European Tour with their Ryder Cup triumphs.

In this way was the high standard set

and while individual fortunes can ebb and flow without too much criticism or alarm, the collective strength of the European sport needed, by rights, to follow a more normal unwavering path.

But the real point was that Europe had laid out its stall, as it were, with those heady successes against the mighty United States in the Ryder Cup by Johnnie Walker match of 1985. That really was the evidence of a kind of corporate class and that the highest standards were to be found among the ranks and not just the major stars. And when it was repeated two years later, and was followed by a tied match at The Belfry in 1989 it seemed the sport had truly emerged.

Two defeats later however, a few questions arose. Would there be a world-wide reputation for Europe once the famous five were past their prime? And, Colin Montgomerie and José Maria Olazábal apart, where were all the new-comers who were supposed to follow in the great tradition and become world conquerors?

There were urgent reasons for believing therefore, that a third consecutive defeat at the hands of the Americans would seriously damage credibility and the hitherto proud parity that existed between Europe and America.

For those reasons, the exploits of the team that skipper Bernard Gallacher led and moulded into an effective fighting force at Oak Hill take on a huge signifi-

Nick Price (above) in the twilight
at St Andrews. Johnnie Walker Classic
winner Fred Couples (right) is interviewed
by Peter Oosterhuis of Sky Sports.

cance far beyond the simple
matter of who played best
on the day. This, in a sense,
was more than just a match.
It was trial and judgement
on the way
professional golf is played in
Europe.

What was proved
beyond doubt with that stir-

8

ring 14½-13½ victory was that Europe could produce a team that had immense depth, but more than this, could unite despite its various nationalities for a common cause and play to the limits because of it. That is the true testimony to the nature and structure of the modern PGA European Tour as it has evolved over the years.

It is an arena that has room for everybody and not only does nurture new talent but can sustain some honest men of toil for long periods until they too emerge as winners. Peter Teravainen had been a consistent middle-order performer for 14 years without actually stepping forward to take the winner's cheque until that honour came to him at last in the Chemapol Trophy Czech Open.

Santiago Luna had been at work for 12 years on the Tour and was rewarded with his first triumph in the Maderia Island Open. Wayne Riley, a proved international competitor and former Australian Open champion, nevertheless only got off the mark for the first time in 11 years of trying when he took the Scottish Open at Carnoustie. Adam Hunter was ticking off the years, 11 of them, wondering when his turn would come until fortune smiled during the Portuguese Open.

In these terms, Jarmo Sandelin, Rookie of the Year in 1995, is a quick developer after his Turespaña Open Canarias win. So too is

All in the eyes for (from top) Jesper Parnevik, Bernard Gallacher, John Daly and José Maria Olazábal.

fellow Swede, Mathias Grönberg after capturing the Canon European Masters in Crans-sur-Sierre against a prestigious field.

At least Robert Karlsson (Turespaña Open Mediterrania), Alexander Cejka (Turespaña Open Andalucia, Hohe Brücke Open, Volvo Masters) as well as André Bossert (Air France Cannes Open) had put in six years of apprenticeship before their winning chances came along.

When Nick Price, another former graduate of the PGA European Tour who has done rather well for himself, was asked to define the quality that made European golfers such formidable opponents at team level he said it stemmed from the close camaraderie that existed between them as they travelled the world together, sharing triumphs and tribulations.

It means to say that even the most serious rivals can remain the best of friends and for that reason Colin Montgomerie and Sam Torrance maintained a personal warmth and spirit that took them, together with young partner Andrew Coltart, to Scotland's first success in the Alfred Dunhill Cup at St Andrews even though at the time both were vying to win the Volvo Order of Merit for their own imperative reasons.

Montgomerie had already established himself as a golfer of supreme class on the world stage and after his performance in the US PGA Championship, when he narrowly lost the play-off, even the Americans acknowledged he was playing the best golf in the world. Moreover, he and Torrance were the dominant figures in European golf throughout the season as Sam took the Collingtree British Masters title and the Murphy's Irish Open and Montgomerie captured the Volvo German Open and Trophée Lancôme, and finally, the Volvo Order of Merit for the third successive year.

Torrance stands as a role model to all other campaigners who might wonder at times whether the price of success is too high, particularly if it takes so long to achieve. The genial Scot has been part of the European scene for almost a quarter of a century yet played perhaps his best golf in 1995, testimony to the enduring technique given to him by his golf professional father Bob.

That said, Bernhard Langer lurked

Santiago Luna (left) is exultant, Bernhard Langer (centre) is doubly exposed, Sandy Lyle (right) re-emerges and Severiano Ballesteros (below) is dominant at the Ryder Cup.

quietly just out of the spotlight but menacingly close after taking the Volvo PGA Championship and the Smurfit European Open, and even Seve Ballesteros, who later took a five-month break to rekindle his desire, did not come away empty handed as he picked up the Peugeot Open de Espana and a share of the Tournoi Perrier de Paris with partner Olazábal, who himself was plagued all season with foot problems.

These and other established campaigners maintained a sense of continuity on the PGA European Tour that included Mark James winning the Moroccan Open,

Greg Turner (Turespaña Open Baleares), Philip Walton (Open Catalonia Turespana and the Murphy's English Open), Peter O'Malley (Benson and Hedges International), Andrew Oldcorn (DHL Jersey Open), Jesper Parnevik (Volvo Scandinavian Masters), Frank Nobilo (BMW International Open), Paul Broadhurst (Peugeot Open de France), and Ernie Els (Lexington SA PGA and Toyota World Match-Play Championship).

There was even room too for visiting Americans to pick up a share of the cake with Fred Couples taking the Dubai Classic and then the Johnnie Walker Classic in Manila and John Daly winning the Open Championship at St Andrews. Scott Hoch won the Heineken Dutch Open and then remarked that he had beaten the best European professionals but was still not good enough for the American Ryder Cup side. It could have been some sort of threat of course. But nobody noticed. And certainly not after Oak Hill.

Michael McDonnell

Painted Wormburner

Checkered Bogeytail

Mulligan's Monarch

Common Slicer

Kills butterflies dead.

You're standing on the tee of a long par 3 when the fluttering in your stomach starts. Butterflies. So what do you do? Chances are you try to kill the ball. And that can really kill your game.

Let the clubs do the work with new Staff Midsize® irons from Wilson®. Our generous sweet spot and patented perimeter weighting give you maximum accuracy and forgiveness, while a moving notch on each club ideally positions the centre of gravity for optimal trajectory and distance.

Wilson also believes in a harmonious balance between form and function, so Staff Midsize irons feature a clean top line, graduated offset and proprietary finish.

But perhaps most telling, most golfers said Staff Midsize irons played better than Ping Zing®, Big Bertha® and King Cobra®. To try out the Staff Midsize visit your Golf Professional. Because the sooner you get rid of the butterflies, the sooner, they'll stop killing your game.

Wilson®
The Right Equipment Makes The Difference™

Montgomerie's marvellous hat-trick

In a pulsating race for the Volvo Order of Merit,

Colin Montgomerie finished ahead

for the third consecutive year

*I*n motor racing it was a rivalry that got out of hand at times and people wondered whether the spat between Damon Hill and Michael Schumacher would result in the ultimate folly.

In golf, an equally fierce rivalry for the Volvo Order of Merit fostered nothing more than increasing respect and a burgeoning friendship. So much so that Colin Montgomerie's first thoughts on finishing top of the money list for a third year in a row were for the vanquished. A week earlier he had been team-mates with Sam Torrance as they had won the Alfred Dunhill Cup. Now he had deprived the European stalwart of a lifetime's ambition. 'I feel for Sam,' Montgomerie said. 'He's played so well, so bravely all year. This is going to be hard for him to take.'

It was, simply, the best year of Torrance's professional life and yet the cruel truth is that it was still not good enough to beat the peerless Montgomerie.

Two other players have won the Order of Merit three years running but Severiano Ballesteros' and Peter Oosterhuis' successes in the 1970s were achieved in the Tour's formative years.

The quality of golf played on the PGA European Tour has taken the breath away at times and those occasions have become much more frequent with the passing of the years. No longer is there just a clutch of players capable of winning a tournament. All the way down the money list one finds golfers who have won events of the highest calibre.

The rewards available mean that each year standards continue to rise as a group of hungry young players appear, each armed with the skill, the determination and that pleasant streak of arrogance necessary to demand a piece of the action. This year it was Alexander Cejka, Jarmo Sandelin, and Michael Campbell who impressed most of all. And then there are the regulars who improve each year on their own incredible standards: players like Torrance, Bernhard Langer, and Costantino Rocca.

Such is Montgomerie's feat to stay at

the summit for three years running, ahead of all these golfers with similar designs, it will probably be another 20 years, if ever, before we witness anything like it again.

It also maintained the Scot's remarkable record since turning professional in 1987 of never regressing in the Order of Merit. It's such a brilliant performance sheet it is worth printing in full: 52nd in 1988, his first full year; 25th in 1989, and then, in order, 14th, fourth, third, first, first and first. No player in the history of the game can boast such a cv.

Montgomerie laid the groundwork for winning the Order of Merit in the middle of the season. His play up to the Open Championship, with five top four finishes in ten starts, was hardly untidy but at St Andrews he suffered the savage disappointment of missing the cut. Clearly, there could have been a reaction. Montgomerie had rightly gone into the Open as one of the favourites: to not even make the last two days would have played on a weaker mind for weeks.

His response? In the six tournaments and 24 rounds of golf that followed he broke 70 on no less than 18 occasions; he earned over £450,000, or more than £1,000 for every hole he played; he won two tournaments, the Volvo German Open and the Trophée Lancôme, and finished second in the Volvo Scandinavian Masters; he took a week off from Europe and finished runner-up in the US PGA Championship, losing a sudden-death play-off to Steve Elkington.

In achieving all that he has, Montgomerie, not surprisingly, has earned the admiration of his fellow professionals. When Severiano Ballesteros, upon learning that José Maria Olazábal would not be playing in the Ryder Cup, was asked who he would like as his new partner, his reply was unhesitating, Montgomerie.

Colin Montgomerie congratulates Steve Elkington at the USPGA.

And here's a view from the other end of the professional spectrum. Stuart Cage, a young player who's had a promising first year and who partnered Montgomerie at the Collingtree British Masters: 'It was great to play with him for the first time. Everyone out here on Tour can play as well as Monty on a given day, but every round? That's just fantastic and every young player should look up to him because of it and try to emulate him.'

Even allowing for all this, it still came down to the final shot of the final round of the final tournament before Montgomerie could claim his glittering prize. He had gone to Valderrama trailing Torrance by just under £4,000, which, given the manner of prize money distribution and how much is on offer at the Volvo Masters, effectively meant one shot.

In the final round, Torrance gave it his very best effort. With so much at stake he rose to the occasion like the proud warrior he is and delivered a concluding 68, which turned out to be the best round of the day.

Montgomerie, who was playing the tenth hole at the time, now knew what he had to do. He had to play the inward nine on arguably the hardest course in Europe in one under par if he was to prevail. And so a microcosm of all the Tour strives to achieve had developed, a standard had been set and marvellous golf had to be played if it was to be realised.

Montgomerie hit a five iron to the par three 12th to eight feet and holed the putt. Six pars needed now. Montgomerie hadn't had a bogey on any back nine hole all week. Some players might have thought about that and allowed negative thoughts to creep in. Montgomerie played for the safe areas of the green and concentrated on his overall target.

By the last hole he was still on course. He hit his second shot to 25 feet. His first putt to three feet. Three feet for the Order of Merit. The putt hit the back of the hole with a resounding thump and disappeared. A clenched fist salute from Montgomerie, a sad slump of the shoulders from Torrance. All Europe held its breath in wonder and marvelled at such a finish.

Derek Lawrenson

We couldn't stop a little boy flexing his grazed knee, but we had to stop an elephant flexing his broken leg.

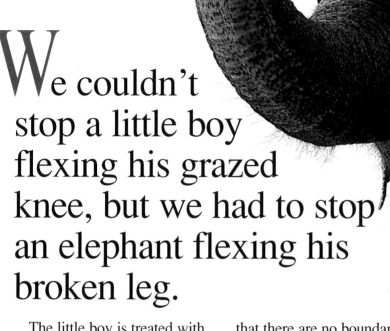

The little boy is treated with new 3M™ Active™ Strips Flexible Foam Bandages, to cushion and protect hard-to-bandage places (like his knees). While the elephant is treated with 3M™ Vetcast™ Plus Veterinary Casting Tape, a strong conformable tape that can bear the animal's huge weight without causing discomfort.

On the face of it the two technologies owe little to the other. But dig deeper and you'll discover their common bond is the spirit of innovation within the company that conceived them. A spirit and culture that runs right through 3M, ensuring

that there are no boundaries to imagination or barriers to co-operation. Scientists and researchers are encouraged to spend time on their own projects and to share ideas between divisions.

In this way the 3M Active Strips Bandages were born. The result of multiple technologies and an amalgam of good ideas. In all, 3M's unique approach has yielded over 60,000 other products thus far for industry, commerce, health care and the home, solving problems both great and small.

Because they're flexible foam strips, 3M Active Strips Bandages stretch in every direction, conforming to the active body's twists and turns.

3M *Innovation*

The search for a future

Apollo Week provided the perfect grounding
for aspiring newcomers to the Tour

Andrew Coltart had a good deal to reflect on as he drove through the gates at The San Roque Club in Southern Spain for the final day of the 1995 Apollo Week. Not least among his thoughts was the manner in which his life had been transformed since graduating from the same Tour training school a mere 12 months before.

The personable Scot has developed enormous belief in himself since the start of the 1994 season, but even he cannot come close to accounting for the progress he has made since taking his first steps on Tour last Spring.

'I have thought about it a lot,' he says. 'There is no simple answer but at least it shows the sort of thing that can be done.'

Coltart's presence at the final day of this season's Apollo Week was ample testament to the huge riches the Tour offers to those fortunate enough to succeed. It is a message reinforced by the fact that the 20 players who attended last year's school made in excess of £1 million during the 1994 season, but one which has to be tempered by the realisation that for each success there are at least a dozen failures.

Coltart's welcome appearance at this year's Apollo Week was propitious as it put into perspective the standards which are required to succeed on the Tour. It also served as a useful reminder that even the most successful amateurs can struggle. Most importantly, however, the young Scot's presence helped to encapsulate what the Apollo Week itself is all about.

Andrew Coltart was a successful graduate
from the 1994 Apollo Week.

'All the youngsters have done well to get here but what they have to do now is move up a gear,' says world renowned coach John Jacobs, who in the 1970s was responsible for digging the foundation on which the Tour is built today, and who for the last two years has been a welcome addition to the Apollo Week teaching panel.

'It's quite simple,' agrees Tommy Horton. 'What we are trying to do is to put old heads on young shoulders. We can't teach them all they need to know in the space of a week, but we can give them advice and the benefit of experience. It's important for them to realise that earning

a Tour Card isn't the end of their problems – for some of them it could well be the start.'

Horton and Jacobs were the two senior figures in an impressive group of people put together to give advice to the Tour School and Challenge Tour graduates selected to attend the week at San Roque. Indeed, Horton's contribution is more fundamental in as much as it was his idea in the first place.

'When I was younger I was fortunate to receive a lot of advice from people like Max Faulkner, Ken Bousfield and Dai Rees; it was invaluable to me. But a lot of youngsters aren't as fortunate as me and it's them we're trying to help.'

The future of the training week was secured with the introduction of commercial sponsors at the start of the 1980s. The event continued to develop and started to take its current shape when the renowned shaft manufacturers TI Apollo assumed overall sponsorship of the week in 1989.

Apollo has now funded the last seven Tour training weeks and as each year passes the event seems to grow in stature. This season a total of 25 Tour School and Challenge Tour graduates travelled to San Roque where they were able to secure advice on a host of subjects from a disparate team of teaching panellists.

Some came with the sole intention to brush up their swing under the guidance of John Jacobs and Denis Pugh, but while there, almost all of them took the opportunity to sharpen their short game at

Horton's around the green clinics and improve their mental approach with help from noted sports psychologist Alan Fine.

Almost all aspects of Tour life were addressed. Tour regulars Steven Richardson and Jamie Spence were on hand to answer questions from a player's perspective. The Tour's Chief Referee, John Paramor, and his team, took time out to help graduates brush up on the Rules and there were seminars set up to

all this information will do this year's graduates, but, if last year's results are indicative, then several are destined to become major forces on Tour.

In the meantime the class of '95 was universal in its praise both for the structure of the week and its instructors.

'It's been tremendous,' says Christian Cevaer, former French amateur champion and the man who finished second behind England's David Carter at the PGA

some of the players too.

'I thought I knew a lot about the short game but Tommy Horton made me feel quite small out there. He made me realise just how much we have to learn if we want to compete. It will be tough but what we have learned this week should put us in good stead.'

But perhaps the last word should go to Coltart. After all, he knows the difficulties involved in making the grade.

offer advice on such specialist areas as personal finance and handling the media.

Last but not least, all manner of fitness advice was on offer from Steve Gregg (nutrition) and Ted Pollard (fitness routines) and also from Guy Delacave, who as head of the Tour's Physio Unit has more idea than most about the physical problems which can afflict Tour golfers.

It remains to be seen how much good

European Tour Qualifying School.

'I'm going to go home and suggest the French Golf Federation send a representative next year because it's the sort of thing which would be a massive help to all our young golfers.'

Holland's Rolf Muntz, who won the 1990 British Amateur title, concurs: 'I've had a wonderful week. I feel a bit more at home now because I've had a chance to meet a lot of the Tour administrators and

'It is a great week and it gives you a wonderful opportunity to practise on courses similar to those we find on Tour,' he says. 'All the same you have got to be careful you do not fill your head with too much information. You have got to be selective. That's something you have to learn on Tour.' Words of wisdom. But Coltart now has an old head on young shoulders.

Colin Callander

John Jacobs (top left) advises Dean Robertson on the practice range. Sports psychologist Alan Fine (top right) in discussion with Antoine Lebouc. David Carter (right) undergoes some short game guidance from Tommy Horton.

Couples makes amends

After missing the cut the previous year,

Fred Couples returned to Dubai

and put the record straight

A year earlier in the Dubai Desert Classic Fred Couples had finished up as a television commentator. It was the least he could do having missed the cut, but embarrassing nonetheless. It was a score to be settled and settle it the American did in the most emphatic manner, under 70 in all his four rounds and, with a winning 20 under par aggregate of 268, equalling the record set by Ernie Els the previous year.

Couples was consequently up the television tower again, but this time facing the camera rather than behind it.

It was, in every way, a compelling start to the new season with all the big names right up there from the start and a leaderboard on the Saturday night after the third round that any of the major championships would have envied.

Couples and Colin Montgomerie shared the lead at 14 under par after 54 holes. A stroke behind came Greg Norman and Ernie Els, they in turn being a shot in front of Nick Price together with the one Swedish outsider, Pierre Fulke. Only Bernhard Langer, of the week's 'big six', was out of it.

Form thus came early, and right across the board as well. The cut had fallen at one under par, unprecedented in the six years of the tournament and surprisingly so for a course the professionals rate as highly as any.

Couples, dogged by a back injury for most of the early part of 1994 which kept him out of, among other things, both the Masters and the Open Championship, had the edge when it mattered. A 65 in the first round left him a stroke behind Norman and a 69 in the second, while bringing him level with the Australian, was nonetheless eclipsed by Montgomerie, whose 63 gave the Scotsman a three stroke lead.

However, Montgomerie was to take 71 in the third round, which brought him back, if not to the field, certainly to Couples. They continued to be deadlocked for the first eight holes of the final round before Couples produced two classic strokes. They won the tournament.

The first came at the ninth, a treacherous par four of 463 yards with water to the left of the dog-legged fairway and then encroaching from the left in front of the green. With the wind against, it was a challenging stroke, one Montgomerie rather avoided as he baled out to the right

19

of the green.

Couples, after much deliberation, that familiar readjustment of his visor and a then windmilling of his arms reminiscent years ago of Michael Bonallack, took the bull by the horns. His six iron from 160 yards never wavered in its flight, came to rest eight feet beyond the flag and he holed the putt for a birdie. It proved a two stroke swing for Montgomerie paid

the price of his caution, chipping and for once missing the putt to save his par.

There was one glimpse more of vintage Couples. The 12th, 467 yards curving gently right to left and uphill is, in amateur handicap terms, stroke two on the card though probably tougher than the eighth, which is stroke one. With the wind now left to right, Couples this time hit a three iron second, right behind the flag again, to four feet. Birdie again.

After that the sailing was plain and Couples coasted in with a 66 to

Colin Montgomerie was in sparkling form in the second round as was Pierre Fulke (above).

21

High finish for the New Zealand newcomer, Michael Campbell (left). Howard Clark (centre) discovers that trees do grow in the desert. Greg Norman is about to get a free drop from Ernie Els (right).

Montgomerie's 69 to win by three, Price, Wayne Riley, of Australia, and a young newcomer from New Zealand, Michael Campbell, tied third. Montgomerie, so often runner-up, just managed it on his own by holing a very missable putt for a birdie on the last green. He deserved it for this had not been as easy week for him.

He was under pressure to perform because this was his first tournament since signing a contract with Callaway after terminating a contract with Wilson, whose clubs had served him so well throughout his professional career. It was in many ways an instant success, particularly in that second round of 63. This equalled a personal best but this was the first time he has scored ten birdies in one round.

The big heads on the irons are not to everyone's liking but Montgomerie declared that they have given him more length, so much so that he felt he now had 'a 15th club in my bag'. His euphoria was not quite so high at the end of the tournament.

Very much on his mind was the fact that he had not made the most of a commanding position. After that second round of 63 he had begun his third with three consecutive birdies – not that it gained him anything since Couples had an eagle and a birdie over the same three holes – and at that point he was 16 under par for 39 holes. The remaining 33 he played in only one under.

Price would have been in stronger contention if he had not missed so many short putts and Norman would have been if he could have demolished, in his normal style, the par fives. Instead they demolished him.

Michael Williams

THE COURSE

If you were blindfolded and plonked down in the middle of it you would never have the faintest idea you were in a desert; it is also a very good one. Some of the professionals regard it as the best on the Tour, both for design and condition. On otherwise arid land, it is kept green and lush by the pumping of almost one million gallons of water per day, desalinated from the Arabian Gulf.

EMIRATES GC, DUBAI, JANUARY 19-22, 1995 · YARDAGE 7100 · PAR 72

Pos	Name	Country	Rnd 1	Rnd 2	Rnd 3	Rnd 4	Total	Prize Money £
1	Fred COUPLES	(USA)	65	69	68	66	268	75000
2	Colin MONTGOMERIE	(Scot)	68	63	71	69	271	50000
3	Michael CAMPBELL	(NZ)	69	71	65	67	272	23243
	Nick PRICE	(Zim)	66	69	69	68	272	23243
	Wayne RILEY	(Aus)	67	71	67	67	272	23243
6	Greg NORMAN	(Aus)	64	70	69	70	273	15750
7	Ernie ELS	(SA)	68	68	67	71	274	13500
8	Wayne WESTNER	(SA)	71	70	70	64	275	10100
	Retief GOOSEN	(SA)	69	68	68	70	275	10100
	Raymond BURNS	(N.Ire)	67	69	70	69	275	10100
11	Samson GIMSON	(Sing)	69	72	70	66	277	7535
	Pierre FULKE	(Swe)	70	66	68	73	277	7535
	Howard CLARK	(Eng)	68	67	72	70	277	7535
	Costantino ROCCA	(It)	70	69	71	67	277	7535
15	Eoghan O'CONNELL	(Ire)	67	70	72	69	278	6600
16	Bernhard LANGER	(Ger)	70	68	73	68	279	5744
	Paul CURRY	(Eng)	69	70	72	68	279	5744
	Stephen AMES	(T&T)	70	72	70	67	279	5744
	Steven RICHARDSON	(Eng)	69	69	71	70	279	5744
	Stuart CAGE	(Eng)	68	68	70	73	279	5744
	Alexander CEJKA	(Ger)	69	71	69	70	279	5744
22	Paul MCGINLEY	(Ire)	72	68	72	68	280	5130
23	Sven STRÜVER	(Ger)	70	70	67	74	281	4590
	Andrew SHERBORNE	(Eng)	73	67	71	70	281	4590
	Joakim HAEGGMAN	(Swe)	73	70	65	73	281	4590
	Steen TINNING	(Den)	67	70	74	70	281	4590
	Paul EALES	(Eng)	71	70	69	71	281	4590
	Jarmo SANDELIN	(Swe)	72	69	68	72	281	4590
	David GILFORD	(Eng)	70	70	71	70	281	4590
30	Michel BESANCENEY	(Fr)	69	73	68	72	282	3858
	Philip WALTON	(Ire)	69	69	74	70	282	3858
	Mark MOULAND	(Wal)	72	68	72	70	282	3858
	Jay TOWNSEND	(USA)	71	69	70	72	282	3858
34	Ross MCFARLANE	(Eng)	71	71	69	72	283	3420
	Darren CLARKE	(N.Ire)	71	68	73	71	283	3420
	Pedro LINHART	(Sp)	71	67	72	73	283	3420
	Mark JAMES	(Eng)	71	67	74	71	283	3420
	Miguel Angel MARTIN	(Sp)	73	70	71	69	283	3420
39	Gavin LEVENSON	(SA)	72	68	72	72	284	2835
	Carl MASON	(Eng)	71	71	71	71	284	2835
	Klas ERIKSSON	(Swe)	69	72	71	72	284	2835
	Andrew MURRAY	(Eng)	70	71	71	72	284	2835
	Craig CASSELLS	(Eng)	68	74	74	68	284	2835
	Mark DAVIS	(Eng)	71	70	71	72	284	2835
	Peter BAKER	(Eng)	67	73	74	70	284	2835
	Ignacio GARRIDO	(Sp)	70	73	71	70	284	2835
47	Tsukasa WATANABE	(Jap)	73	69	69	74	285	2295
	Mark ROE	(Eng)	73	70	73	69	285	2295
	Gordon J BRAND	(Eng)	67	73	71	74	285	2295
	Stephen MCALLISTER	(Scot)	71	70	74	70	285	2295
51	Barry LANE	(Eng)	70	73	73	70	286	2025
	Jeremy ROBINSON	(Eng)	70	73	71	72	286	2025
53	Scott WATSON	(Eng)	71	71	70	75	287	1800
	David CARTER	(Eng)	70	72	75	70	287	1800
	Steven BOTTOMLEY	(Eng)	71	67	74	75	287	1800
56	Mats LANNER	(Swe)	70	69	71	78	288	1530
	Richard BOXALL	(Eng)	69	73	71	75	288	1530
	Jeff HAWKES	(SA)	70	73	74	71	288	1530
59	Malcolm MACKENZIE	(Eng)	69	73	70	77	289	1327
	Andrew OLDCORN	(Eng)	70	70	73	76	289	1327
	Fredrik LINDGREN	(Swe)	75	68	74	72	289	1327
	Ricky WILLISON	(Eng)	69	71	76	73	289	1327
63	Anders GILLNER	(Swe)	71	72	74	74	291	1192
	Peter HEDBLOM	(Swe)	69	73	74	75	291	1192
65	Mats HALLBERG	(Swe)	70	73	77	72	292	786
	David WILLIAMS	(Eng)	73	70	74	75	292	786
	Christian CEVAER	(Fr)	71	72	74	75	292	786
	Paul MOLONEY	(Aus)	71	70	70	81	292	786
69	Jean VAN DE VELDE	(Fr)	71	70	75	77	293	669

SHOT OF THE WEEK

It is not only the winner who produces a shot to be remembered. Just as good was Greg Norman's second to the 463 yard ninth in the first round when he had a 64 to lead the field. As he had started at the tenth, it was his finishing hole. Attempting to carry the bunker at the corner of the left-to-right dog-leg he instead found the sand. Water eating into the green from the left threatened. With his ball lying clean, Norman (below) hit a five iron from 183 yards to 15 feet and holed the putt for a birdie.

Couples at the double

Fred Couples completed
a classic double after the first
two events of the 1995 Tour

The Orchard Golf and Country Club in the Philippines is a sporting haven which boasts two eye-catching courses, a quite astonishing clubhouse and, in the words of its own publicity material, 'perpetual serenity broken only by the chirping of birds atop fruit-bearing mango trees swaying languidly and spreading their leaves and branches in worshipful homage to the sun above'.

The serenity was suspended for one week in January, however, as the Johnnie Walker Classic and its star-studded cast came to town for a show which brought the people of Manila out in their thousands and which brought 'Asia's best-kept secret' out into the open.

There were rich pickings to be found in The Orchard and Fred Couples, Nick Price, Greg Norman, Ernie Els, Bernhard Langer and Colin Montgomerie had all moved on from Dubai to do battle again. With Seve Ballesteros and David Frost joining them, eight of the world's top 13

were present for Norman's defence of the title he had lifted in Phuket a year earlier.

All were agreed that the Arnold Palmer-designed Legacy course, only a few months old and with firm greens bordered by Bermuda-grass rough, would present the stern challenge envisaged by Palmer, present himself for the pre-tournament celebrity shoot-out in which

Filipino President Ramos and his First Lady also took part.

In Dubai the big guns had fired their bullets from day one. They were to do so eventually here too, but in the opening round they took cover and it was others who came out shooting.

Confronted by an unfriendly-sound-ing Siberian wind whipping in from the north-east only a dozen of the 144-strong field broke par, the three under 69 of Swede Mats Hallberg giving him a one-stoke lead over his compatriot Joakim Haeggman, Andrew Coltart, Paul Eales, Silvio Grappasonni and Malaysia's Marimuthu Ramayuah.

Conditions were kinder for the second round and the ratio of birdies to bogeys changed dramatically. So did the leaderboard. Couples, resuming on level par, turned in 34 and then reduced the 521-yard second – his 11th – to a drive and five iron and rolled in from a putt from 20 feet for an eagle three.

Robert Allenby (top), and Nick Price (above), both had to give best to Fred Couples.

The Dubai champion finished with a 67 to set a target of 139, five under par, and then sat back to see first Robert Karlsson catch him with a sparkling 65 – it was to earn the 25-year old the first £3,000 Johnnie Walker Course Record Award of the season – and then Nick Price overtake him by one with a 67 of his own.

Price's wish for his 38th birthday the following day was to build on his advantage, but it was not granted. The Zimbabwean managed only a 71 and fell back into a tie for third with Colin Montgomerie and Robert Allenby, one behind Kiwi Michael Campbell and two adrift of Couples.

If the American had brought his confidence with him from Dubai, so had Campbell. A member of the four-man side which won the world amateur team title in 1982, this 25-year old PGA European Challenge Tour qualifier had not just been joint third in Dubai, but had also filled the same position in the New Zealand Open the previous week.

The great-great-great grandson of a Scot who emigrated in 1864 and married into the Maori community, Campbell had originally wanted to be an All Black rugby star and played for Wellington at Under-16 level. 'Then one day a guy punched me out and I thought this game is too hard for me. I switched to golf.'

The whalebone charm he wore round

Greg Norman was looking for a repeat victory.

his neck looked lucky indeed as he began the final round by pitching to under a foot at the first and then making an outrageous eagle putt of 60 feet on the next. When he added another birdie on the sixth Campbell was ahead, but his hopes of a dream victory were effectively ended two holes later. His second shot found water and when he three-putted as well a triple bogey seven had to go on his card.

It put Couples and Allenby out in front and, with Price and Scots Coltart and Montgomerie making mistakes too when poised to challenge, the pair were still locked together with four to play.

The 427-yard 15th and 206-yard 16th were to decide the duel. Allenby bogeyed them both, finding horrid lies just off the green on each occasion, while Couples, after salvaging a magnificent par on the 14th, got up and down again at the 15th, then struck a superb three iron to ten feet for a two.

As he had shown in Dubai, Couples was not the type to toss away such an advantage. Twenty years after the 'Thriller in Manila' between Muhammad Ali and Joe Frazier another American had left his mark on the Filipino capital – and, for the second week running, on the Tour as well. A Classic double from a classy golfer.

Mark Garrod

THE COURSE

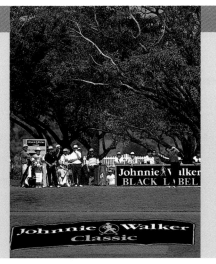

Row upon row of 60-year old mango trees frame the Orchard Golf and Country Club, a brand new 36-hole development with one course (The Legacy) designed by Arnold Palmer and the other (The Tradition) by Gary Player.

Palmer's lay-out, which has water in play at all but five of its holes, was the one chosen for the Johnnie Walker Classic. More than 100,000 bags of white beach sand, shipped from an atoll in the Pacific Ocean, were needed to fill the 127 bunkers, some of which fall directly into lakes.

The longest hole is the 583-yard 18th, alongside which runs a truly spectacular clubhouse complex incorporating 150-seater cinema, 12-lane bowling alley, tennis, badminton, squash and basketball courts, half-size Olympic pool, five restaurants, fitness centre, library and 500-seater Grand Ballroom.

SHOT OF THE WEEK

Fred Couples, one of the longest hitters in golf, won the Johnnie Walker Classic not with his power, but with his gentle touch on and around the greens. In danger of losing the lead to Robert Allenby entering the final straight, Couples saved a vital par at the long 14th with a superb chip from the clinging Bermuda rough. Opening the blade of his sand wedge he swung as though in a bunker and the ball came down 18 inches from the hole like a butterfly landing on a leaf. The shot of a master.

THE ORCHARD GOLF & COUNTRY CLUB, MANILA, JANUARY 26-29, 1995 • YARDAGE 7016 • PAR 72

Pos	Name	Country	Rnd 1	Rnd 2	Rnd 3	Rnd 4	Total	Prize Money £
1	Fred COUPLES	(USA)	72	67	67	71	277	100000
2	Nick PRICE	(Zim)	71	67	71	70	279	66660
3	Robert ALLENBY	(Aus)	71	70	68	71	280	37560
4	Andrew COLTART	(Scot)	70	72	69	70	281	25466
	Greg NORMAN	(Aus)	72	70	70	69	281	25466
	Michael CAMPBELL	(NZ)	74	68	66	73	281	25466
7	Colin MONTGOMERIE	(Scot)	73	68	68	74	283	18000
8	Peter SENIOR	(Aus)	71	72	71	70	284	15000
9	David FROST	(SA)	74	71	71	69	285	12720
	Darren CLARKE	(N.Ire)	72	69	72	72	285	12720
11	Philip WALTON	(Ire)	73	73	70	70	286	11020
12	Robert KARLSSON	(Swe)	74	65	72	76	287	9485
	Per-Ulrik JOHANSSON	(Swe)	71	73	73	70	287	9485
	Mats HALLBERG	(Swe)	69	73	74	71	287	9485
	Sven STRÜVER	(Ger)	73	71	72	71	287	9485
16	Brandt JOBE	(USA)	76	70	69	73	288	8100
	Andrew SHERBORNE	(Eng)	74	73	71	70	288	8100
	Mats LANNER	(Swe)	74	73	70	71	288	8100
19	Mike CLAYTON	(Aus)	75	73	70	71	289	7125
	Pedro LINHART	(Sp)	75	70	74	70	289	7125
	Ignacio GARRIDO	(Sp)	74	72	71	72	289	7125
	Mike MCLEAN	(Eng)	75	74	68	72	289	7125
23	Costantino ROCCA	(It)	73	69	74	74	290	6300
	Bernhard LANGER	(Ger)	74	70	71	75	290	6300
	Sam TORRANCE	(Scot)	71	71	72	76	290	6300
	Silvio GRAPPASONNI	(It)	70	73	73	74	290	6300
	Jean Louis GUEPY	(Fr)	78	71	69	72	290	6300
28	Mark DAVIS	(Eng)	72	70	74	75	291	5400
	Ian PALMER	(SA)	73	72	79	67	291	5400
	Peter FOWLER	(Aus)	75	69	74	73	291	5400
	Peter O'MALLEY	(Aus)	74	70	73	74	291	5400
	Roger CHAPMAN	(Eng)	71	73	73	74	291	5400
33	Russell CLAYDON	(Eng)	75	73	70	74	292	4740
	Alexander CEJKA	(Ger)	76	71	67	78	292	4740
	Stephen AMES	(T&T)	76	71	73	72	292	4740
	Stephen MCALLISTER	(Scot)	74	69	74	75	292	4740
37	Peter HEDBLOM	(Swe)	76	73	72	72	293	4260
	Brian WATTS	(USA)	75	72	73	73	293	4260
	Isao AOKI	(Jap)	72	70	78	73	293	4260
	Joakim HAEGGMAN	(Swe)	70	76	76	71	293	4260
41	Paul BROADHURST	(Eng)	73	74	75	72	294	3900
	Scott WATSON	(Eng)	72	77	75	70	294	3900
43	Paul EALES	(Eng)	70	73	76	76	295	3480
	Ross DRUMMOND	(Scot)	74	74	76	71	295	3480
	Ernie ELS	(SA)	78	71	75	71	295	3480
	Tze-Chung CHEN	(Tai)	76	72	73	74	295	3480
	Cassius CASAS	(Phil)	73	74	71	77	295	3480
	Chiao-YU HONG	(ROC)	74	75	71	75	295	(Am)
48	Seve BALLESTEROS	(Sp)	73	73	74	76	296	3000
	Don WALSWORTH	(USA)	76	72	79	69	296	3000
	Jeev Milkha SINGH	(Ind)	75	74	74	73	296	3000
51	Lee WESTWOOD	(Eng)	75	69	72	81	297	2460
	Craig CASSELLS	(Eng)	74	74	75	74	297	2460
	Marimuthu RAMAYAH	(Mal)	70	74	75	78	297	2460
	Danilo CRUZ	(Phil)	77	72	72	76	297	2460
	Zhang LIAN-WEI	(Chi)	77	72	73	75	297	2460
	Steve FLESCH	(USA)	74	73	73	77	297	2460
57	Miguel Angel MARTIN	(Sp)	73	76	71	78	298	1808
	Wayne RILEY	(Aus)	75	74	75	74	298	1808
	Boonchu RUANGKIT	(Thai)	73	72	78	75	298	1808
	Kyi Hla HAN	(Bur)	78	71	72	77	298	1808
	Anders SØRENSEN	(Den)	73	74	78	73	298	1808
	Gordon J BRAND	(Eng)	72	74	77	75	298	1808
	Carl MASON	(Eng)	76	73	74	75	298	1808
64	Jung-Duck KIM	(Kor)	75	72	76	76	299	1214
	Yu Shu HSIEH	(Tai)	76	71	75	77	299	1214
	Periasamy GUNASAGARAN	(Mal)	74	74	77	74	299	1214
	Paul WAY	(Eng)	76	73	73	77	299	1214
68	Lee PORTER	(USA)	74	74	76	76	300	892
	Stuart CAGE	(Eng)	74	75	76	75	300	892
	Mathias GRÖNBERG	(Swe)	74	75	78	73	300	892
	Samson GIMSON	(Sing)	73	74	76	77	300	892
	Rodger DAVIS	(Aus)	78	70	76	76	300	892
73	Mike HARWOOD	(Aus)	74	71	76	81	302	885
	Philip TALBOT	(Eng)	73	76	76	77	302	885
75	Neal BRIGGS	(Eng)	77	72	76	78	303	882
76	Daniel WESTERMARK	(Swe)	76	72	79	77	304	880
77	David RAY	(Eng)	77	70	77	82	306	878

CELLNET.

THE NET

THAT SETS

YOU FREE.

Cellnet is the official supplier of mobile communication services to the PGA European Tour.

Luna puts in stellar performance

Leading from start to finish, Santiago Luna secured

his maiden victory after ten years on Tour

The 18th hole at the Campo de Golfe course in Madeira rises gradually to a peak that rewards the player who scales it with sublime views over this gorgeous island. As Santiago Luna, with victory certain, made his way up this hill to the 72nd green, the symbolism of the moment was too great to ignore.

For here was a first Tour success that was a testament to the player's perseverance and dedication, and for always trying to progress even when the gradient appeared too steep. And yes, the view from the top was splendid. A Luna landscape you might say. 'I'm having difficulty putting into words what victory means to me,' the Spaniard said. 'For three years I have worked hard mentally for this. I have tried to learn how to put out of my mind all the distractions, all the pressures, to worry about nothing but winning. So you can imagine how I feel having finally achieved that.'

For a player who went into the last round with a reputation for succumbing to distractions like the pressure of the moment it was the most impressive performance imaginable. The back nine of this fine course has been armoured with all the tricks of an architect's trade. Anyone familiar with the work of Robert Trent Jones Junior would have recognised some characteristically devilish touches: tight tree-lined fairways; sloping greens; plunging ravines; spectacular hazards. Luna negotiated them all without a bogey on that final day. His driving was arrow-straight. He attacked the pins with his iron shots when this option was readily available and played for the safe parts of the greens when necessary.

Leading from start to finish and protecting a big lead are perhaps the two most difficult skills in the game. Luna demonstrated both. He averaged 68 shots per round which represented golf of the highest order. And he negotiated the back nine with the same four shots advantage with which he had begun it, protecting his gains with all the self-assurance of a grand master. It was the sort of performance which establishes new reputations.

This tournament bore out fully the Tour's attempts to offer as many playing opportunities as possible to its members. Many of the entrants were tomorrow's potential stars who were desperate for just such a chance to learn their trade. Many were like Luna, who sensed that the event offered them a marvellous opportunity to finally enter the winner's circle.

Of the newcomers, no-one impressed more than Christian Cevaer, the 24-year old Frenchman who was playing in just

the putts that mattered. At the end he showed a refreshing candour when asked about his £500 fine for slow play on the second day. Was he bitter about it? Did he think it unfair? He thought neither of these things. He said he was slow and he needed to quicken his approach. 'I don't want to be a burden and I shall be going

ogy degree, was there almost straight out of college. Luna went to the PGA European Tour's qualifying school on no fewer than five occasions and this was the start of his 11th year on Tour. It took a psychologist, Mariano Espinsosa, to finally convince him he could do it, although Severiano Ballesteros, who had been

Former Walker Cup players Iain Pyman and Liam White were well in the money.

his fifth Tour event. On the final day it looked more like his 50th as he played with seemingly no inhibitions. Over the last six or seven holes it had become clear that he was duelling for second place with his playing companion, Paul Curry.

Would experience win out? Not on this occasion as it was Cevaer who holed

out in future practice rounds with a stop-watch until I have learned to be quicker', he said.

At the prize presentation, Cevaer's smile almost matched that of Luna's. It was hard not to think of the contrasting ways in which they had reached such heights. Cevaer, armed with his psychol-

telling him for year that he had the game to win, deserved some credit as well.

Below these two, in joint fourth place, were Iain Pyman and Dean Robertson, who were Walker Cup colleagues just a couple of years ago. For all four, it was a week to cherish.

Derek Lawrenson

THE COURSE

There cannot be many more scenic venues in Europe than this one, perched 2,300 ft above sea level, and containing a number of memorable holes. Many are lined with pine, mimosa, and eucalyptus trees, though not the signature hole, the par five 12th, which is reachable in two – provided the player is courageous enough to dice with an enormous ravine.

Campo de Golfe da Madeira, February 2-5, 1995 · Yardage 6606 · Par 72

Pos	Name	Country	Rnd 1	Rnd 2	Rnd 3	Rnd 4	Total	Prize Money £
1	Santiago LUNA	(Sp)	67	67	68	70	272	41660
2	Christian CEVAER	(Fr)	70	69	68	69	276	27770
3	Paul CURRY	(Eng)	73	67	68	71	279	15650
4	Olle KARLSSON	(Swe)	72	66	75	68	281	9120
	Dean ROBERTSON	(Scot)	73	70	68	70	281	9120
	José COCERES	(Arg)	72	67	71	71	281	9120
	Iain PYMAN	(Eng)	75	68	66	72	281	9120
	Steen TINNING	(Den)	74	65	67	75	281	9120
9	John HAWKSWORTH	(Eng)	72	72	71	67	282	5066
	Ruben ALVAREZ	(Arg)	71	70	72	69	282	5066
	Mathias GRÖNBERG	(Swe)	71	72	69	70	282	5066
12	David J RUSSELL	(Eng)	75	71	71	66	283	3782
	Paul MAYO	(Wal)	74	68	72	69	283	3782
	David WILLIAMS	(Eng)	70	74	70	69	283	3782
	Dennis EDLUND	(Swe)	73	67	73	70	283	3782
	Paul LAWRIE	(Scot)	68	72	71	72	283	3782
	Paul AFFLECK	(Wal)	72	71	67	73	283	3782
18	Robert KARLSSON	(Swe)	75	69	70	70	284	3020
	Andrew SHERBORNE	(Eng)	68	71	73	72	284	3020
	Neal BRIGGS	(Eng)	71	71	68	74	284	3020
	Kenny CROSS	(Swe)	72	67	70	75	284	3020
	Liam WHITE	(Eng)	69	67	70	78	284	3020
23	Juan PIÑERO	(Sp)	70	74	73	68	285	2662
	David R JONES	(Eng)	75	69	70	71	285	2662
	Mark LITTON	(Wal)	76	70	64	75	285	2662
	Rolf MUNTZ	(Hol)	72	66	71	76	285	2662
27	Scott WATSON	(Eng)	74	70	71	71	286	2221
	Peter MITCHELL	(Eng)	70	76	71	69	286	2221
	Jay TOWNSEND	(USA)	72	73	69	72	286	2221
	Carlos LARRAIN	(Ven)	71	72	69	74	286	2221
	Eamonn DARCY	(Ire)	69	71	71	75	286	2221
	Bill MALLEY	(USA)	68	72	71	75	286	2221
	John MCHENRY	(Ire)	75	66	70	75	286	2221
	Lee WESTWOOD	(Eng)	68	72	69	77	286	2221
35	Andrew COLTART	(Scot)	69	74	72	72	287	1800
	Michael ARCHER	(Eng)	70	72	73	72	287	1800
	Paul BROADHURST	(Eng)	69	72	74	72	287	1800
	Brian MARCHBANK	(Scot)	69	71	75	72	287	1800
	Joakim GRONHAGEN	(Swe)	72	72	72	71	287	1800
	Mats HALLBERG	(Swe)	74	71	72	70	287	1800
	Jesus Maria ARRUTI	(Sp)	68	77	69	73	287	1800
42	Brian BARNES	(Scot)	71	71	73	73	288	1500
	Mark JAMES	(Eng)	69	75	73	71	288	1500
	Andrew CLAPP	(Eng)	74	71	73	70	288	1500
	Eoghan O'CONNELL	(Ire)	72	72	70	74	288	1500
	Jamie SPENCE	(Eng)	72	67	74	75	288	1500
47	John MELLOR	(Eng)	71	72	72	74	289	1250
	Gordon BRAND JNR.	(Scot)	73	72	71	73	289	1250
	José Manuel CARRILES	(Sp)	74	72	72	71	289	1250
	Emanuele CANONICA	(It)	71	74	69	75	289	1250
	Wayne RILEY	(Aus)	73	70	68	78	289	1250
52	Jeremy ROBINSON	(Eng)	71	72	74	73	290	1050
	Keith WATERS	(Eng)	73	70	74	73	290	1050
	Ian SPENCER	(Eng)	72	71	75	72	290	1050
55	Jon ROBSON	(Eng)	77	69	72	73	291	900
	Des SMYTH	(Ire)	72	71	71	77	291	900
	Jarmo SANDELIN	(Swe)	69	70	72	80	291	900
58	Frédéric REGARD	(Fr)	69	72	73	78	292	762
	Adam MEDNICK	(Swe)	72	73	71	76	292	762
	Peter BAKER	(Eng)	72	71	73	76	292	762
	Phil GOLDING	(Eng)	70	73	78	71	292	762
62	Gary EMERSON	(Eng)	70	74	71	78	293	675
	Thomas GÖGELE	(Ger)	73	71	74	75	293	675
	Heinz P THÜL	(Ger)	72	74	75	72	293	675
65	Martyn ROBERTS	(Wal)	73	71	74	76	294	625
66	Jonathan WILSHIRE	(Eng)	71	72	75	77	295	399
	Stephen AMES	(T&T)	73	73	75	74	295	399
68	Michael JONZON	(Swe)	73	70	76	77	296	395
	Gordon J BRAND	(Eng)	72	68	82	74	296	395
	José CORREIA	(Port)	73	72	74	82	301	(Am)
70	Daren LEE	(Eng)	74	72	75	82	303	392

SHOT OF THE WEEK

Christian Cevaer still had a ravine and 180 yards to negotiate as he lined up his fourth shot on the final day to the long 12th. All the week's good work could have been undone had he lost his nerve at that point but he didn't panic. He played the bravest of four irons, his ball finishing 12 feet from the hole. He sank the putt for a remarkable par.

33

Sandelin sings sweetest in the Canaries

Jarmo Sandelin outlasted none other than Severiano Ballesteros for victory in only his fourth Tour event

Who do you know that can give Severiano Ballesteros six shots with 14 holes to play in the last round of a golf tournament and beat him? Nobody, right? Wrong. It happened in a weird and wonderful week in the sunshine off the coast of North Africa in February, a week that started with a funeral, included several big songs by a Fat Lady and ended with a baptism after the aforesaid diva forgot the tune.

To be strictly accurate, it was not the funeral that opened proceedings, just the news of it, with a small and happy wake thrown in for a few family friends. Of the

Fat Lady, more later, but the baptism was one of fire that came four days later when Ballesteros was taken on and beaten at his own game by a little-known Swede by the name of Jarmo Sandelin.

Jarmo Who? A perfectly understandable question, and one over which not even Sandelin would take umbrage. He was playing only his fourth Tour event as a fully-fledged card-carrying member of the Tour having finished ninth in the previous year's PGA European Challenge Tour money list, and here he was handing out a lesson in coolness to one of golf's greatest pressure players to win with a total of 282, six under par, a shot in front of Ballesteros and the workmanlike Paul Eales.

Sandelin, 27, was born of Finnish parents in a small town two miles from the Soviet border, but moved to Sweden in 1974 and later took out Swedish nationality. He cut his golfing teeth on pitch-and-putt courses, where he refined the short game that was revealed at Maspalomas as one of his strengths.

Life had been pretty tough for much of the seven years that he had been a professional. He had ground out a living on the Swedish mini-tour, then graduated to the Challenge Tour, and finally made his breakthrough in 1994, when his big moment was victory in the Challenge Novotel the previous September.

Now here he was being recognised as a name to be reckoned with on the Tour, and it was obviously all a touch overwhelming. 'I don't have the word to express what this means', he said, his eyes wide with would-you-believe-it incredulity. 'Only my fourth tournament after getting my card and beating the big hero in Spain.' Ballesteros was as gracious in defeat as only he can be. 'He got more confident as the last round went on', he said. 'He didn't make a single mistake on the back nine; he played very well.'

He did, too. Not one to be conventional for its own sake, Sandelin carries four wedges in his bag and has a 50-inch driver, some six inches longer than normal. He used all those clubs to haul himself back from the brink of disaster when he had two sixes in the first four holes of the last day.

'I was very nervous at the start, and I got the sixes because I was hitting the ball too soft', he said .'I decided then to hit the ball as hard as I could, and it came off.'

That did it. He had five birdies in the next ten holes, including a two at the 229-yard eighth from seven feet while Ballesteros bogeyed the hole for the fourth day running. That was crucial enough, but the final blow came when he pulled out his 65-degree wedge and chipped in for a birdie from 20 yards on

35

Big impact from Severiano Ballesteros.

the 15th, where Ballesteros dropped another shot after diving into a bush.

It was a sad moment for Ballesteros, going for his 54th European victory, but after making sweet music with the Fat Lady putter given him a few weeks before in Manila by Nick Price in opening rounds of 68 and 69, he slipped badly on the last two days with a pair of undistinguished 73s, finding, like many of his fellow competitors, the grainy greens at Maspalomas difficult to read and the fairways even more difficult to find. Even so, he had a chance to take the tournament into a sudden-death play-off when faced with a seven foot putt for a birdie on the 72nd hole. He missed.

It was all a bit of an anti-climax for Ballesteros, who had arrived in Gran Canaria in rare high spirits having just completed a 15,000-mile round trip to visit Mac O'Grady, his coach, in California.

Nobody but the eccentric O'Grady would have dreamed up the ploy of gathering together a bunch of pictures of Ballesteros's bad habits, putting them in a shoe-box, driving out into the desert and burying them. 'We conducted a funeral, and then prayed for two minutes that I should catch my second wind in my career,' Ballesteros said with the ghost of a smile playing on his lips. Quite why he was seeking his second wind after winning something like £590,000 the previous year was anybody's guess. Perhaps only he and O'Grady could answer that one.

Ballesteros was happy as Larry as he sat, relaxed, and talked about what he was expecting from his season, and the members of the Fourth Estate who sat with him smiled at the old ham's braggadoccio. He played beautifully for two days, and all was right with the world. That he slipped in the closing acts did little to lessen the impact he had made on the tournament. Jarmo Who, meanwhile, was becoming Jarmo Sandelin, tournament winner: at last, a man with a name.

Mel Webb

THE COURSE

Maspalomas was not an easy proposition for the players. Narrow landing areas on already-tight fairways put a premium on accuracy off the tee, a demand that brought about the demise of Severiano Ballesteros in the final two rounds. Difficult-to-read greens made constant demands on the players' skills when they drew out their putters. Not an easy course, as was evinced by the winner's total of only six under par for 72 holes.

CAMPO DE GOLFE DA MASPALOMAS, GRAN CANARIA, FEBRUARY 9-12, 1995 · YARDAGE 6904 · PAR 36

Pos	Name	Country	Rnd 1	Rnd 2	Rnd 3	Rnd 4	Total	Prize Money £
1	Jarmo SANDELIN	(Swe)	74	72	66	70	282	40719
2	Paul EALES	(Eng)	68	72	72	71	283	21219
	Seve BALLESTEROS	(Sp)	68	69	73	73	283	21219
4	Anders FORSBRAND	(Swe)	72	69	72	71	284	12216
5	Sven STRÜVER	(Ger)	70	72	73	70	285	8746
	Darren CLARKE	(N.Ire)	72	69	71	73	285	8746
	Gary EMERSON	(Eng)	69	72	71	73	285	8746
8	Paolo QUIRICI	(Swi)	76	70	73	68	287	6108
9	John MCHENRY	(Ire)	74	72	74	68	288	4448
	Paul CURRY	(Eng)	71	74	70	73	288	4448
	Gordon BRAND JNR.	(Scot)	71	72	74	71	288	4448
	Pedro LINHART	(Sp)	76	68	73	71	288	4448
	Gary ORR	(Scot)	68	75	71	74	288	4448
	Derrick COOPER	(Eng)	74	69	75	70	288	4448
15	Phillip PRICE	(Wal)	73	69	73	74	289	3591
16	Paul R SIMPSON	(Eng)	70	75	69	76	290	3026
	Steen TINNING	(Den)	72	72	74	72	290	3026
	Paul LAWRIE	(Scot)	72	77	68	73	290	3026
	Jamie SPENCE	(Eng)	69	75	74	72	290	3026
	Raymond BURNS	(N.Ire)	73	72	74	71	290	3026
	Des SMYTH	(Ire)	75	69	72	74	290	3026
	Steven BOTTOMLEY	(Eng)	72	73	73	72	290	3026
	Brian MARCHBANK	(Scot)	76	68	74	72	290	3026
24	Robert KARLSSON	(Swe)	69	75	74	73	291	2345
	Anders GILLNER	(Swe)	74	72	74	71	291	2345
	José Maria CAÑIZARES	(Sp)	75	71	72	73	291	2345
	Manuel PIÑERO	(Sp)	76	71	70	74	291	2345
	Mike MCLEAN	(Eng)	74	73	71	73	291	2345
	Stuart CAGE	(Eng)	72	73	77	69	291	2345
	Christy O'CONNOR JNR	(Ire)	74	69	75	73	291	2345
	Eamonn DARCY	(Ire)	72	73	74	72	291	2345
	Paul WAY	(Eng)	74	73	74	70	291	2345
33	Steven RICHARDSON	(Eng)	73	74	74	71	292	1881
	Philip WALTON	(Ire)	68	76	75	73	292	1881
	Joakim GRONHAGEN	(Swe)	74	73	71	74	292	1881
	Peter BAKER	(Eng)	71	74	77	70	292	1881
	Richard BOXALL	(Eng)	73	70	73	76	292	1881
	Jon ROBSON	(Eng)	72	72	71	77	292	1881
39	Francisco VALERA	(Sp)	76	71	74	72	293	1563
	José COCERES	(Arg)	74	71	76	72	293	1563
	Ruben ALVAREZ	(Arg)	76	70	76	71	293	1563
	Mark NICHOLS	(Eng)	76	72	74	71	293	1563
	Per HAUGSRUD	(Nor)	74	73	73	73	293	1563
	David GILFORD	(Eng)	78	71	70	74	293	1563
	John BICKERTON	(Eng)	74	71	75	73	293	1563
46	Anders SØRENSEN	(Den)	72	72	77	73	294	1172
	Michael ARCHER	(Eng)	72	74	72	76	294	1172
	Mark MOULAND	(Wal)	75	71	72	76	294	1172
	Alexander CEJKA	(Ger)	74	73	74	73	294	1172
	Peter MITCHELL	(Eng)	74	72	72	76	294	1172
	Santiago LUNA	(Sp)	72	71	74	77	294	1172
	Miguel Angel MARTIN	(Sp)	72	73	77	72	294	1172
	John MELLOR	(Eng)	74	75	73	72	294	1172
	Dean ROBERTSON	(Scot)	72	75	71	76	294	1172
55	Michel BESANCENEY	(Fr)	72	75	73	75	295	835
	David RAY	(Eng)	71	75	76	73	295	835
	Iain PYMAN	(Eng)	74	72	74	75	295	835
	Jesus Maria ARRUTI	(Sp)	76	68	71	80	295	835
	Fabrice TARNAUD	(Fr)	76	72	77	70	295	835
60	Juan QUIRÓS	(Sp)	73	72	79	72	296	708
	Rolf MUNTZ	(Hol)	75	72	72	77	296	708
	Carl SUNESON	(Eng)	76	72	71	77	296	708
63	Andrew SHERBORNE	(Eng)	73	74	71	79	297	576
	Stephen MCALLISTER	(Scot)	75	72	73	77	297	576
	Mark LITTON	(Wal)	73	76	73	75	297	576
	Fredrik JACOBSON	(Swe)	76	72	73	76	297	576
	Oscar SANCHEZ	(Sp)	71	73	74	80	298	(Am)
67	Juan PIÑERO	(Sp)	76	71	76	76	299	398
68	José ROZADILLA	(Sp)	78	68	73	81	300	396
69	Keith WATERS	(Eng)	77	72	78	74	301	394

SHOT OF THE WEEK

Jarmo Sandelin, third shot, 15th hole, final round. The blow that all but killed off Ballesteros's hopes. Sandelin, a short-iron specialist, pulled out his 65-degree lobbing wedge and, from 20 yards, chipped in for a birdie three. It bounced twice, then rolled and rolled before falling into the hole almost at the last gasp. It was a stroke of which even Ballesteros, the master escape artist, would have been proud. As it was, he was forced to look on in admiration, knowing that his chance of victory was breathing its last gasps.

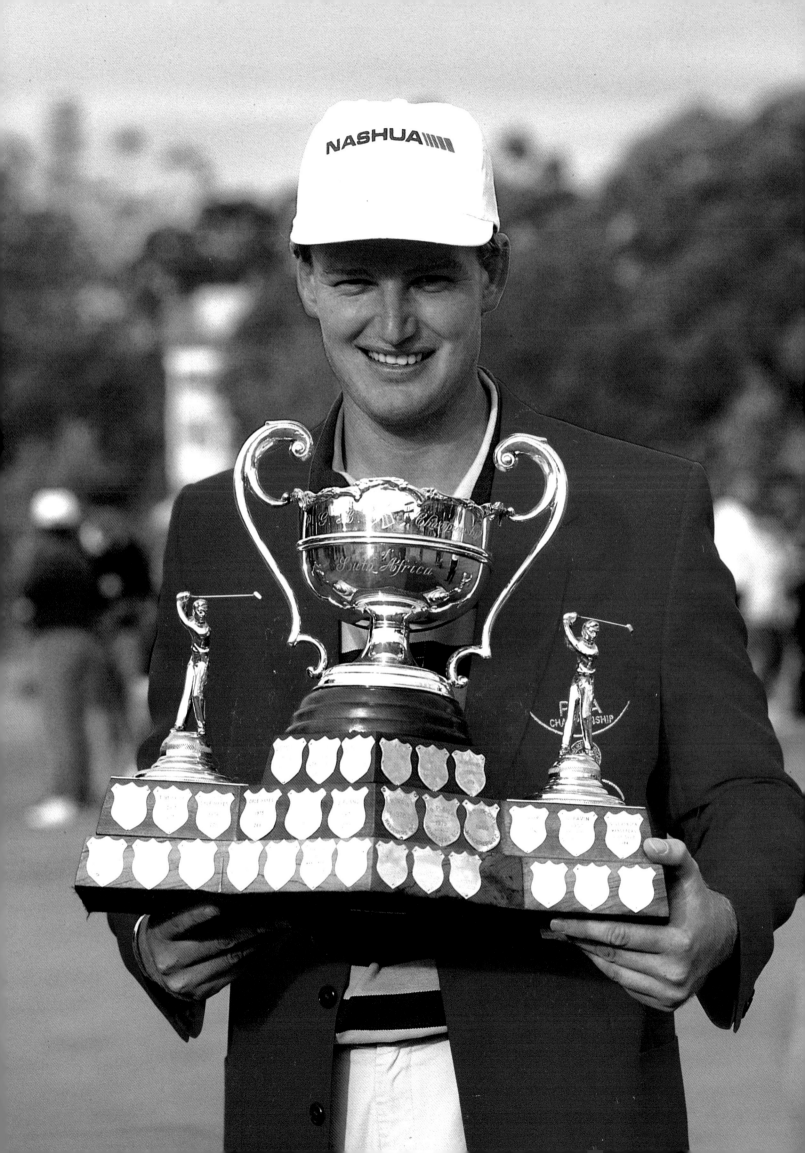

Els is right at home

The first PGA European Tour event

in South Africa resulted in

a home win for Ernie Els

You can never give Ernie Els an inch because he's sure to take a mile. Even in the best company he takes some holding so when most of Europe's elite opted to by-pass the Lexington SA PGA Championship at the Wanderers in Johannesburg, the young man was firm favourite. He certainly didn't disappoint his many fans, not only chalking up his second South African PGA Championship but completing his fifth victory in as many months.

Having already tucked away the 1994 US Open, the victory parade began the previous October when he won the Toyota World Match-Play Championship at Wentworth. In November it was the Gene Sarazen World Championship in Atlanta. December brought the Johnnie Walker World Championship in Jamaica, and January the Bell's Cup in Cape Town. Now, in mid-February, also in his native South Africa, he proved once again what an exciting player he is.

Perhaps it was fitting that Els should come out on top as the Tour stretched its boundaries to its most southerly outpost yet. With prize money of £250,000 on offer, the largest offered to the South African FNB Tour men, Mark James, Darren Clarke and Andrew Coltart were the main British and Irish challengers.

Others, such as Vijay Singh and Frank Nobilo used the event as a warm-up for the following week's inaugural Alfred Dunhill Challenge between Southern Africa and Australasia at nearby Houghton. At mile-high Wanderers – now the highest destination on Tour at almost 6,000 feet, Els was a cut above the rest, a closing 64 giving him a winning nine under par 271 and a two shot victory over fellow South African Roger Wessels, who also closed with a 64.

The European challenge, in fact, came from an unexpected source in Vanslow Phillips, the former Walker Cup man, who failed to earn his Tour card at last November's PGA European Tour Qualifying School. The 22-year old from Slough closed with a brilliant 66 for 274 and joint third place with such experienced campaigners as Zimbabweans Tony Johnstone and Mark McNulty and another

'It was raining when we teed-off but I got a great start with a birdie three at the first.'

It was just the ticket. As Dodds found little going his way, apart from an eagle three at the long fifth, in a closing 70 to drop to seventh, Els reeled in three successive birdies from the fifth to be out in 31, the best of the day.

Although he dropped shots at two par threes, the 12th and 15th, four more birdies came his way to make eight in all which was enough to keep McNulty and Johnstone at bay. The Zimbabweans didn't help their cause by both three-putting

Tony Johnstone (left) pointed the way to third place. David Carter (below) returned to his birthplace.

SHOT OF THE WEEK

When Els came to the par three 17th on Sunday he needed something special to shake off his pursuers. It came with a birdie putt of 25 feet on a sloping green which he just knocked in. 'It had a break of two feet and I read it perfectly,' he said. 'Only then did I feel the tournament was mine because Mark could still birdie the last two holes.' But unbeknown to Els, McNulty had bogeyed the 16th to put himself out of the hunt.

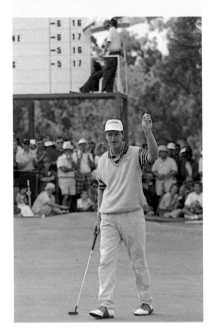

South African, Warren Schutte.

Not only did Phillips collect £12,190, his biggest ever pay day, but a wealth of experience, especially from partnering Els on the final two days. 'To play two rounds with Ernie was brilliant. He's so good it's unbelievable. And he's such a nice bloke, too,' said Phillips. 'He told me he enjoyed playing with me and to keep it going. I've had a lot of doors shut in my face since I turned professional and have had a lot of bad luck, too (like the 67 opening round at the Tour School which was rubbed out when the round was cancelled). I know I can play to the standard required. It's just having the opportunity.' Third place earned him a spot in the following week's Turespaña Open Mediterrania in Valencia but he confirmed he would concentrate on the PGA European Challenge Tour in 1995 as the best chance of earning his Tour card. 'I'm determined to get it,' he added.

Els on the other hand was equally determined especially after completing a third round one over par 71. It left him to start the final day two shots adrift of Namibian Trevor Dodds and alongside Johnstone, McNulty and Schutte. 'Going into the last round I thought that if the weather was fine, I would need to shoot 63 with Mark and Tony so close,' said Els.

the 16th to be overtaken by Wessels, who matched Els's 64, as did young Swede Michael Jonzon to finish joint eighth.

But this was yet another week that belonged to Els. After collecting the tournament's red jacket, he said with classic understatement: 'It's not been a bad year so far. But it's going to be hard to have one like the last.'

David Hamilton

WANDERERS CLUB, JOHANNESBURG, FEBRUARY 16-19, 1995 · YARDAGE 6960 · PAR 70

Pos	Name	Country	Rnd 1	Rnd 2	Rnd 3	Rnd 4	Total	Prize Money £
1	Ernie ELS	(SA)	65	71	71	64	271	39478
2	Roger WESSELS	(SA)	68	72	69	64	273	28748
3	Vanslow PHILLIPS	(Eng)	66	71	71	66	274	12190
	Tony JOHNSTONE	(Zim)	68	70	69	67	274	12190
	Warren SCHUTTE	(SA)	68	71	68	67	274	12190
	Mark MCNULTY	(Zim)	68	72	67	67	274	12190
7	Trevor DODDS	(Nam)	66	71	68	70	275	7386
8	Mats HALLBERG	(Swe)	73	68	69	66	276	5789
	Michael JONZON	(Swe)	71	71	70	64	276	5789
10	Nic HENNING	(SA)	69	66	74	68	277	4385
	Robbie STEWART	(SA)	69	70	70	68	277	4385
	Jay TOWNSEND	(USA)	67	74	70	66	277	4385
	Mark JAMES	(Eng)	71	71	69	66	277	4385
14	Wayne WESTNER	(SA)	62	75	73	68	278	3643
	Jimmy JOHNSON	(USA)	68	74	68	68	278	3643
16	Alexander CEJKA	(Ger)	66	72	74	67	279	3306
	James KINGSTON	(SA)	71	69	71	68	279	3306
	Michael SCHOLZ	(SA)	73	69	71	66	279	3306
	Mike CHRISTIE	(USA)	72	72	70	65	279	3306
20	Francis QUINN	(USA)	69	71	69	71	280	2863
	De Wet BASSON	(SA)	71	70	70	69	280	2863
	Sammy DANIELS	(SA)	72	70	69	69	280	2863
	Marc FARRY	(Fr)	70	74	66	70	280	2863
24	Jeff HAWKES	(SA)	71	69	71	70	281	2515
	Richard KAPLAN	(SA)	71	70	68	72	281	2515
	PH HORGAN	(USA)	74	68	70	69	281	2515
	David CARTER	(Eng)	69	74	68	70	281	2515
	Ricky WILLISON	(Eng)	72	72	67	70	281	2515
29	Deane PAPPAS	(SA)	69	72	70	71	282	2229
	Wayne RILEY	(Aus)	70	71	71	70	282	2229
	Mark WILTSHIRE	(SA)	71	70	72	69	282	2229
32	André BOSSERT	(Swi)	71	69	71	72	283	1996
	John MCHENRY	(Ire)	69	72	74	68	283	1996
	Michael ARCHER	(Eng)	70	73	74	66	283	1996
	John BLAND	(SA)	72	72	70	69	283	1996
	Mike HARWOOD	(Aus)	70	75	71	67	283	1996
	Ian LEGGATT	(CAN)	71	75	68	69	283	1996
38	Wayne BRADLEY	(SA)	68	73	69	74	284	1721
	Kevin STONE	(SA)	73	69	71	71	284	1721
	Vijay SINGH	(Fij)	73	72	69	70	284	1721
	David FROST	(SA)	70	75	69	70	284	1721
	Andrew COLTART	(Scot)	74	72	69	69	284	1721
43	Ron WHITTAKER	(USA)	66	73	73	73	285	1522
	John MELLOR	(Eng)	70	73	72	70	285	1522
	Craig RONALD	(Scot)	73	71	71	70	285	1522
46	Bobby LINCOLN	(SA)	68	73	72	73	286	1322
	Michael GREEN	(SA)	71	71	71	73	286	1322
	Schalk VAN DER MERWE	(SA)	71	73	68	74	286	1322
	Chris WILLIAMS	(Eng)	71	73	70	72	286	1322
	Retief GOOSEN	(SA)	73	73	68	72	286	1322
51	Marco GORTANA	(USA)	72	70	72	73	287	1023
	Brian MARCHBANK	(Scot)	74	69	71	73	287	1023
	Greg REID	(SA)	69	74	72	72	287	1023
	Greg TURNER	(NZ)	68	75	73	71	287	1023
	Bill LONGMUIR	(Scot)	72	72	71	72	287	1023
	Philip JONAS	(SA)	71	75	73	68	287	1023
	Andrew CLAPP	(Eng)	70	76	73	68	287	1023
58	Dennis EDLUND	(Swe)	71	70	74	73	288	798
	Frank NOBILO	(NZ)	70	71	72	75	288	798
	Steve VAN VUUREN	(SA)	69	75	70	74	288	798
61	Mike BOARD	(USA)	68	71	72	78	289	648
	Clinton WHITELAW	(SA)	71	72	77	69	289	648
	Jonathan HODGSON	(Eng)	68	75	70	76	289	648
	Fulton ALLEM	(SA)	72	71	76	70	289	648
	Dean ROBERTSON	(Scot)	72	73	72	72	289	648
	Darren CLARKE	(N.Ire)	71	75	72	71	289	648
67	Jannie LE GRANGE	(SA)	74	72	74	70	290	397
	Adilson DA SILVA	(Bra)	73	73	78	66	290	397
69	John MASHEGO	(SA)	76	70	74	71	291	394
70	Russell FLETCHER	(SA)	70	73	78	72	293	392
71	Nico VAN RENSBURG	(SA)	69	77	71	77	294	390
72	Brett LIDDLE	(SA)	72	74	78	71	295	388
73	Wilhelm WINSNES	(SA)	73	72	75	76	296	386

THE COURSE

The Wanderers is a splendid parkland course situation in the heart of Johannesburg's exclusive residential belt. Designed by Robert Grimsdell, it was completed in 1939 on pleasant rolling terrain, with generous fairways but small, closely guarded greens. For the PGA the course was played back-to-front, the back nine becoming the front nine, while the regular par of 71 became 70 with the 290 yard 17th being reduced to 238 yards.

Karlsson leads Swedish assault

Swedish golfers dominated in Valencia and in the end

Robert Karlsson was head and shoulders above the rest

Y ou would always know if Robert Karlsson approached from behind and spoke to you on a dark night. His would be the voice that was coming from some way above your ears. At 6ft 5in, the tallest player on the Tour, the Swede is in more danger than most of having his head in the clouds, but his extreme altitude did not prevent him from staying in solid contact with terra firma on a windy Sunday in Spain in February.

When Karlsson arrived to play in the Turespaña Open Mediterrania he was one of a group of seven youthful Swedes who had finished second in Tour events. A few days later there were only six left as Karlsson completed a gun-to-tape victory with a score of 276, 12 under par. Not even an occasionally jittery final round of 72 in blustery and difficult conditions could take the gloss off a triumph for maturity far beyond his 25 years.

Of that seven-man group, Pierre Fulke and Fredrik Lindgren were on a final leaderboard at Escorpion that gave eloquent proof of the burgeoning influence of Swedish players on the Tour. There were six of them in the top eight, only Sam Torrance and Miguel Angel Jiménez, who joined Anders Forsbrand and Jarmo Sandelin in second place three strokes behind the winner, breaking the Swedish monopoly.

On another day Karlsson's closing round might have left him still frustratedly pawing the ground outside the winner's circle, but as it was a surprising lack of challenge from the pursuing pack left him to win more or less as he liked.

Trying, not always totally successfully, to hide the shredding nerves that were doing their best to betray him, Karlsson went through more than one crisis of confidence, most notably when he bogeyed three holes in succession from the 12th. He looked then what he was then – a young man inexperienced in the ways of winning. Churning stomach controlled at last, four holes after he had re-established contact with planet Earth he had learnt a lesson that would stay with him for the rest of his days.

Karlsson's closing ride was a switchback affair. He birdied the first from 30 feet and did not make a mistake until he bogeyed the ninth. He birdied the tenth and 11th to put him five shots clear, but then failed to get up and down at the

43

12th, put his ball into the trees at the 13th and went into the water at the 14th. If anybody was going to catch him, this was the moment, but his pursuers failed to take advantage of his errors, and when he birdied the 16th with a putt from ten feet, he had the tournament won.

In many ways, the final 18 holes of the best week in Karlsson's life was the least convincing of the 72 he played. He produced a course-record round of 64 on the first day, the only debit against nine birdies being one bogey. The key to his round was his play over Escorpion's four par-fives, including a monster that is 597-yards along – not so much as a golf hole, more a full-blown country walk. He got a birdie there and picked up shots at two of the other three long holes for good measure. He finished with a surge of birdies, four in the last five holes pushing him out of the pack and into the lead.

Day two brought more modest brilliance, a 69 giving him a one-stroke advantage over Lindgren, who had a 68. The Swedes were on the march, with their only enemies a gaggle of Tour greybeards. Sharing third place with Ross McFarlane and Costantino Rocca two shots off the

Joint second place for Anders Forsbrand.

pace were Sam Torrance and Vicente Fernandez, while a further shots behind lurked Mark James and the grand-daddy of them all, Brian Barnes.

Torrance, Fernandez, James and Barnes, all fortysomethings who were living proof that ageism has no place on today's Tour, had a European victory tally of precisely 50 between them. The race in the approaching weekend might yet go to the young cubs, but there were a few old lions around who could still handle themselves pretty handily in a scrap.

The status quo was more or less maintained in the third round, and after a one under par 71 Karlsson went into the final day three shots clear. For a long while he had no challengers among the Brits, and in the end it took a remarkable few minutes from Torrance on the last

hole of the tournament to put him within sight of the leader.

Torrance was not at his best in spite of recovering from a bout of food poisoning that had kept him from his bed throughout the Friday night. He had two bogeys on the front nine, and when he three-putted the 14th he was back to seven under par and out of contention.

He redeemed himself in a big way on the 18th, however, covering the 492-yard par five with an immense drive downwind across water and a nine-iron to two feet for a show-stopping eagle three. It was a spectacular finale for the veteran Scot in an otherwise disappointing 73.

Meanwhile, Karlsson was playing the last in par with the aplomb of a seasoned campaigner. As he raised his arms in triumph he was engulfed and thrown aloft several times by a gang of his compatriots who had been urging him on from the sidelines. Even as he was hurtling skywards, Karlsson might have been thanking his lucky stars that amid the emotion and the turmoil he had managed, gloriously, to keep his feet firmly on the ground.

Mel Webb

THE COURSE

Escorpion was at once a tiger and a pussycat. The course record had stood for 15 years, but only because it was that long since a Tour event had been held there. The course was a test for the best back then, and was again on the last day when the wind blew, but with the weather at its most benign in the early stages of the tournament its flat terrain and wide-open fairways were ripe for the plucking. Karlsson's 64 on the first day proved it.

ESCORPION, VALENCIA, FEBRUARY 23-26, 1995 • YARDAGE 6909 • PAR 72

Pos	Name	Country	Rnd 1	Rnd 2	Rnd 3	Rnd 4	Total	Prize Money £			Pos	Name	Country	Rnd 1	Rnd 2	Rnd 3	Rnd 4	Total	Prize Money £
1	Robert KARLSSON	(Swe)	64	69	71	72	276	50000				Silvio GRAPPASONNI	(It)	70	72	71	74	287	2040
												Roger WESSELS	(SA)	72	71	73	71	287	2040
2	Miguel Angel JIMÉNEZ	(Sp)	73	69	69	68	279	19952				Darren CLARKE	(N.Ire)	70	73	76	68	287	2040
	Anders FORSBRAND	(Swe)	69	71	67	72	279	19952				Mike MCLEAN	(Eng)	71	70	71	75	287	2040
	Jarmo SANDELIN	(Swe)	68	71	71	69	279	19952				John BICKERTON	(Eng)	69	71	73	74	287	2040
	Sam TORRANCE	(Scot)	68	67	71	73	279	19952			44	Mark ROE	(Eng)	68	73	67	80	288	1500
6	Pierre FULKE	(Swe)	74	68	68	70	280	9000				Steven RICHARDSON	(Eng)	73	69	74	72	288	1500
	Per-Ulrik JOHANSSON	(Swe)	69	71	69	71	280	9000				Richard BOXALL	(Eng)	69	73	75	71	288	1500
	Fredrik LINDGREN	(Swe)	66	68	77	69	280	9000				David WILLIAMS	(Eng)	69	73	73	73	288	1500
9	Lee WESTWOOD	(Eng)	68	72	69	72	281	5640				José RIVERO	(Sp)	73	69	73	73	288	1500
	Paul AFFLECK	(Wal)	71	69	69	72	281	5640				Steven BOTTOMLEY	(Eng)	74	68	73	73	288	1500
	Diego BORREGO	(Sp)	70	69	70	72	281	5640				Joakim HAEGGMAN	(Swe)	70	73	71	74	288	1500
	Wayne RILEY	(Aus)	69	70	72	70	281	5640				Sandy LYLE	(Scot)	73	70	75	70	288	1500
	Ross MCFARLANE	(Eng)	65	70	75	71	281	5640				Barry LANE	(Eng)	72	71	73	72	288	1500
14	Ian PALMER	(SA)	71	70	70	71	282	4230				Mark LITTON	(Wal)	70	70	72	76	288	1500
	David GILFORD	(Eng)	69	74	72	67	282	4230				Phil GOLDING	(Eng)	69	71	72	76	288	1500
	Andrew SHERBORNE	(Eng)	66	72	72	72	282	4230			55	Jon ROBSON	(Eng)	71	71	69	78	289	1005
	Mark JAMES	(Eng)	69	67	73	73	282	4230				Iain PYMAN	(Eng)	72	71	72	74	289	1005
	Costantino ROCCA	(It)	69	66	74	73	282	4230				Adam HUNTER	(Scot)	74	69	71	75	289	1005
19	Malcolm MACKENZIE	(Eng)	69	72	74	68	283	3288				Eamonn DARCY	(Ire)	70	73	70	76	289	1005
	Derrick COOPER	(Eng)	72	69	73	69	283	3288				Paul BROADHURST	(Eng)	69	72	73	75	289	1005
	Howard CLARK	(Eng)	70	71	71	71	283	3288				José COCERES	(Arg)	73	66	75	75	289	1005
	Alberto BINAGHI	(It)	71	70	68	74	283	3288			61	Manuel CALERO	(Sp)	72	70	73	75	290	840
	Liam WHITE	(Eng)	71	69	70	73	283	3288				Scott WATSON	(Eng)	70	71	76	73	290	840
24	José Maria CAÑIZARES	(Sp)	67	73	71	72	283	3288				Russell CLAYDON	(Eng)	69	71	74	76	290	840
	Manuel PIÑERO	(Sp)	71	68	72	72	283	3288			64	Miguel Angel MARTIN	(Sp)	71	72	76	72	291	765
	Peter BAKER	(Eng)	68	70	71	74	283	3288				Gordon BRAND JNR.	(Scot)	69	72	75	75	291	765
	Brian BARNES	(Scot)	71	65	74	73	283	3288			66	Peter TERAVAINEN	(USA)	72	70	76	74	292	445
	Vicente FERNANDEZ	(Arg)	68	67	71	77	283	3288				Niclas FASTH	(Swe)	72	70	76	74	292	445
29	Stuart CAGE	(Eng)	72	68	70	74	284	2745				Emanuele CANONICA	(It)	73	70	78	71	292	445
	Paul CURRY	(Eng)	69	70	72	73	284	2745				Paul MAYO	(Wal)	75	68	71	78	292	445
31	Olle KARLSSON	(Swe)	73	67	75	70	285	2565				Gary ORR	(Scot)	74	69	76	73	292	445
	Paul WAY	(Eng)	69	69	70	77	285	2565				Bernard GALLACHER	(Scot)	71	72	75	74	292	445
33	Peter MITCHELL	(Eng)	72	69	73	72	286	2370				Sergio GARCIA	(Sp)	73	70	73	76	292	(Am)
	Des SMYTH	(Ire)	69	73	73	71	286	2370			72	Mats HALLBERG	(Swe)	71	72	73	77	293	438
	Roger CHAPMAN	(Eng)	71	72	71	72	286	2370			73	Mats LANNER	(Swe)	74	69	75	76	294	436
	Gary EMERSON	(Eng)	70	68	74	74	286	2370			74	Eoghan O'CONNELL	(Ire)	71	72	74	81	298	434
37	Mike MILLER	(Scot)	70	72	72	73	287	2040			75	John MELLOR	(Eng)	71	71	81	76	299	432
	Alexander CEJKA	(Ger)	71	71	72	73	287	2040			76	Yago BEAMONTE	(Sp)	71	72	79	80	302	430

SHOT OF THE WEEK

Robert Karlsson, second shot, 16th hole, final round. On another day it might have been regarded as just another shot, but it was made vitally important by the three bogeys that had preceded it. Karlsson had dropped shots at the 12th, 13th and 14th to see his lead narrowed to two, but the nine iron he hit to ten feet from 122 yards set up the birdie that put clear daylight between him and the pursuing pack again. It was the shot that effectively won the tournament.

TURESPAÑA
OPEN Mediterrania
COMUNITAT VALENCIANA

ESPAÑA ESPAÑA
Passion for Golf

Alexander the Great

Alexander Cejka showed that

Bernhard Langer isn't the only German golfer

capable of winning on the Tour

Christopher Columbus made Huelva the departing point for his voyage of discovery in 1492. A little over 500 years later, it is where Alexander Cejka 'arrived'. The journey, in its own way, was equally adventurous; the story, in golfing terms, as extraordinary.

Cejka won the Turespaña Open Andalucia, at Islantilla, just along the Costa de la Luz from the port town of Huelva, by three shots from Italy's Costantino Rocca. 'This is a dream come true,' the 24-year old said in time-honoured fashion for those achieving their maiden Tour victories.

But this was a triumph Cejka never dared dream when growing up in communist Czechoslovakia. Golf meant hanging round while his father, an engineer and 16-handicapper, played at their local course in Marianske Lazne, the oldest golf club in the country. Royalty, premiers, the cream of high society played here in the heyday of the famous spa town. But the club barely made it through the communist era, and when Cejka patted a ball around the fringes with a cut down club, it must have seemed an improbable future

venue for a Tour event.

In 1980, aged nine, Cejka and his father escaped a bleak future, first going on holiday to Yugoslavia, then fleeing through Italy and Switzerland to Germany. Two years after arriving in Frankfurt, Cejka had been gripped by the game. When the German Open came to town, he had eyes for one man, Bernhard Langer. 'I remember one day, he walked right by me and I looked up to him as a big star,' said Cejka.

'He is still my hero. It is hard to believe that I now play in the same tournaments and play practice rounds with him. You can learn so much from just watching. Bernhard was on his own for many, many years, but now I have won, Sven Strüver has come close and there are

others waiting to come through. Hopefully German golf will move on again.'

Cejka was a scratch amateur at 16, but took his time like many others to make it through the PGA European Tour Qualifying School, his fifth attempt being successful in 1993. Up to then he had won four times on the Challenge Tour, including the Czech Open twice in 1990 and 1992. In 1994, a promising year was interrupted all too often, for five weeks in August due to sunstroke, by missing his tee-time after being caught in traffic when doing well at German Masters, and then by food poisoning, meaning that he spent the week of the Czech Open, now a fully-fledged tournament, in hospital.

Nothing of his early 1995 form sug-

47

SHOT OF THE WEEK

The problem hole all week was the par four 13th, which most played as a par five as the narrow entrance to the green was best negotiated with a pitch. Cejka laid up in just the right spot, 60 yards back and then hit his wedge to six feet and holed the putt for his first par of the week there. A possible mishap avoided, he celebrated by pumping his arm in the air. 'That was the moment I thought I could win,' Cejka said. 'That changed my whole round and my mind.'

gested a win was around the corner, but neither was he playing badly. It was by cutting out the mistakes that he won his first tournament. 'I made a few good saves and a few good putts,' he said. 'Few' was the wrong word, as he showed remarkable consistency with rounds of 71, 68, 70, 69. No-one else managed to avoid straying over par for all four days.

The Islantilla course, on the hills over looking the ocean, proved an exacting test, especially as the sea breeze constantly blew and swirled through the pine trees. Des Smyth plotted his way round on Thursday morning for a three under par 68, on which mark he was joined by Santigao Luna, the only man not to have a bogey on the day.

Rocca found a golden touch with his putter on Friday, taking just 12 putts in the last ten holes in his 65. But this was a course on which you went low only once. On Saturday he had the worse score of the day, a 78. 'Everything went wrong' he said. Instead, Anders Forsbrand caught up in a hurry with 29 to the turn, 11 putts, and then protecting his score superbly on the potentially disastrous back nine for a new record 64.

The Swede, who lives on the Costa del Sol, found himself sharing the lead with Cejka going into the final round. Against theory, the experienced winner bogeyed the first, while the rookie birdied it. Another at the third put Cejka three in front. 'I was not nervous at all, especially after such a good start,' said Cejka. Forsbrand finally got into gear with birdies at the eighth and the ninth, but was still two behind. Then he collapsed.

Three bogeys in a row starting at the 11th only brought a double bogey at the 14th. No-one else was making a charge, only a resurgent Rocca, who was just too far back. 'When I saw Rocca had bogeyed the 17th, I knew I just had to keep cool,' Cejka added.

A free spirit, you can imagine the young man on his motorbike, his flowing locks – he occasionally sports a ponytail – streaming out as he rides over the Bavarian plains near his Munich home. Cejka became a German citizen three years ago, making him the second Tour winner from that country after Langer. But what of the country of his birth, where he still regularly visits family. 'Maybe they will claim me as the first Czech to win on Tour,' he said.

Andrew Farrell

THE COURSE

Designed by Luis Recasens and Enrique Canales, whose son José is the club's director, the Islantilla course sits in the hills above the coast, winding its way through a pine forest. The narrow fairways put a premium on long iron play, while the short game must also be in top condition. Avoiding disaster on the back nine, and at the 13th in particular, is essential to post a good score. Only four players finished under par for four rounds. The club also features Spain's only women head professional, Macerena Tey.

ISLANTILLA GC, SPAIN, MARCH 2-5, 1995 · YARDAGE 6677 · PAR 71

Pos	Name	Country	Rnd 1	Rnd 2	Rnd 3	Rnd 4	Total	Prize Money £
1	Alexander CEJKA	(Ger)	71	68	70	69	278	49344
2	Costantino ROCCA	(It)	71	65	78	67	281	32893
3	Paul MCGINLEY	(Ire)	71	74	69	69	283	16668
	Wayne RILEY	(Aus)	70	73	68	72	283	16668
5	Olle KARLSSON	(Swe)	72	76	69	67	284	11448
	Anders FORSBRAND	(Swe)	73	72	64	75	284	11448
7	Paolo QUIRICI	(Swi)	71	71	69	74	285	8882
8	Des SMYTH	(Ire)	68	71	76	71	286	6093
	Fabrice TARNAUD	(Fr)	70	72	73	71	286	6093
	Mark MOULAND	(Wal)	70	75	70	71	286	6093
	Barry LANE	(Eng)	74	70	70	72	286	6093
	Jon ROBSON	(Eng)	71	69	72	74	286	6093
13	José RIVERO	(Sp)	75	72	71	69	287	4187
	Andrew SHERBORNE	(Eng)	72	75	70	70	287	4187
	Pedro LINHART	(Sp)	72	73	71	71	287	4187
	David WILLIAMS	(Eng)	74	72	69	72	287	4187
	Peter MITCHELL	(Eng)	73	73	69	72	287	4187
	Phillip PRICE	(Wal)	69	71	74	73	287	4187
	Marc FARRY	(Fr)	72	71	69	75	287	4187
20	John BICKERTON	(Eng)	71	72	74	71	288	3286
	José Maria OLAZÁBAL	(Sp)	72	76	70	70	288	3286
	Juan PIÑERO	(Sp)	72	72	74	70	288	3286
	Russell CLAYDON	(Eng)	72	72	74	70	288	3286
	Ian PALMER	(SA)	70	74	75	69	288	3286
	Mike MCLEAN	(Eng)	75	73	68	72	288	3286
	John MELLOR	(Eng)	72	74	70	72	288	3286
27	Mathias GRÖNBERG	(Swe)	73	74	71	71	289	2631
	Tomas Jesus MUNOZ	(Sp)	72	72	74	71	289	2631
	Peter HEDBLOM	(Swe)	71	72	75	71	289	2631
	Ross MCFARLANE	(Eng)	73	71	73	72	289	2631
	José Maria CAÑIZARES	(Sp)	72	76	69	72	289	2631
	Peter BAKER	(Eng)	76	71	70	72	289	2631
	Santiago LUNA	(Sp)	68	73	74	74	289	2631
	Jonathan LOMAS	(Eng)	74	71	69	75	289	2631
35	Ignacio GARRIDO	(Sp)	77	69	73	71	290	2125
	Paul R SIMPSON	(Eng)	73	70	76	71	290	2125
	Sam TORRANCE	(Scot)	70	74	73	73	290	2125
	John MCHENRY	(Ire)	73	74	69	74	290	2125
	Domingo HOSPITAL	(Sp)	70	74	71	75	290	2125
	Eoghan O'CONNELL	(Ire)	71	75	69	75	290	2125
	David CARTER	(Eng)	73	66	75	76	290	2125
42	Stephen MCALLISTER	(Scot)	73	71	74	73	291	1776
	Alberto BINAGHI	(It)	74	72	73	72	291	1776
	Paul WAY	(Eng)	76	72	72	71	291	1776
	Daren LEE	(Eng)	74	70	76	71	291	1776
	André BOSSERT	(Swi)	72	76	73	70	291	1776
47	Stephen DODD	(Wal)	76	72	70	74	292	1421
	Roger CHAPMAN	(Eng)	74	71	74	73	292	1421
	Miguel Angel JIMÉNEZ	(Sp)	72	75	74	71	292	1421
	Jesus Maria ARRUTI	(Sp)	74	71	71	76	292	1421
	Mats HALLBERG	(Swe)	72	75	69	76	292	1421
	Carl MASON	(Eng)	75	72	68	77	292	1421
	Paul MAYO	(Wal)	72	71	71	78	292	1421
54	Mark LITTON	(Wal)	81	67	72	73	293	1184
55	Philip TALBOT	(Eng)	76	71	74	73	294	1065
	Vicente FERNANDEZ	(Arg)	72	75	74	73	294	1065
	Diego BORREGO	(Sp)	72	72	73	77	294	1065
58	Liam WHITE	(Eng)	72	72	73	78	295	947
59	Derrick COOPER	(Eng)	73	74	72	77	296	903
	Silvio GRAPPASONNI	(It)	74	72	74	76	296	903
61	Mark DAVIS	(Eng)	72	73	74	78	297	799
	Francisco VALERA	(Sp)	70	75	75	77	297	799
	Steen TINNING	(Den)	74	73	74	76	297	799
	Sandy LYLE	(Scot)	73	71	77	76	297	799
	Joakim GRONHAGEN	(Swe)	75	73	74	75	297	799
66	Manuel MORENO	(Sp)	74	74	76	74	298	444
67	Lee WESTWOOD	(Eng)	73	74	73	81	301	442

Wayne Riley's bid for victory came up short again.

49

James sweeps in with new putter

A recent convert to the broomhandle putter,

Mark James used it to telling effect

for his 17th Tour victory

The PGA European Tour is all about the pursuit of excellence and one of its most eagerly anticipated events is the annual visit to Agadir, not least because its members rarely experience the level of exclusivity provided by their Moroccan hosts.

And when they returned to the superbly conditioned Royal links inside the salmon-pink walls of the King's palace for the third year running, nothing had changed – even to the extent that all 18 flagsticks were in precisely the same positions in which they had been placed for the final round 12 months previously.

The colourful Bedouin-style tents housing clubhouse amenities and restaurants were sited as usual around the lake to provide surely the most exotic backdrop to any practice ground: and the sun shone warmly on the Sahara Cup preamble in which Europe's team led by Sam Torrance trounced Africa 4-0 in a better-ball contest.

All was thus set fair on and off the course and the Tour's newest champion Alexander Cejka contributed to the air of continuity by following up his Turespaña Open Andalucia victory with a record equalling first round 66 containing only 26 putts to lead Torrance by one shot. To no one's surprise Moroccan specialist Robert

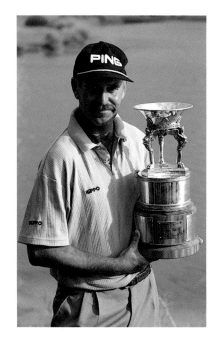

Karlsson who had won the Open Mediterrania in Valencia from Torrance, was in the group a stroke further back.

Yet odd things were afoot that were to have a profound influence on the destiny of the title. First came the decision by Mark James, the new chairman of the Tournament Committee, and veteran of six Ryder Cup by Johnnie Walker contests, to transfer his allegiance to a broomhandle putter which he was using for the first time in competition. Then Cejka announced that the legacy of his

exploits on the hard ground at Islantilla was a bad case of water on the knee. Within a few hours everyone else was also struggling to cope with a surfeit of H20.

For the whole of the second round it rained, and it rained, and it rained. And the tournament was played out in the wettest weather Agadir had experienced for more than two years. It spoke volumes for the quality of the course that play was uninterrupted, although many competitors, were ill-equipped to cope with the unexpected desert storm.

Torrance was among those who did best, after removing his saturated slacks in a tent behind the sixth green, and wearing only his waterproof over-trousers for the remainder of the damp and chilly second stage. Others soldiered on as best they could and the halfway leaderboard reflected the efforts of those who showed the most resolve.

Torrance and Robert Karlsson, both at seven under par, led the field into the third day, with Cejka just behind. David Gilford, winner of the title on his last two appearances was within striking distance, and so was James, playing with growing confidence after starting with two rounds of 70.

Although he had been among Europe's top ten on six occasions in his 19

Sam Torrance led after three rounds.

previous seasons, James had rarely been satisfied with the quality of his putting. It had caused him particularly anguish during the 1993 match against the USA and he had experimented during the winter break with a long putter that had been in his possession for almost two years. The success that his contemporary Torrance had achieved with a similar club as he

SHOT OF THE WEEK

Two players shared the distinction of rare birdies at the ninth in the final round: David Gilford (below, centre) and Robert Karlsson (below, left). From almost identical positions in the heart of the fairway Gilford first struck a four wood from around 200 yards which pitched five feet short of the flag. Karlsson stuck his three iron approach with such accuracy that it flew straight over the flag to land five feet above the hole. Both then converted the birdie chances their precision had created.

entered the autumn of his career was an additional spur for a golfer who had gone almost two years without adding to his 16 Tour victories. But although his mind was made up, he had not mastered the technique of consistently accurate stroking with the 48-inch club despite hours of practice on a putting carpet at home.

It was a tip from Torrance who advised James to change his grip and clasp the club to his chest rather than hold it under his chin, that provided the key. After completing his third successive round of 70 the Englishman knew he had rediscovered the means to capitalise on the strength of his driving and iron play.

Torrance still had the edge at the start of the final round having birdied the 18th for the third day running to head James, Karlsson and Cejka by one stroke with Gilford in fifth place after a third day 69.

The stage was therefore set for a 'High Noon' shoot-out between the long handles of sharp-shooting Sam and marksman Jesse, and the rivalry intensified when the latter had four birdies in the first six holes to get out in 33.

The lofty Karlsson, who had been second, fourth and third in his previous Moroccan Opens was looking for the missing number, and Gilford, shortly to make his first appearance in the US Masters, was also at home in the persistent rain. Karlsson charged to the turn in 32 to displace Torrance (35) as leader and

Gilford was hot on the trail of a personal hat-trick after also getting out in 33. The Midlander looked likely to achieve it when he set a new course record of 65 after making four more birdies in the last six holes, that from 25 feet at the 18th enabling him to post a 12 under par target of 276.

Gilford described his round as 'one of the best 18 holes I have ever played' and Karlsson was highly satisfied with his quality of striking in his 67 to finish one behind, declaring that he had played 'better than on any day in my win at Valencia', but without holing three birdie putts under ten feet in the last three holes.

James however, was on target every time he pulled the broomstick out of his bag. The long putt he holed on the ninth to escape with a bogey after an adventure in the trees, sent his confidence soaring. He birdied the 11th and 12th, snapped up the birdie fours on offer at the 15th and 17th and in between sank a crucial par saver from five feet.

He counted only 26 putts after the most solid of par fours at the 18th to be home in 32, taking a share of the course record and victory by one stroke from Gilford, with Karlsson and the fast-finishing Cejka. 'My new putter felt reasonable from the moment I holed from six feet on the first green in the first round,' said James. 'In the last round it was brilliant and I could not believe how well I putted under pressure in the closing stages. I have putted poorly for 18 years so I don't expect to suddenly become a great putter after all this time, just better and more consistent.'

Torrance, relegated to fifth place alongside Adam Hunter and Phillip Price, had mixed feelings after being swept aside by the birdie avalanche from old rival James. 'I am delighted for him,' he said. 'The only surprise to me is that it has taken so long for others to appreciate the benefit of the long putter.'

Mike Britten

ROYAL GOLF LINKS AGADIR, MARCH 9-12, 1995 · YARDAGE 6657 · PAR 72

Pos	Name	Country	Rnd 1	Rnd 2	Rnd 3	Rnd 4	Total	Prize Money £
1	Mark JAMES	(Eng)	70	70	70	65	275	58330
2	David GILFORD	(Eng)	71	71	69	65	276	38880
3	Robert KARLSSON	(Swe)	68	69	73	67	277	21910
4	Alexander CEJKA	(Ger)	66	72	72	68	278	17500
5	Phillip PRICE	(Wal)	71	72	69	68	280	13540
	Sam TORRANCE	(Scot)	67	70	72	71	280	13540
7	Adam HUNTER	(Scot)	75	68	69	71	283	9625
	Russell CLAYDON	(Eng)	69	75	69	70	283	9625
9	Andrew COLTART	(Scot)	70	72	72	70	284	7820
10	Anders GILLNER	(Swe)	68	73	73	71	285	6272
	Roger CHAPMAN	(Eng)	74	70	69	72	285	6272
	Jeff HAWKES	(SA)	73	70	72	70	285	6272
	Howard CLARK	(Eng)	70	77	70	68	285	6272
14	David CARTER	(Eng)	69	73	71	73	286	4833
	Eamonn DARCY	(Ire)	68	74	70	74	286	4833
	Malcolm MACKENZIE	(Eng)	68	72	73	73	286	4833
	Paul AFFLECK	(Wal)	73	70	72	71	286	4833
	Antoine LEBOUC	(Fr)	72	75	66	73	286	4833
	Per-Ulrik JOHANSSON	(Swe)	73	70	73	70	286	4833
20	Neal BRIGGS	(Eng)	73	74	69	71	287	4042
	Olle KARLSSON	(Swe)	74	70	69	74	287	4042
	Mike MCLEAN	(Eng)	73	70	73	71	287	4042
	Anders FORSBRAND	(Swe)	75	71	70	71	287	4042
24	Paul MCGINLEY	(Ire)	70	74	75	69	288	3570
	Paolo QUIRICI	(Swi)	72	72	71	73	288	3570
	Michael JONZON	(Swe)	70	74	76	68	288	3570
	Costantino ROCCA	(It)	72	70	71	75	288	3570
	Per HAUGSRUD	(Nor)	75	72	72	69	288	3570
29	Mats LANNER	(Swe)	71	76	73	69	289	3010
	André BOSSERT	(Swi)	69	74	74	72	289	3010
	Peter MITCHELL	(Eng)	71	72	75	71	289	3010
	Pedro LINHART	(Sp)	71	75	69	74	289	3010
	José COCERES	(Arg)	74	70	68	77	289	3010
	Steven BOTTOMLEY	(Eng)	77	69	72	71	289	3010
35	Rolf MUNTZ	(Hol)	71	73	77	69	290	2485
	Liam WHITE	(Eng)	73	74	71	72	290	2485
	Raymond BURNS	(N.Ire)	71	74	73	72	290	2485
	Paul R SIMPSON	(Eng)	72	74	74	70	290	2485
	Steven RICHARDSON	(Eng)	70	71	75	74	290	2485
	Peter BAKER	(Eng)	77	70	71	72	290	2485
	Gordon BRAND JNR.	(Scot)	70	77	74	69	290	2485
	Vicente FERNANDEZ	(Arg)	69	75	74	72	290	2485
43	Paul EALES	(Eng)	69	78	72	72	291	2100
	Gavin LEVENSON	(SA)	69	71	77	74	291	2100
	Ross DRUMMOND	(Scot)	77	69	70	75	291	2100
46	Dennis EDLUND	(Swe)	74	72	74	72	292	1855
	Gary ORR	(Scot)	70	74	75	73	292	1855
	Brian MARCHBANK	(Scot)	72	73	78	69	292	1855
	Jeremy ROBINSON	(Eng)	70	73	74	75	292	1855
50	Barry LANE	(Eng)	71	75	74	73	293	1505
	Tony JOHNSTONE	(Zim)	72	72	76	73	293	1505
	Michel BESANCENEY	(Fr)	68	75	74	76	293	1505
	Martyn ROBERTS	(Wal)	75	72	72	74	293	1505
	Ian SPENCER	(Eng)	72	70	80	71	293	1505
	Jay TOWNSEND	(USA)	71	76	74	72	293	1505
56	Anders SØRENSEN	(Den)	75	69	76	74	294	1190
	David RAY	(Eng)	71	72	75	76	294	1190
	Nicolas VANHOOTEGEM	(Bel)	72	73	78	71	294	1190
59	David WILLIAMS	(Eng)	71	73	77	74	295	1067
	Ross MCFARLANE	(Eng)	74	72	76	73	295	1067
61	George RYALL	(Eng)	72	73	80	72	297	997
	David R JONES	(Eng)	69	75	78	75	297	997
63	Jean Louis GUEPY	(Fr)	71	73	75	79	298	945
64	Joakim GRONHAGEN	(Swe)	74	71	79	75	299	892
	Stephen AMES	(T&T)	73	73	73	80	299	892
66	Jonathan LOMAS	(Eng)	72	74	80	76	302	525
67	Emanuele CANONICA	(It)	73	74	75	83	305	523

THE COURSE

One of the masterpieces of Robert Trent Jones, the Royal links is a truly regal test of shot-making with the emphasis on straight driving and positional play, particularly on the par fives where nests of bunkers threaten those who put power before accuracy. The short 12th and 14th provide challenging variety for both tee shots are played over water to undulating greens. But the most difficult hole is the 457 yards ninth, a sharp right hand dog-leg among eucalyptus trees where the drive has to avoid two bunkers guarding the angle and a long iron second shot has to find a relatively small elevated green.

Hunter comes home

After ten years of trying
Adam Hunter finally broke through
for his maiden Tour victory

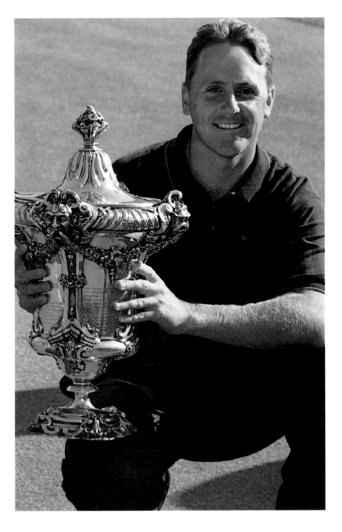

Behind every successful man there is a good woman. It's the same in golf, just ask Adam Hunter.

The 31-year old Scot was on the point of turning his back on tournament golf in January 1994 after a decade of toil, disappointment and frustration with his morale at rock bottom. Something had to be done, so he applied for the coaching job with the Scottish Golf Union. 'I wasn't getting anywhere and I thought it was time to hang my sticks up,' he said.

If successful it would mean a 'steady job' at home in Glasgow with his family, away from the weekly hustle and bustle of chasing prize money around Europe. But again he was out of luck. The job went to fellow pro Bill Lockie, leaving Hunter's career clearly at the crossroads.

It was then that his wife Caroline took a hand. She told him he was good enough, that he should carry on and redouble his efforts at building a solid playing career. Even then it wasn't plain sailing. A few months later during the 1994 Volvo PGA Championship at Wentworth, Hunter's will was questioned again when Caroline, who was expecting their second child, was rushed into hospital. 'She lost the baby and I wanted to pull out and go home,' he said, 'but she told me to stay and play well. It focused my mind and I did well, finishing eighth to win £20,000.'

That wasn't the end of his problems. The rest of the season was fairly uneventful and at the end he finished up 69th on the money list. The future didn't look bright. 'I was fed up with just making up the numbers for so long. I felt I was working harder at my game than anyone else but I was getting nowhere,' Hunter explained. Then he remembered Caroline's words.

The examples of Nick Faldo and Nick Price impressed Hunter and he felt what was good for them, could be good for him. He decided to fly to Florida and seek out coaching guru David Leadbetter to work on his game and he also did something about his fitness. 'All the top guys are superbly fit and I wasn't.' he said. 'I had to get myself into shape.' So it was off to see Paul Darby, the former Wolverhampton Wanderers physiotherapist, and the result was a new slimline Hunter who was destined for greater things.

55

SHOT OF THE WEEK

Adam Hunter's second shot on the 542-yard 72nd hole with a driver from the fairway, fully 275 yards to eight feet. It should have set up an eagle three, but the putt never threatened the hole and he had to settle for a birdie. 'I totally misread it,' he admitted.

way. Both hit good drives but Hunter looked in trouble when he found a greenside bunker with his second shot, a driver from the fairway. Clarke's approach finished left, just off the green in thick rough, but he fluffed his chip and took two putts from 30 feet for his par.

Hunter, on the other hand, played masterfully from the sand to eight feet

Paul McGinley came close again.

All that hard work was destined to bear fruit and all was gathered in over the testing Penha Longa course near the holiday resort of Estoril when Hunter won the Portuguese Open Championship at the first hole of sudden death against Ulsterman Darren Clarke.

The Celtic rivals had finished on 11 under-par 277, Hunter with a closing 68, thanks to a birdie four at the last, and Clarke with 70. With Clarke just back from finishing runner-up in the previous week's Malaysian Open, he was favoured to take the £50,000 first prize.

But when they returned to the 542-yard 18th it didn't quite work out that and calmly swept in the putt for his second birdie at that hole within a matter of minutes, but for victory this time.

'I expected Adam to make that putt,' said Clarke. 'He made a great four but I played well. My second shot was about five yards from being perfect. Then the lie was bad and I couldn't get my club to the

56

back of the ball.'

Clarke was not the only Irishman lamenting his luck. Paul McGinley began the final round as joint leader on nine under par 207 with Clarke and Italy's Costantino Rocca. Hunter was one of seven players two shots back.

While Rocca crashed out with a 75, McGinley looked to have a first tournament win in his grasp. With six holes to play he was 12 under and two ahead with no one mounting a challenge. But sud-

Darren Clarke had to give best to Adam Hunter in the play-off.

denly it began to go wrong.

Bogeys at the 14th and the 16th saw McGinley slip behind and another at the 17th left him two adrift. Then to compound his demise he three-putted the 18th for another bogey to finish 73 for 280 and three shots out of the play off.

With Hunter in the clubhouse on 11 under, Clarke still had a chance to snatch

victory on his own if he could birdie the 18th. He drove poorly, chose to hit his second down the adjacent first fairway, wedged over the greenside bunkers and took two putts for a par five and 70 to match Hunter's mark.

Minutes later Clarke redeemed himself by finding the middle of the 18th fairway, but it was to prove in vain as Hunter's day had come and few would deny him that sweet taste of victory.

Dave Hamilton   57

PENHA LONGA GC, SINTRA, LISBON, MARCH 16-19, 1995 · YARDAGE 6864 · PAR 72

Pos	Name	Country	Rnd 1	Rnd 2	Rnd 3	Rnd 4	Total	Prize Money £
1	Adam HUNTER	(Scot)	73	65	71	68	277	50000
2	Darren CLARKE	(N.Ire)	72	69	66	70	277	33330
3	José COCERES	(Arg)	69	72	68	69	278	18780
4	Jon ROBSON	(Eng)	70	71	68	71	280	12733
	Tony JOHNSTONE	(Zim)	71	68	71	70	280	12733
	Paul MCGINLEY	(Ire)	74	65	68	73	280	12733
7	Fredrik LINDGREN	(Swe)	71	73	69	68	281	7730
	Paul CURRY	(Eng)	68	70	73	70	281	7730
	Miguel Angel JIMÉNEZ	(Sp)	68	66	75	72	281	7730
10	Russell CLAYDON	(Eng)	70	74	69	69	282	4962
	Carl MASON	(Eng)	72	71	71	68	282	4962
	Paul LAWRIE	(Scot)	75	67	68	72	282	4962
	Ross MCFARLANE	(Eng)	70	71	70	71	282	4962
	Jamie SPENCE	(Eng)	74	67	69	72	282	4962
	Mark DAVIS	(Eng)	71	67	72	72	282	4962
	Costantino ROCCA	(It)	68	69	70	75	282	4962
17	Peter MITCHELL	(Eng)	75	69	67	72	283	3880
	Ian PALMER	(SA)	77	66	66	74	283	3880
	Paul BROADHURST	(Eng)	69	71	71	72	283	3880
20	Mike CLAYTON	(Aus)	76	70	66	72	284	3465
	Jean VAN DE VELDE	(Fr)	72	69	68	75	284	3465
	Peter HEDBLOM	(Swe)	72	69	74	69	284	3465
	David RAY	(Eng)	72	68	74	70	284	3465
24	Christian CEVAER	(Fr)	71	74	70	70	285	3105
	Jeff HAWKES	(SA)	75	70	70	70	285	3105
	Andrew SHERBORNE	(Eng)	70	71	73	71	285	3105
	David GILFORD	(Eng)	69	70	75	71	285	3105
28	Gordon BRAND JNR.	(Scot)	76	68	71	71	286	2700
	André BOSSERT	(Swi)	75	69	71	71	286	2700
	Barry LANE	(Eng)	74	71	73	68	286	2700
	David J RUSSELL	(Eng)	76	69	71	70	286	2700
	David CARTER	(Eng)	72	69	74	71	286	2700
33	Mike HARWOOD	(Aus)	78	68	70	71	287	2370
	Ignacio GARRIDO	(Sp)	76	67	72	72	287	2370
	Paul WAY	(Eng)	70	72	75	70	287	2370
	Richard BOXALL	(Eng)	72	69	72	74	287	2370
37	Mark JAMES	(Eng)	72	73	72	71	288	2100
	Malcolm MACKENZIE	(Eng)	71	72	74	71	288	2100
	Eamonn DARCY	(Ire)	74	68	71	75	288	2100
	Andrew MURRAY	(Eng)	68	73	71	76	288	2100
	John BICKERTON	(Eng)	72	68	74	74	288	2100
42	Antonio SOBRINHO	(Port)	76	69	70	74	289	1770
	Robert KARLSSON	(Swe)	76	69	73	71	289	1770
	Mathias GRÖNBERG	(Swe)	74	72	70	73	289	1770
	Craig CASSELLS	(Eng)	73	73	70	73	289	1770
	Paolo QUIRICI	(Swi)	75	67	67	80	289	1770
	Neal BRIGGS	(Eng)	71	69	73	76	289	1770
48	Santiago LUNA	(Sp)	73	72	73	72	290	1500
	Daniel WESTERMARK	(Swe)	73	72	72	73	290	1500
	Andrew OLDCORN	(Eng)	74	72	71	73	290	1500
51	José Maria CAÑIZARES	(Sp)	74	71	71	75	291	1290
	Liam WHITE	(Eng)	74	72	75	70	291	1290
	Pedro LINHART	(Sp)	72	74	69	76	291	1290
	Howard CLARK	(Eng)	71	70	73	77	291	1290
55	Alberto BINAGHI	(It)	77	68	72	75	292	1110
	Ronan RAFFERTY	(N.Ire)	72	72	76	72	292	1110
57	Jay TOWNSEND	(USA)	77	67	76	73	293	990
	Mark ROE	(Eng)	74	72	73	74	293	990
59	Gavin LEVENSON	(SA)	69	76	75	75	295	930
60	Wayne RILEY	(Aus)	71	73	77	75	296	870
	Darrell KESTNER	(USA)	73	73	76	74	296	870
	Michel BESANCENEY	(Fr)	73	71	80	72	296	870
63	Wayne WESTNER	(SA)	75	70	75	79	299	795
	Keith ASHDOWN	(Eng)	73	73	76	77	299	795
65	Daniel SILVA	(Port)	76	70	75	79	300	600
	Scott WATSON	(Eng)	73	71	80	76	300	600

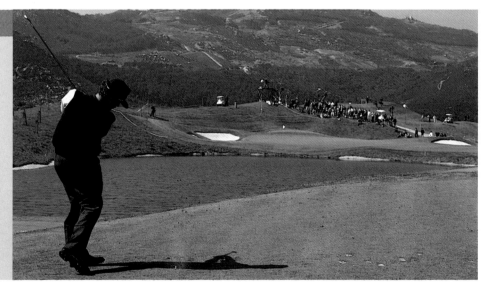

THE COURSE

Penha Longa, or Long Rock, is a Robert Trent Jones Junior design, built on the site of a 14th century monastery and situated in the Sintra Hills, half an hour from the Portuguese capital of Lisbon and just inland from the holiday resort of Estoril. The par 72 course occupies a hilly terrain where the wind can be a crucial factor.

Breakthrough victory for Adam Hunter.

Turner surprises himself

When Greg Turner made his first

appearance on the 1995 Tour

victory was the last thing on his mind

When New Zealand's Greg Turner put the 'gone fishing' sign above his door in Dunedin at the end of the 1994 golf season he was a contented man. For the second year running he had finished in the top 30 on the PGA European Tour, made his fifth appearance in the Alfred Dunhill Cup at St Andrews, and represented his country for the ninth successive year in the World Cup in Puerto Rico where he and Frank Nobilo were a creditable fourth behind runaway winners USA. He therefore had every justification for taking a four months break during which he fished for trout, indulged his passion for modern political literature, and played golf when he felt like it.

So when he arrived in Majorca in mid-March for his first European appearance of 1995 in the Turespaña Open Baleares it was more a question of removing the rust from his swing rather than harbouring serious ambitions of a winning start to his tenth PGA European Tour season.

Certainly Turner thought as much when he took four putts on the opening green of the unfamiliar Santa Ponsa No 2 course to start his first round with a triple bogey seven. And there seemed little cause for great optimism when his opening 74 left him sharing 47th place with 14 other golfers, seven shots behind Welshman Mark Mouland and Canary Islander Pedro Linhart.

Yet such is the glorious uncertainty of golf that three days later Turner was celebrating a two stroke victory having played the subsequent 54 holes in 16 under par and netted a Johnnie Walker Tour Course Record Award in the process.

Six birdies and an eagle three at the 17th on the second day enabled the tall Kiwi to establish a record for this new Tour venue, but although it elevated him to third place with Ross McFarlane, Turner was still three shots behind the revitalised Mouland at the halfway mark.

In between was the formidable figure of Costantino Rocca, already a runner-up in the Turespaña Open Andalucia.

Mouland, a former Dutch Open champion, was reaping the benefit of a new approach to tournament golf, enforced he declared by the level of fitness and dedication being achieved by ambitious younger rivals. "Their lifestyle of regular work-outs in the gym, no alcohol and early nights might be boring," he remarked, "but they are getting the job done". Mouland had not been in serious contention for a title since he lost a play-off for the 1990 Tenerife Open. Indeed he had struggled to retain his Tour card in two of the previous four seasons. But in the early months of 1995 he was a more frequent visitor to the practice ground and in Majorca he saw the first benefits. "I am working harder and I am feeling happier with myself," he declared after opening rounds of 67 and 69 had put him in command of the leaderboard. "Professional golf is all about consistency and not missing cuts. You cannot make a living sitting at home watching golf on television at the weekend."

Eleven birdies in his first 28 holes reflected the quality of his driving and iron play, but his putting was unable to keep pace. It had been his Achilles heel in the previous four seasons, and when Mouland missed a string of chances at the end of his second round and throughout the third, the rest of the field took fresh heart.

They came to terms with the eccentricities of a course that meandered through olive trees, some of them in the middle of narrow fairways, for 12 holes,

SHOT OF THE WEEK

This was played by Swede Jarmo Sandelin, who beat Seve Ballesteros to win the Open Canarias, at the 518-yard 17th. Not with the 56-inch 'broomhandle' driver he unveiled at Santa Ponsa, but with a six iron from a gravel path on a steep bank of the island fairway. From 165 yards he put his ball within ten feet of the hole for an eagle three.

Barry Lane put up a stout defence of the title.

and then opened out into an expanse of lakes and streams. And they knew that the best chance of making progress lay in posting a low score before a boisterous sea breeze arrived early in the afternoon.

Ireland's Darren Clarke was the first to launch a charge with a third round 66 containing nine birdies, and Spain's Miguel Angel Jiménez followed suit by playing the last eleven holes in seven under par, getting home in 31. Clarke however had begun with 76 and Jiménez had been five over par after his first six holes on the opening day and neither was able to ruffle Turner's composure.

The New Zealander laid the founda-tion of victory with his expert handling of the afternoon wind over the closing holes for the 67 that gave him a three shot advantage for the last stage. His play of the 17th in particular stamped him as a player of quality and courage.

Twin fairways separated by a lake which almost surrounds the green, pro-vide alternative routes of approach at the par five. The safest tee shot leaves the longer second shot, and into the wind Turner needed a driver to take on the challenge of getting to the front of the green 226 yards away. His aim was true and the resultant birdie four brought him home in 32 for ten under par 206. Only

Rocca, who was back in 34 for 71 was now a threat, although the English trio of defending champion Barry Lane, Paul Eales, and Ross McFarlane were all at six under par, along with Mouland whose only success on the greens in a 74 was to eagle the ninth from a mere two feet after two stupendous wood shots.

Although Rocca went to the turn in 33 in the last round, Turner's careful golf over the same stretch kept him two ahead, and he was four clear after the 11th where he made a birdie three after a six iron recovery from the woods put him six feet from the flag. Answering birdies from the Italian Ryder Cup player at the 12th and 13th kept the issue alive but Turner com-pleted a flawless 68 to win by two strokes with Jiménez third, just ahead of France's Jean Van de Velde and Lane. Mouland forfeited a share of fourth place when he put two balls into the water at the last. A 75 meant that he had taken 13 extra shots to play his second 36 holes.

Turner was delighted how well he had played at critical times having arrived with no greater expectation than a top 20 place from a much needed week of com-petition. Perhaps it is because he is now taking a more philosophical view of the trials and tribulations of touring.

"I have been reading Nelson Mandela's autobiography,' he said. 'It reminds me that no matter how bad a spot you might be in on the golf course, it is a lot better than Robben Island".

Mike Britten

Santa Ponsa II, Majorca, March 23-26, 1995 · Yardage 6620 · Par 72

Pos	Name	Country	Rnd 1	Rnd 2	Rnd 3	Rnd 4	Total	Prize Money £
1	Greg TURNER	(NZ)	74	65	67	68	274	40478
2	Costantino ROCCA	(It)	71	67	71	67	276	26983
3	Miguel Angel JIMÉNEZ	(Sp)	72	73	66	69	280	15204
4	Jean VAN DE VELDE	(Fr)	70	72	71	68	281	11221
	Barry LANE	(Eng)	71	70	69	71	281	11221
6	Ross MCFARLANE	(Eng)	70	69	71	72	282	8500
7	Sven STRÜVER	(Ger)	75	69	68	71	283	7286
8	Jarmo SANDELIN	(Swe)	70	70	75	69	284	5448
	Fredrik LINDGREN	(Swe)	69	72	70	73	284	5448
	Paul EALES	(Eng)	73	69	68	74	284	5448
11	Michael JONZON	(Swe)	77	70	70	68	285	3965
	Andrew COLTART	(Scot)	74	69	70	72	285	3965
	Darren CLARKE	(N.Ire)	76	71	66	72	285	3965
	Peter MITCHELL	(Eng)	76	68	68	73	285	3965
	Mark MOULAND	(Wal)	67	69	74	75	285	3965
16	Gary EMERSON	(Eng)	68	72	76	70	286	3152
	Keith WATERS	(Eng)	75	72	68	71	286	3152
	Mike CLAYTON	(Aus)	74	69	71	72	286	3152
	Iain PYMAN	(Eng)	71	70	71	74	286	3152
	Phil GOLDING	(Eng)	70	73	68	75	286	3152
21	Anders SØRENSEN	(Den)	76	70	70	71	287	2768
	Mark JAMES	(Eng)	73	69	73	72	287	2768
	Pierre FULKE	(Swe)	77	68	69	73	287	2768
24	Stephen MCALLISTER	(Scot)	71	73	72	72	288	2550
	Adam HUNTER	(Scot)	73	73	69	73	288	2550
	Francisco VALERA	(Sp)	73	70	70	75	288	2550
27	Jonathan LOMAS	(Eng)	72	75	71	71	289	2189
	Roger CHAPMAN	(Eng)	73	73	73	70	289	2189
	José ROZADILLA	(Sp)	68	74	77	70	289	2189
	Daniel WESTERMARK	(Swe)	72	68	77	72	289	2189
	Fabrice TARNAUD	(Fr)	75	71	71	72	289	2189
	Anders GILLNER	(Swe)	74	73	69	73	289	2189
	Pedro LINHART	(Sp)	67	74	74	74	289	2189
34	José Manuel CARRILES	(Sp)	73	71	72	74	290	1894
	Lee WESTWOOD	(Eng)	75	71	70	74	290	1894
	Marco GORTANA	(It)	72	75	66	77	290	1894
37	Scott WATSON	(Eng)	70	76	72	73	291	1724
	Ignacio GARRIDO	(Sp)	75	70	73	73	291	1724
	Des SMYTH	(Ire)	70	71	80	70	291	1724
	Peter HEDBLOM	(Swe)	75	70	71	75	291	1724
41	Paul AFFLECK	(Wal)	71	72	75	74	292	1578
	John HAWKSWORTH	(Eng)	77	69	71	75	292	1578
43	Mark DAVIS	(Eng)	74	72	72	75	293	1432
	Mike MCLEAN	(Eng)	78	70	75	70	293	1432
	Eoghan O'CONNELL	(Ire)	77	71	75	70	293	1432
	André BOSSERT	(Swi)	70	73	74	76	293	1432
47	Christian CEVAER	(Fr)	77	71	70	76	294	1214
	Andrew OLDCORN	(Eng)	76	71	73	74	294	1214
	Stephen AMES	(T&T)	68	80	72	74	294	1214
	Paul MOLONEY	(Aus)	79	69	79	67	294	1214
	Steven RICHARDSON	(Eng)	70	77	70	77	294	1214
52	David R JONES	(Eng)	74	72	73	76	295	1020
	Paul MAYO	(Wal)	74	72	74	75	295	1020
	Jean Louis GUEPY	(Fr)	75	71	75	74	295	1020
55	Carl SUNESON	(Eng)	78	69	72	77	296	813
	Miguel Angel MARTIN	(Sp)	74	73	74	75	296	813
	Martyn ROBERTS	(Wal)	73	75	74	74	296	813
	Juan QUIRÓS	(Sp)	74	74	75	73	296	813
	Paul MCGINLEY	(Ire)	71	74	78	73	296	813
	José RIVERO	(Sp)	71	74	81	70	296	813
61	Alexander CEJKA	(Ger)	76	71	71	79	297	582
	Mark LITTON	(Wal)	71	73	74	79	297	582
	Thomas LEVET	(Fr)	74	72	74	77	297	582
	Mathias GRÖNBERG	(Swe)	74	74	73	76	297	582
	José Maria CAÑIZARES	(Sp)	74	74	75	74	297	582
	Fredrik JACOBSON	(Swe)	75	72	77	73	297	582
	Ross DRUMMOND	(Scot)	76	72	76	73	297	582
68	Brian NELSON	(USA)	77	70	76	75	298	395
	Daren LEE	(Eng)	76	72	77	73	298	395
70	Robert LEE	(Eng)	75	71	77	76	299	392
71	Carlos LARRAIN	(Ven)	70	72	75	83	300	390
72	Mark NICHOLS	(Eng)	74	70	75	82	301	387

THE COURSE

Former Spanish amateur champion Pepe Gancedo has been dubbed the Picasso of golf course architecture because of the surrealistic nature of his designs. Santa Ponsa's No 2 course features a double dog-leg par five (third), another with a stream dividing twin fairways (eighth) and a par four (sixth) with three olive trees set at an angle across the fairway. Feature hole is the 182 yards 18th, where the green in the shape of the island of Majorca, is set in the middle of a lake and reached by a stone causeway.

Walton wins in surreal weather

At a venue near the home of Salvador Dali,

Philip Walton mastered some stern weather conditions

for the second Tour title of his career

Who wants to be a millionaire? Philip Walton joined the Tour's elite seven-figure career prize money winners with his Open Catalonia Turespaña Series victory at Peralada near Figueres, where the celebrated painter Salvador Dali lived and worked. And the 33-year old Irishman's Costa Brava breakthrough, after a patient five-year wait since his Peugeot French Open success, was achieved in a style familiar to fellow 'Millionaires' Club' members of the calibre of Faldo, Ballesteros, Olazábal, Langer, Woosnam and Montgomerie.

The Malahide man kept his head when all around him others were losing their's as the 'tramontana' blew in on the nearby snow capped Pyrennean peaks to put together coolly skilful rounds of 68, 74, 71, 68 for a seven below par 281 score and a three strokes victory over young Scot Andrew Coltart, with experienced Ryder Cup man Howard Clark ending a stroke further back.

Typically, the modest man with the choirboy voice sang the praises at the finish of Scots father and son – Bob Torrance, his coach, for the 18 hours hard work he had put in with him on his swing the previous week in Ireland, and tournament veteran Sam, for persuading him to switch to a 48-inch 'broomhandle' putter.

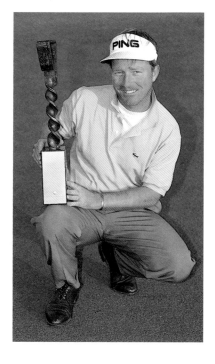

But the tenacity and nerve he displayed in bouncing back after four painful missed halfway cuts to prove his French victory after a play-off against Bernhard Langer was no fluke were the qualities that separated him from the chasing pack.

Victory lifted Walton, ten years on Tour, from 51st place in the Volvo Order of Merit to tenth and he admitted: 'When Coltart, a fine player and a very good putter, eagled the 71st to get within a stroke I knew I had to rip my drive up the final

fairway, fully expecting him to make a birdie. I left myself with only a nine iron to the green and I laid it stiff'.

It set up his fifth birdie of a fighting last round – three, including two twos, coming at successive holes from the 12th in a homeward 33 – but perhaps the real key to his second Tour triumph was his flying start to a third round which had to be aborted after only six holes when winds gusting up to 50 miles an hour began blowing balls about on the greens.

Walton pitched to three feet for a birdie three at the first, then followed up with a spectacular eagle two at the 384 yards third, a sharp left-hand dog-leg where most pros cut off 100 yards or so by opting for the direct line to the flag over rough ground. Walton hit a four wood off the tee and chipped in from 30 feet at a hole on which there were 45 birdies and two eagles on the first day alone. When play was suspended Walton, having been four behind Philip Price at halfway, found himself sharing the lead with the Welshman at five under par.

An attempt to restart late in the day, after heroic efforts by Tournament Director Mike Stewart, officials and staff, had to be called off when the wind suddenly blew up to storm force again, and when the 35 players left on the course

**Andrew Coltart lined up
a second place finish.**

resumed next morning Price slipped to a 76 to end on 214 with Coltart, round in 68, as Walton edged past him on 213 to finish only one behind new leader Clark.

The powerful Yorkshireman, second three times in 1994, had little luck with the putter as he faltered with a closing 73, while poor Price, who had shared the first round lead on 67 with South African Retief Goosen, crashed to an 81 after a 12 at the par five 17th, which included five penalty strokes, two for grounding his club in a hazard.

Victory tasted especially sweet for Walton, who had underlined his fighting

qualities with six wins in eight matches on his two Walker Cup outings in the early 1980s, after he drove out of bounds at the 18th to lose out to Mark Davis in Austria's Hohe Brücke Open the previous summer after leading the second and third rounds. Walton explained: 'I was hopeful of more successes after following my play-off defeat by Ian Woosnam in the Irish Open in 1989 with that victory in Paris the following year, but it didn't happen and I began to struggle, slipping to 92nd in the Order of Merit in 1993.'

'After Sam Torrance gave me a 'broomhandle' putter at the start of 1994

things improved dramatically on the greens. I eventually acquired a new version of the putter but it's essentially the same as the original and I lost count of the number of crucial four footers I holed in Spain.'

'Bob Torrance has worked wonders on my swing and he flew over to Dublin the week before Peralada and we worked for six hours a day for three days on getting more width in my backswing. He told me to try and feel as if I was casting the clubhead at the ball. I started swinging the club well and I've never hit it so far off the tee.'

Sad that the weather was not kinder to the Catalonian event. The region, which boasts 26 courses, has become one of Spain's most important tourist areas and Angel Gallardo, Vice-Chairman of the PGA European Tour, revealed the new course he designed with Neil Coles at nearby Caldas, which will become the Tour's new winter headquarters, has applied to stage the 1997 World Cup. It should be open for play by the summer of 1996 and the Catalonian Tourist Authority, which hopes to host a Seniors Tour event soon, mounted promotions at ten Tour stops in 1995.

Gordon Richardson

SHOT OF THE WEEK

Ronan Rafferty's two at the 16th – he holed a 120 yards sand-iron shot- was one of an amazing seven eagles at four different par fours on day three, but after Andrew Coltart hit a three wood to two feet to eagle the long 71st and get within a stroke of the lead the shot of the week had to be winner Philip Walton's precision nine iron to within 12 inches of the hole at the last to slam the door tight shut on his challengers.

Peralada, Girona, April 14-17, 1995 · Yardage 6839 · Par 72

Pos	Name	Country	Rnd 1	Rnd 2	Rnd 3	Rnd 4	Total	Prize Money £
1	Philip WALTON	(Ire)	68	74	71	68	281	50000
2	Andrew COLTART	(Scot)	72	74	68	70	284	33330
3	Howard CLARK	(Eng)	70	70	72	73	285	18780
4	Mark DAVIS	(Eng)	71	72	74	71	288	15000
5	Paul AFFLECK	(Wal)	73	73	73	70	289	11600
	Retief GOOSEN	(SA)	67	75	75	72	289	11600
7	Sam TORRANCE	(Scot)	73	72	73	72	290	9000
8	Michael CAMPBELL	(NZ)	70	75	76	70	291	6730
	Pierre FULKE	(Swe)	74	76	70	71	291	6730
	Dean ROBERTSON	(Scot)	73	74	71	73	291	6730
11	David WILLIAMS	(Eng)	73	76	71	72	292	5340
	Stuart CAGE	(Eng)	69	74	72	77	292	5340
13	Ross MCFARLANE	(Eng)	74	76	71	72	293	4242
	Russell CLAYDON	(Eng)	70	73	77	73	293	4242
	Fabrice TARNAUD	(Fr)	69	74	77	73	293	4242
	Silvio GRAPPASONNI	(It)	76	72	72	73	293	4242
	Roger WESSELS	(SA)	72	78	70	73	293	4242
	Wayne RILEY	(Aus)	74	69	75	75	293	4242
	Ronan RAFFERTY	(N.Ire)	78	71	69	75	293	4242
20	Frank NOBILO	(NZ)	73	71	79	71	294	3420
	Vicente FERNANDEZ	(Arg)	78	72	72	72	294	3420
	Paul EALES	(Eng)	69	73	79	73	294	3420
	Mats LANNER	(Swe)	74	73	74	73	294	3420
	Joakim HAEGGMAN	(Swe)	73	77	66	78	294	3420
25	Richard BOXALL	(Eng)	72	78	73	72	295	2716
	Barry LANE	(Eng)	73	76	74	72	295	2716
	Peter HEDBLOM	(Swe)	73	69	81	72	295	2716
	Andrew SHERBORNE	(Eng)	73	77	74	71	295	2716
	Anders GILLNER	(Swe)	74	76	74	71	295	2716
	Gordon BRAND JNR.	(Scot)	68	78	78	71	295	2716
	Steven RICHARDSON	(Eng)	75	75	75	70	295	2716
	Stephen DODD	(Wal)	72	71	78	74	295	2716
	José Maria CAÑIZARES	(Sp)	73	77	71	74	295	2716
	Santiago LUNA	(Sp)	72	72	76	75	295	2716
	Phillip PRICE	(Wal)	67	71	76	81	295	2716
36	Paul CURRY	(Eng)	75	75	74	72	296	2070
	David CARTER	(Eng)	71	74	79	72	296	2070
	Robert KARLSSON	(Swe)	73	75	77	71	296	2070
	Peter MITCHELL	(Eng)	69	74	79	74	296	2070
	Gary ORR	(Scot)	74	71	77	74	296	2070
	Christian CEVAER	(Fr)	73	73	76	74	296	2070
	David R JONES	(Eng)	73	72	76	75	296	2070
	George RYALL	(Eng)	71	73	75	77	296	2070
44	Adam HUNTER	(Scot)	70	76	79	72	297	1710
	Peter O'MALLEY	(Aus)	75	75	77	70	297	1710
	José RIVERO	(Sp)	74	75	78	70	297	1710
	Martyn ROBERTS	(Wal)	72	74	74	77	297	1710
48	Paul MAYO	(Wal)	72	76	76	74	298	1530
	Ruben ALVAREZ	(Arg)	72	78	77	71	298	1530
50	José Manuel CARRILES	(Sp)	77	73	76	73	299	1350
	Lee WESTWOOD	(Eng)	72	75	79	73	299	1350
	Miguel Angel MARTIN	(Sp)	74	70	82	73	299	1350
	Mathias GRÖNBERG	(Swe)	75	71	76	77	299	1350
54	Stephen AMES	(T&T)	72	77	75	76	300	1055
	Paul MOLONEY	(Aus)	71	73	80	76	300	1055
	Jon ROBSON	(Eng)	76	72	77	75	300	1055
	Ignacio GERVAS	(Sp)	73	77	77	73	300	1055
	David GILFORD	(Eng)	69	75	83	73	300	1055
	Paul R SIMPSON	(Eng)	69	79	80	72	300	1055
60	Paul WAY	(Eng)	76	73	74	79	302	840
	Gary EMERSON	(Eng)	72	77	77	76	302	840
	Carl SUNESON	(Eng)	74	75	78	75	302	840
	Carlos LARRAIN	(Ven)	76	74	82	70	302	840
	Michael JONZON	(Swe)	75	74	72	81	302	840
65	Neal BRIGGS	(Eng)	70	80	74	79	303	549
	Jarmo SANDELIN	(Swe)	70	79	79	75	303	549
	Ignacio GARRIDO	(Sp)	76	74	80	73	303	549
68	Øyvind ROJAHN	(Nor)	75	75	77	78	305	446
69	Anders SØRENSEN	(Den)	72	77	79	80	308	444
70	Peter BAKER	(Eng)	74	72	84	80	310	442

THE COURSE

Designed on old dry marshes and pools bordering the lake at Castello by Jordi Soler, Peralada opened for play in 1993. A gently sloping par 72 set among olive, oak and elm trees against a dramatic Pyrennean backdrop, it measures 6839 yards (6253 metres) and has four par threes, four par fives and ten par fours, including the 384-yard third, where most pros went straight for the green, cutting out a left-hand dog-leg over a stream.

Bossert becomes role model for the Swiss

André Bossert made history by becoming the first Swiss golfer to win on the Tour

When the Swiss Golf Federation signed up Stockholm-based Jan Blomqvist to co-ordinate their golf programme they hoped he could do for Swiss golf what he had done a decade earlier for Swedish golf. The job was far-reaching, involving every aspect of Swiss golf. But one priority was to produce a golfer talented enough as a professional to give Switzerland a high-profile victory on the Tour.

There were already several candidates – Paoli Quirici was one. Former All-American college golfer André Bossert, brought up in Johannesburg was another. Indeed, Bossert had been so enthusiastic himself about putting Swiss golf on the map that, using his degree in Business Administration from Tulsa University, he had tried but failed to find the sponsorship to start up a contingent along the lines Blomqvist had done so successfully in Sweden.

When Blomqvist came on board three years ago, he and Bossert were to prove the perfect team and on the French Riviera one wet weekend they saw the

dream they both held most dear come true. In the Air France Cannes Open played round Royal Mougins over just 36 holes because of a two-day deluge that flooded the valley course, Bossert made history.

The event may have been restricted because of the weather and he may, as a result, have received only 75 per cent of what he would have won under the rules and regulations covering weather-affected events, but Bossert took the trophy with genuine and justified pride by two shots from Frenchman Jean Van de Velde, back in action after having been sidelined for

five weeks by a ski-ing accident on the way to the slopes at Colorado, and Norwegian Øyvind Rohan.

'This victory gives the Swiss golf programme credibility,' said the delighted Bossert in his strong South African accent. 'Hopefully we shall see more sponsors coming forward in Switzerland to support the game and more people taking it up.' The stage belonged to Bossert but in the background, out of camera range, and equally satisfied Blomqvist nodded vigorously.

Earlier in the year Bossert had hurt his back. While playing at The Wanderers,

Après la deluge at Royal Mougins (left). Another solid display from David Gilford (right).

home of the South African PGA Championship, he slipped a disc and, until Blomqvist made arrangements for him to see a Scandinavian back specialist, he had been uncertain about operating with full power. His fears assuaged, Bossert arrived in Cannes as confident as he has always been that he could win but aware, too, that winning on the Tour these days is far more difficult than it was in the late 1970s. Standards are continually rising and there are more potential winners around. There is a depth of talent today that once was missing.

It turned out to be his week. He felt he was ready to win but knew he needed a slice of luck to help him achieve that. Every winner does and the rain helped in this respect. He likes to think that he would have gone on to win over 72 holes

and most certainly would have preferred to do so but in becoming the sixth first-time winner of the season and the first Swiss to win, Bossert was neither complaining nor apologising. He had no need.

In fact the 31-year old winner made a slice of personal history when he toured the Robert Von Hagge course on the second day in 67 without dropping a shot – the first time he had done that in his six-year Tour career.

Apart from the weather the week was notable for the way in which the players handled greens as undulating and, it seemed, almost as fast as those that face the players at the US Masters each year. They needed to be handled with care. The wrong line could sometimes prove costly as highlighted on the first day by Colin Montgomerie who powered two great

shots on to the front edge of the water-protected green at the par five last. As a putter with touch and feel and imagination, Montgomerie is in the Ballesteros class but on this occasion he got it wrong. For this roller-coaster from 60 feet he chose an inappropriate line and hit the ball a fraction too hard. He stood transfixed as he watched the ball roll over two humps, gather speed as it passed the hole, bounce drunkenly through the back fringe and drop embarrassingly into the lake.

Course designer Von Hagge was watching the action at the time from behind the green at the last. He had come down from the splendid clubhouse to introduce himself to Europe's number one but decided it was neither the time nor place for such a meeting. He was right.

Renton Laidlaw

THE COURSE

Royal Mougins, built in a valley in the hills above Cannes, is rich not only in challenging holes but in delightful views. Because of the terrain the course is tight and by modern standards short, but what it lacks in length is compensated for by undulating greens that can be made to roll as fast as those at Augusta.

ROYAL MOUGINS, APRIL 20-23RD, 1995 · YARDAGE 6566 · PAR 72

Pos	Name	Country	Rnd 1	Rnd 2	Rnd 3	Rnd 4	Total	Prize Money £
1	André BOSSERT	(Swi)	65	67			132	37500
2	Øyvind ROJAHN	(Nor)	67	67			134	19541
	Jean VAN DE VELDE	(Fr)	64	70			134	19541
4	David GILFORD	(Eng)	70	65			135	10387
	Andrew COLTART	(Scot)	66	69			135	10387
6	Domingo HOSPITAL	(Sp)	66	70			136	6316
	Jon ROBSON	(Eng)	67	69			136	6316
	Mathias GRÖNBERG	(Swe)	64	72			136	6316
	Ove SELLBERG	(Swe)	66	70			136	6316
10	Dean ROBERTSON	(Scot)	68	69			137	4170
	Adam HUNTER	(Scot)	68	69			137	4170
	Richard BOXALL	(Eng)	67	70			137	4170
13	Ross DRUMMOND	(Scot)	70	68			138	3247
	Ignacio GARRIDO	(Sp)	69	69			138	3247
	Alberto BINAGHI	(It)	67	71			138	3247
	Peter HEDBLOM	(Swe)	69	69			138	3247
	Roger CHAPMAN	(Eng)	68	70			138	3247
	Colin MONTGOMERIE	(Scot)	68	70			138	3247
19	Iain PYMAN	(Eng)	72	67			139	2745
	Niclas FASTH	(Swe)	67	72			139	2745
21	Paul MOLONEY	(Aus)	68	72			140	2396
	John BICKERTON	(Eng)	71	69			140	2396
	Mike MILLER	(Scot)	70	70			140	2396
	Costantino ROCCA	(It)	74	66			140	2396
	Ian PALMER	(SA)	68	72			140	2396
	Ian WOOSNAM	(Wal)	67	73			140	2396
	David CURRY	(Eng)	70	70			140	2396
	Emanuele CANONICA	(It)	69	71			140	2396
29	Tony JOHNSTONE	(Zim)	73	68			141	1935
	Peter O'MALLEY	(Aus)	69	72			141	1935
	Frank NOBILO	(NZ)	69	72			141	1935
	John BLAND	(SA)	66	75			141	1935
	Sven STRÜVER	(Ger)	71	70			141	1935
	Jeff REMESY	(Fr)	71	70			141	1935
35	Paul MCGINLEY	(Ire)	71	71			142	1620
	Peter MITCHELL	(Eng)	70	72			142	1620
	Joakim HAEGGMAN	(Swe)	68	74			142	1620
	Sam TORRANCE	(Scot)	70	72			142	1620
	Robert KARLSSON	(Swe)	71	71			142	1620
	Eric GIRAUD	(Fr)	68	74			142	1620
	Michael CAMPBELL	(NZ)	69	73			142	1620
42	Howard CLARK	(Eng)	71	72			143	1170
	Greg TURNER	(NZ)	70	73			143	1170
	Jeff HAWKES	(SA)	74	69			143	1170
	Eamonn DARCY	(Ire)	67	76			143	1170
	Russell CLAYDON	(Eng)	72	71			143	1170
	Jonathan LOMAS	(Eng)	67	76			143	1170
	Miguel Angel MARTIN	(Sp)	70	73			143	1170
	Retief GOOSEN	(SA)	71	72			143	1170
	Fabrice TARNAUD	(Fr)	72	71			143	1170
	Stephen MCALLISTER	(Scot)	68	75			143	1170
	Silvio GRAPPASONNI	(It)	73	70			143	1170
	Anders GILLNER	(Swe)	72	71			143	1170
	Gary ORR	(Scot)	71	72			143	1170
55	Manuel PIÑERO	(Sp)	69	75			144	633
	Christian CEVAER	(Fr)	71	73			144	633
	Jarmo SANDELIN	(Swe)	69	75			144	633
	Steen TINNING	(Den)	70	74			144	633
	Fredrik JACOBSON	(Swe)	74	70			144	633
	Vicente FERNANDEZ	(Arg)	72	72			144	633
	Mark MOULAND	(Wal)	73	71			144	633
	Fredrik ANDERSSON	(Swe)	75	69			144	633
	Paul WAY	(Eng)	71	73			144	633
	Ronan RAFFERTY	(N.Ire)	70	74			144	633
	Pierre FULKE	(Swe)	69	75			144	633
	Gavin LEVENSON	(SA)	73	71			144	633
	David RAY	(Eng)	72	72			144	633

SHOT OF THE WEEK

There were three of them and one did not count. Ove Sellberg (below) and Retief Goosen both had holes in one on the first day, Sellberg at the eighth and Goosen at the 17th, but Paul McGinlay's ace at the tenth does not appear in the record books. He achieved the feat on the third day when play was eventually abandoned and the round wiped out because of flooding on the course.

Effervescent Spaniards rise to the top

Severiano Ballesteros and José Maria Olazábal

proved that they have no peers in team golf

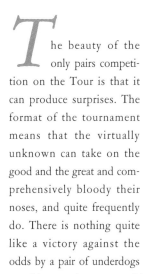

The beauty of the only pairs competition on the Tour is that it can produce surprises. The format of the tournament means that the virtually unknown can take on the good and the great and comprehensively bloody their noses, and quite frequently do. There is nothing quite like a victory against the odds by a pair of underdogs – and in 1995 there was nothing like a victory by a pair of underdogs.

Instead the laurels went to two of world golf's undisputed overdogs. Severiano Ballesteros and José Maria Olazábal are beyond doubt one of the best partnerships in the history of the game; a mere two defeats in Ryder Cup outings together as things got under way tells the story in one simple statistic.

When Ballesteros and Olazábal arrived at St Cloud in the leafy suburbs of Paris at the end of April for the Tournoi Perrier de Paris they were, almost as of right, the favourites. Before the tournament started their most obvious challengers were the scratch but powerful pairing of Colin Montgomerie and Ian Woosnam. By the time it ended they had

left the Woosie-Monty axis and the rest gasping in their wake as they won by three shots with a total of 264, 24 under par, after a classic rendition of a symphony in four movements.

For Olazábal and, especially, Ballesteros, the pursuit of victory was the pursuit of a holy grail that extended beyond the mere acquisition of £35,000 apiece. It was, above all, a demonstration that they remained the pre-eminent two-man golfing force on the planet. There was little doubt where they were sending their message, either; United States Ryder Cup captain Lanny Wadkins and his men would have ignored this triumph at their peril.

Lest there be any confusion, Ballesteros spelt it out. 'We didn't play

just to win the tournament, but also for our prestige,' he said. 'It's important to have the respect of other people. We keep proving that every time we play together. Plus, we are great competitors.

'Send a fax immediately,' he added, leaving no room for misunderstanding that the message should have an American destination. 'Tell them we want the Cup back as soon as possible – and we're ready.' It was said with a smile, but its message was chilling in its intensity. It somehow did not matter that the big match was at the time five months away, or, even what would happen when it did take place. It was a matter of simple but enormous pride, nothing more complicated than that.

But do not let us end before we have begun. If things had gone to plan, the first round of the tournament, played in rain and cold, would have featured one of the two big-name partnerships. Instead, they found themselves being put in the shade by two players who would be flattered by being described as little-known.

Bickerton and Lee sounded a little like something out of 1930s provincial music

73

Daren Lee and John Bickerton stole the early headlines.

hall, the sort of old-time troupers who hawked their comedian-and-straight-man act around such outposts of British vaudeville as the Birmingham Hippodrome and the Croydon Empire.

There was nothing remotely comic about the deeds of John Bickerton and Daren Lee on the golf course, though. They had a 59, a score that would have sent the statisticians scurrying for their record books were it not for the better-ball format of the day.

Whether walking the fairways or treading the boards, the secret of success is timing, and the precocious duo had had their lines off pat. Of their 11 birdies, Bickerton got six and Lee five. Not unnaturally, they had a job to keep a smile off their faces, and it was not long before they stopped trying. Fame having being tasted, they promptly returned to respectable obscurity.

On day two the format turned to foursomes, and with it came the inexorable rise to the top of the golfing vat of *la crème de la crème.* The 64 recorded by Montgomerie and Woosnam on the first day had left them languishing in a comparatively modest share of 17th place. Not for long, as they proved that there is little substitute for experience and innate class by producing a 65 to take the lead on 129, 11 under par. Nobody was very surprised that Ballesteros and Olazábal were lurking

a shot behind, sharing second place with Richard Boxall and Derrick Cooper.

The unspoken but nonetheless cardinal rule of foursomes golf is 'Never say sorry', but Montgomerie was shamed into ignoring the maxim when he put his partner into all sort of bother with his tee shot on the short 13th. At the same time he revealed the precision with which these people play the game.

He was 189 yards from the flag, which for Montgomerie means an easy six iron, but 'easy' suddenly became 'hard' as he put the ball through the green and into a bush. A few minutes later they walked away after a humbling double-bogey five.

'There was no excuse,' Montgomerie said. 'I just hit it 11 yards too hard. I know you're never meant to apologise to your partner in foursomes, but I was saying 'sorry' all the way up the next fairway.

Woosie was very good about it, but he must have been muttering to himself.'

They regrouped after that, and put a fine gloss on their round with birdies on the last three holes. Ballesteros and Olazábal also had a powerful finish as they picked up shots on the last two holes, while the Boxall-Cooper partnership, twice winners of the charmingly old-fashioned Sunningdale Foursomes, celebrated Boxall's 34th birthday with a 68 that contained five birdies and three bogeys.

Montgomerie and Woosnam had a dead-eye-straight day on greensomes Saturday, hitting every fairway and every green in regulation, but had only three birdies in their 67. In contrast, Ballesteros and Olazábal were all over the place, but ended up with nine birdies in their 64. Funny old game, golf.

So dawned the final day and back to

GOLF DE SAINT-CLOUD, APRIL 27 - 30, 1995 · YARDAGE 6,539 · PAR 70

Pos	Name	Rnd 1	Rnd 2	Rnd 3	Rnd 4	Total	Prize Money £ (Per Team)
1	Seve BALLESTEROS & José Maria OLAZÁBAL	63	67	64	62	256	70000
2	Mike CLAYTON & Peter O'MALLEY	66	70	63	60	259	50000
3	Colin MONTGOMERIE & Ian WOOSNAM	64	65	67	64	260	35000
4	Gavin LEVENSON & Ian PALMER	66	66	70	60	262	21500
	Darren CLARKE & Paul MCGINLEY	63	69	68	62	262	21500
6	Russell CLAYDON & Paul EALES	63	74	66	61	264	10625
	Paul BROADHURST & Ross MCFARLANE	63	71	67	63	264	10625
	Malcolm MACKENZIE & David RAY	63	69	68	64	264	10625
	Stuart CAGE & Iain PYMAN	63	69	65	67	264	10625
10	Frédéric CUPILLARD & Fabrice TARNAUD	61	72	70	62	265	7750
	Ignacio GARRIDO & Miguel Angel MARTIN	67	68	68	62	265	7750
	Ruben ALVAREZ & José COCERES	66	66	69	64	265	7750
	Raymond BURNS & Carl MASON	63	68	69	65	265	7750
14	Fredrik ANDERSSON & Jean Charles CAMBON	67	70	67	62	266	6100
	John BLAND & Jeff HAWKES	65	70	68	63	266	6100
	José Manuel CARRILES & Juan PIÑERO	67	66	66	67	266	6100
17	Barry LANE & Mark ROE	65	72	69	62	268	5200
	Stephen DODD & Mark LITTON	66	68	70	64	268	5200
	Phil GOLDING & Ricky WILLISON	66	68	69	65	268	5200
	Richard BOXALL & Derrick COOPER	62	68	70	68	268	5200
	John BICKERTON & Daren LEE	59	72	69	68	268	5200
22	Emanuele CANONICA & Costantino ROCCA	66	70	69	64	269	4400
	Michel BESANCENEY & Vicente FERNANDEZ	64	73	67	65	269	4400
	Peter BAKER & David J RUSSELL	64	68	71	66	269	4400
25	Roger CHAPMAN & Paul WAY	64	72	71	63	270	3700
	Rolf MUNTZ & Martyn ROBERTS	66	71	68	65	270	3700
	Carlos LARRAIN & Daniel WESTERMARK	65	69	70	66	270	3700
	Paul MOLONEY & Terry PRICE	65	70	69	66	270	3700
29	Alexander CEJKA & Heinz P THÜL	62	74	72	64	272	3100
	Jon ROBSON & Scott WATSON	62	72	70	68	272	3100
31	Mark DAVIS & David WILLIAMS	68	67	69	69	273	1050
32	John MELLOR & Jonathan WILSHIRE	67	70	72	68	277	1044
	Dean ROBERTSON & Craig RONALD	63	70	72	72	277	1044

Le style de Colin Montgomerie.

four-ball, and the sun was seen for the first time in the two years of this tournament. The sensation of warmth on their backs was the prompt for the Australian pairing of Peter O'Malley and Mike Clayton to complete a weekend that they played in 17 under par, ending with a 60 to post a challenging target.

The Aussies played beyond them-selves, and on another day might have even have won. But in the end it went as it was written, and the aristocratic blood-lines prevailed. Ballesteros and Olazábal completed their final, triumphant lap in 62 with Ballesteros holing five shot-gaining putts and Olazábal three, but on a couple of occasions one beat the other to the birdie by only a matter of seconds.

Before the third round was completed the trophy had their names on it. The race does not always go to the swiftest, human frailty sees to that. This time class and blue-blooded pedigree brought its deserved reward.

Mel Webb

Torrance makes the right decision

On the verge of pulling out through injury,

Sam Torrance decided to stay on and captured

the second Italian Open title of his career

*S*am Torrance owes a great debt of gratitude to the Italian Golf Federation whose support for the Italian Open, a tournament dating back to 1925, was just as significant as the Scot's two-shot victory over José Rivero.

The recession has not been kind to professional golf in Italy but the Italian Federation boldly showed its faith by putting up the one billion lire (approximately £370,000) prize fund.

That gave confidence for sponsors to support the event, the clothing manufacturer Conte of Florence taking the title sponsorship and Nissan putting forward a car for a hole in one at the 17th. Their insurance plan was called into action when Rivero drove off with the prize in the first round.

So one of the most stylish events on the Tour was back on to continue its 70-year history. For the first time, though, it would be staged at a public golf course, Le Rovedine, in the southern Milan suburb of Opera. A fine public facility, with a magnificent driving range and an academy course, this is just what Italy needs. And thanks to visits from Alberto Binaghi, a member of the Tour's Tournament Committee, during the preparations, it was brought up to the required condition. The test was too severe for many, includ-

Emanuele Canonica (left) was home challenger at the picturesque La Rovedine course (above).

ing Binaghi, who missed the cut.

The other requirement from the Federation was that spectators would be let in free. Now all they needed was for Costantino Rocca to be in contention.

Italy's first Ryder Cup player rose to the occasion, bringing with him a couple of thousand from his home town of Bergamo. He may not have led in the first

round – that was the province of the young Englishman Neal Briggs on seven under – or after 36 holes, when Ireland's Ronan Rafferty showed a welcome return to form to be nine under. But Rocca was only a shot behind and the crowds did come out over the weekend to support him.

Only that was when Torrance took

over. Perhaps he was inspired by cancelling that bet on himself just moments before he teed off on Thursday. The £61,716 first prize would, after all, dwarf his winnings from the £100 bet at odds 16-1. But half-an-hour before he was due to tee off, he wasn't going to play. 'I wasn't in the tournament and phoned my bookmaker to cancel the bet because I was

SHOT OF THE WEEK

When José Rivero stood on the 17th tee in the first round he was two under for the day. Two holes later he was six under, having finished eagle-one, eagle-three. At the 155-yard penultimate hole, the Spaniard hit a seven iron. 'It was a good shot that pitched two feet right of the flag and then kicked left into the hole', he said. It was his first hole in one on Tour and earned him a £25,000 Maxima QX Nissan car.

pulling out,' said the 41-year old Torrance. The problem was soreness in his upper thigh tendon, which appeared mysteriously that morning. 'No-one knows what it is, but there were too many of us for the taxi last night so I walked home from the restaurant and got lost. I have had all these niggles in the last few years – maybe it's my age. But I'm glad I made the effort to play.'

That was after a first round 69. He added a 70 on Friday, then broke the course record with a nine-birdie round of 63 in the third round. Five birdies in the first seven holes, were followed by three in the last four. 'It was a magnificent round, as good as it could be,' he said.

Suddenly, Torrance had rocketed to the top of the leaderboard at 14 under and Rocca had to produce a round of 67, with only 24 putts, and Rafferty a 68, picking four shots in the last four holes, to remain

Mark Litton drove into joint third place.

one behind. Rocca, though, could just not find the hole with his putter on the Sunday, and Torrance's main challenger turned out to be Rivero.

The veteran Spaniard had picked up four shots in the last two holes on day one and no leader would have felt safe knowing someone could do something similar on Sunday. But Rivero could only get within one shot, after he had played 16 holes, and knew Torrance, playing behind him, would have plenty of opportunities.

The Scot had birdied the third, fourth and fifth to gain a handy cushion and not even a bogey at the 11th could halt his progress. His broomhandle putter came into its own on the back nine, as he saved from sand at the 12th and from off the green at the 14th. Then the birdies started

to flow again. He two-putted the par five 15th, got up and down again at the short par four 16th and two-putted the par five last. 'I continued from where I left off yesterday,' he said. 'I didn't panic at any time.'

It was his second Italian win, the first ironically coming after a play-off with Rivero in 1987, but the Ryder Cup points – he was then up to fifth place on the table – meant most to him. 'I want to be in the team again', he said 'It's important to me. I felt a bit useless last time not being able to play with my toe injury.'

Joint third place also boosted Rocca's Ryder Cup prospects, but there were more immediate thoughts. The big hitting rookie Emanuele Canonica was also third and Silvio Grappasonni was tied in the top ten. Said Rocca. 'It was a good week for me and for Italian golf.'

Andrew Farrell

Le Rovedine Golf Club, Milan, May 4-7, 1995 • Yardage 6845 • Par 72

Pos	Name	Country	Rnd 1	Rnd 2	Rnd 3	Rnd 4	Total	Prize Money £
1	Sam TORRANCE	(Scot)	69	70	63	67	269	61716
2	José RIVERO	(Sp)	66	70	69	66	271	41119
3	Ronan RAFFERTY	(N.Ire)	67	68	68	73	276	16299
	Emanuele CANONICA	(It)	68	69	73	66	276	16299
	Paul BROADHURST	(Eng)	69	67	71	69	276	16299
	Costantino ROCCA	(It)	68	68	67	73	276	16299
	Mark LITTON	(Wal)	68	68	72	68	276	16299
8	Tony JOHNSTONE	(Zim)	70	69	69	69	277	7946
	Neal BRIGGS	(Eng)	65	73	70	69	277	7946
	Peter BAKER	(Eng)	71	68	71	67	277	7946
	Silvio GRAPPASONNI	(It)	71	68	69	69	277	7946
12	Peter HEDBLOM	(Swe)	73	66	69	70	278	6001
	Ross DRUMMOND	(Scot)	72	70	66	70	278	6001
	Øyvind ROJAHN	(Nor)	72	67	68	71	278	6001
15	Anders FORSBRAND	(Swe)	71	67	71	70	279	5112
	Greg TURNER	(NZ)	72	69	72	66	279	5112
	Andrew SHERBORNE	(Eng)	71	68	68	72	279	5112
	Gary ORR	(Scot)	69	71	70	69	279	5112
19	Stephen DODD	(Wal)	68	70	72	70	280	4457
	Mark JAMES	(Eng)	70	73	68	69	280	4457
	Vicente FERNANDEZ	(Arg)	69	72	67	72	280	4457
22	Carl MASON	(Eng)	70	73	70	68	281	3945
	Phil GOLDING	(Eng)	71	70	71	69	281	3945
	Fredrik ANDERSSON	(Swe)	71	68	74	68	281	3945
	Andrew COLTART	(Scot)	68	71	71	71	281	3945
	Stephen AMES	(T&T)	74	70	70	67	281	3945
	Keith WATERS	(Eng)	72	68	73	68	281	3945
28	Stephen MCALLISTER	(Scot)	68	70	68	76	282	3445
	Jarmo SANDELIN	(Swe)	68	69	72	73	282	3445
	Michel BESANCENEY	(Fr)	70	72	71	69	282	3445
31	Gavin LEVENSON	(SA)	70	73	68	72	283	3083
	Terry PRICE	(Aus)	70	73	74	66	283	3083
	Richard BOXALL	(Eng)	70	74	67	72	283	3083
	José Manuel CARRILES	(Sp)	69	74	68	72	283	3083
35	Ricky WILLISON	(Eng)	68	71	71	74	284	2667
	Steen TINNING	(Den)	69	71	72	72	284	2667
	Christian CEVAER	(Fr)	69	73	69	73	284	2667
	Carlos LARRAIN	(Ven)	71	73	69	71	284	2667
	Jon ROBSON	(Eng)	69	72	72	71	284	2667
	Fredrik LINDGREN	(Swe)	73	71	69	71	284	2667
	John MCHENRY	(Ire)	70	72	70	72	284	2667
42	Rolf MUNTZ	(Hol)	71	73	71	70	285	2148
	Paolo QUIRICI	(Swi)	70	74	72	69	285	2148
	Michael JONZON	(Swe)	72	72	67	74	285	2148
	Wayne RILEY	(Aus)	70	74	70	71	285	2148
	Derrick COOPER	(Eng)	72	68	72	73	285	2148
	Andrew OLDCORN	(Eng)	68	72	72	73	285	2148
	Ian SPENCER	(Eng)	70	70	78	67	285	2148
49	David R JONES	(Eng)	75	69	70	72	286	1778
	Michael ARCHER	(Eng)	71	69	76	70	286	1778
	Fabrice TARNAUD	(Fr)	72	71	72	71	286	1778
52	Martyn ROBERTS	(Wal)	69	74	73	71	287	1444
	Jim PAYNE	(Eng)	72	71	74	70	287	1444
	Michele REALE	(It)	66	71	77	73	287	1444
	Paul R SIMPSON	(Eng)	77	67	74	69	287	1444
	Marco DURANTE	(It)	67	73	73	74	287	1444
	Joakim GRONHAGEN	(Swe)	72	68	71	76	287	1444
58	Heinz P THÜL	(Ger)	71	72	73	72	288	1074
	Stuart CAGE	(Eng)	68	72	70	78	288	1074
	Fredrik JACOBSON	(Swe)	73	71	72	72	288	1074
	André BOSSERT	(Swi)	75	65	73	75	288	1074
	Manuel PIÑERO	(Sp)	70	70	74	74	288	1074
	Jonathan LOMAS	(Eng)	72	72	73	71	288	1074
	Marc FARRY	(Fr)	70	71	72	75	288	1074
65	Daren LEE	(Eng)	71	72	71	75	289	604
	Malcolm MACKENZIE	(Eng)	67	73	75	74	289	604
	Marcello SANTI	(It)	71	70	74	74	289	604
	Juan QUIRÓS	(Sp)	73	71	70	75	289	604
	Gary EMERSON	(Eng)	69	74	76	70	289	604
	Mike HARWOOD	(Aus)	71	69	76	73	289	604
	Gabriel HJERTSTEDT	(Swe)	70	73	74	72	289	604
72	Steven BOTTOMLEY	(Eng)	72	72	72	74	290	542
	Massimo FLORIOLI	(It)	75	68	73	74	290	542
	Giuseppe CALI	(It)	71	70	75	74	290	542
75	Jeremy ROBINSON	(Eng)	73	71	73	74	291	538
76	Antoine LEBOUC	(Fr)	72	70	75	75	292	536
77	Tierri CORTE	(It)	71	71	78	73	293	534
78	Rodger DAVIS	(Aus)	74	70	72	78	294	532
79	Retief GOOSEN	(SA)	70	74	77	75	296	530

THE COURSE

Le Rovedine began life as a nine-hole public course in 1976 and was extended to 18 in 1992. The first six and last three holes are the original work, weaving in and out of the trees, while the middle nine constitutes the newer, more open part of the layout where the main problem is avoiding the water. A driveable par four, a par three and reachable par five makes for an exciting finish over the final three holes.

O'Malley out of the doldrums

Peter O'Malley ended a

long wait for victory

with a sterling effort at St Mellion

*T*o the left of the 18th green, nestling proudly on a bank, was a battleship grey MGB Roadster. It was the prize for anybody lucky enough to get an eagle two. The registration number was BNH 25, marking Benson and Hedges' 25th anniversary of the International Open, and the way the 18th was playing the car could be there for another 25 years.

At 472 yards, the 18th is the longest par four on the course and the green, full of humps and borrows, is made all the more treacherous by having a duck pond as a neighbour. Since the Benson and Hedges moved from Fulford in York to Cornwall only one name has had a two at the last, Glyn Davies in 1992. Had he done it in 1991 he would have won £5,000. In 1992 there was nothing on offer.

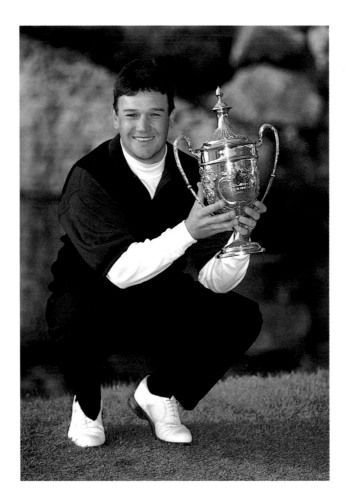

Despite the fact that the majority of players were more in danger of hitting the car than the green – in the first round only one of the 150 players, the young Scottish amateur Gordon Sherry, managed to get a birdie three at the 18th where sixes and sevens were prevalent – the bookmakers were of the opinion that an eagle could be landed. The odds they offered against it were 30-1 which, even by their parsimonious standards, were laughably mean.

Even so, in terms of outrageous gambles, if somebody had said choose a player winning the MGB or Peter O'Malley winning the tournament, William Hill himself would have had a sporting bet on the sports car. O'Malley's record had been so abysmal at St Mellion he had made the halfway cut only once, in 1992, the year he won the Scottish Open. In between he had won nothing and had lost his sponsors.

O'Malley's victory in Scotland came at Gleneagles where he deprived Colin Montgomerie by finishing eagle, birdie, birdie, birdie, eagle. Such a sequence is impossible at St Mellion although O'Malley, over the first two days, played the Cornish wrecker as well, if not better, than it has ever been played.

Had the championship been held a week earlier, as it normally was, the field

would have complained of heat exhaustion. Instead they had the umbrellas, the bobble hats and the mittens out. Colin – 'I'd led here before but I blew it on the Saturday with an 85' – Montgomerie shot 67 in the first round and was pursued by, amongst other, O'Malley and Paul Broadhurst.

'I've never known a course like this,' Broadhurst said. 'There's potential disaster on every shot.' In some cases on some putts. Seve Ballesteros, the defending champion, had a level par 72 in the first round that included a double bogey six at the fifth. From 15 feet he took four putts and this is one greenkeeper who was knocked off the Spaniard's Christmas card list.

The rain relented but the wind did not. Nor did O'Malley. By the halfway stage he had set sail for home and out of a sea of blue figures, signifying scores above par, his score was remarkable. 'I get on a streak sometimes.' O'Malley said. In previous appearances at

Costantino Rocca was hurting after missing a putt.

St Mellion the Australian, with a touch of Cork ancestry and a home in Berkshire, was 62 over par for 12 rounds.

On day two he equalled the course record of 65-the number of players under par could have been counted on two hands- and at 11 under par led by five strokes from Monty. 'That was a tremendous effort,' Montgomerie said of O'Malley's score. 'He's not frightened to go low. Some people are.' Ballesteros said 'It was a very unpleasant day to play golf. I was very impressed with O'Malley's round. It looks like he was playing a computer rather than a golf course.'

O'Malley had nine birdies, two bogeys and in two rounds had missed one fairway. Then the computer started to play rough. O'Malley shot 74 but still held a two-stroke lead going into the last round. He won by a shot and it could well have been by the stroke of luck he had at the second hole on the final day when he blocked his drive so far right his ball clattered into the garden wall of a private house. Flying into out-of-bounds

THE COURSE

Like no other in Cornwall, Devon or anywhere else. The Bond brothers, Hermon and Martin, part-time golfers, full-time farmers and property developers, had a dream and converted 450 acres into St Mellion International. They enlisted the services of Jack Nicklaus who gave the impression of moving bits of heaven and earth in creating a uniquely confounding inland, uphill, and down dale course. Tough and uncompromising? Their name is Bond.

SHOT OF THE WEEK

A five at the 18th is almost respectable. Eamonn Darcy described the hole as a 'bitch'. Darcy, in fact, played it beautifully in the second round, hitting a five iron approach to within three feet of the pin and he made the putt for a birdie three. 'It's an animal.' the Irishman said. 'If you try to steer it around you'll end up in a straitjacket'.

Talented amateur Gordon Sherry (above). New course record from Carl Mason (below).

territory, the ball recoiled from the wall into play and O'Malley salvaged par.

He began and finished with bogeys but birdies at the 12th and 13th were sufficient to keep him on course. O'Malley had laid the foundations of his victory with his opening rounds and it is a measure of the toughness of St Mellion that he could win with final scores of 74 and 73. At various stages his lead evaporated to either Carl Mason, who set a course record of 63 in the third round; Mark James and Costantino Rocca. It was Rocca, who got his noble Italian nose in front over the back nine, who had the best chance of depriving O'Malley but he missed shortish putts at the last three holes. O'Malley, on eight under for the tournament, finished one ahead of Rocca and James.

Sandy Lyle, despite hitting more banks than Butch Cassidy and the Sundance Kid, had just 24 putts in a round of 65 and was four strokes off the lead. At the 18th he came within four feet of the flag, a nine iron following a huge drive. Nobody, however, could get their hands on the best drive of all-a battleship grey MGB Roadster with a V8 engine.

Tim Glover   85

St Mellion G & CC, Plymouth, May 11-14, 1995 • Yardage 7054 • Par 72

Pos	Name	Country	Rnd 1	Rnd 2	Rnd 3	Rnd 4	Total	Prize Money £
1	Peter O'MALLEY	(Aus)	68	65	74	73	280	108330
2	Mark JAMES	(Eng)	71	68	71	71	281	56450
	Costantino ROCCA	(It)	72	73	64	72	281	56450
4	Andrew OLDCORN	(Eng)	70	74	73	65	282	27593
	Colin MONTGOMERIE	(Scot)	67	71	75	69	282	27593
	Carl MASON	(Eng)	71	75	63	73	282	27593
7	Wayne WESTNER	(SA)	74	73	71	66	284	16753
	Sandy LYLE	(Scot)	71	77	71	65	284	16753
	Steen TINNING	(Den)	68	78	70	68	284	16753
10	José Maria OLAZÁBAL	(Sp)	70	74	71	70	285	12480
	Eamonn DARCY	(Ire)	69	73	74	69	285	12480
12	Raymond BURNS	(N.Ire)	76	67	73	70	286	10526
	Paul BROADHURST	(Eng)	68	77	70	71	286	10526
	Gary EVANS	(Eng)	70	73	71	72	286	10526
15	Michael CAMPBELL	(NZ)	78	70	67	72	287	8967
	Roger WESSELS	(SA)	73	73	71	70	287	8967
	Peter SENIOR	(Aus)	69	74	71	73	287	8967
	José COCERES	(Arg)	73	73	71	70	287	8967
19	Barry LANE	(Eng)	74	71	73	70	288	7518
	Derrick COOPER	(Eng)	76	73	69	70	288	7518
	Bernhard LANGER	(Ger)	74	70	70	74	288	7518
	Frank NOBILO	(NZ)	73	71	73	71	288	7518
	Sven STRÜVER	(Ger)	73	73	71	71	288	7518
	Richard BOXALL	(Eng)	68	73	73	74	288	7518
25	Sam TORRANCE	(Scot)	71	73	75	70	289	6727
	Marc FARRY	(Fr)	75	72	71	71	289	6727
27	Paul AFFLECK	(Wal)	71	77	69	73	290	6240
	Miguel Angel JIMÉNEZ	(Sp)	75	73	70	72	290	6240
	Andrew SHERBORNE	(Eng)	74	75	72	69	290	6240
30	Seve BALLESTEROS	(Sp)	72	76	70	73	291	5573
	Christian CEVAER	(Fr)	71	75	73	72	291	5573
	Scott WATSON	(Eng)	74	71	77	69	291	5573
	Lucas PARSONS	(Aus)	73	74	76	68	291	5573
34	Darren CLARKE	(N.Ire)	71	74	72	75	292	4875
	Gavin LEVENSON	(SA)	72	73	73	74	292	4875
	Martin GATES	(Eng)	69	78	71	74	292	4875
	Greg TURNER	(NZ)	72	71	72	77	292	4875
	Domingo HOSPITAL	(Sp)	71	75	73	73	292	4875
	Jamie SPENCE	(Eng)	75	73	70	74	292	4875
40	Russell CLAYDON	(Eng)	74	73	73	73	293	4160
	Mark MOULAND	(Wal)	76	72	72	73	293	4160
	Gary EMERSON	(Eng)	74	70	78	71	293	4160
	Steven RICHARDSON	(Eng)	76	72	71	74	293	4160
	Andrew MURRAY	(Eng)	73	76	73	71	293	4160
45	Stephen MCALLISTER	(Scot)	74	74	73	73	294	3640
	Philip WALTON	(Ire)	72	77	73	72	294	3640
	Gordon BRAND JNR.	(Scot)	71	77	73	73	294	3640
48	Steven BOTTOMLEY	(Eng)	77	70	75	73	295	3250
	Ignacio GARRIDO	(Sp)	73	76	71	75	295	3250
	Mike HARWOOD	(Aus)	73	75	75	72	295	3250
51	David WILLIAMS	(Eng)	74	74	73	75	296	2990
52	Eoghan O'CONNELL	(Ire)	75	73	74	75	297	2665
	Jeremy ROBINSON	(Eng)	75	73	76	73	297	2665
	Andrew COLTART	(Scot)	75	73	74	75	297	2665
	Alberto BINAGHI	(It)	73	74	80	70	297	2665
56	David CURRY	(Eng)	72	76	78	72	298	1971
	Adam HUNTER	(Scot)	72	76	75	75	298	1971
	Alexander CEJKA	(Ger)	74	72	80	72	298	1971
	Mark ROE	(Eng)	73	74	71	80	298	1971
	Emanuele CANONICA	(It)	71	75	75	77	298	1971
	David R JONES	(Eng)	74	75	80	69	298	1971
	Paul WAY	(Eng)	75	74	75	74	298	1971
	Mats HALLBERG	(Swe)	74	69	78	77	298	1971
	Bernard GALLACHER	(Scot)	74	72	77	75	298	1971
65	Jarmo SANDELIN	(Swe)	74	75	74	76	299	1625
66	Antonio GARRIDO	(Sp)	76	73	75	77	301	975
67	Pierre FULKE	(Swe)	74	74	77	79	304	973

Defending champion Severiano Ballesteros (left) was in golden mood. Botanic problems for Gary Emerson (right) on the 18th.

All packs contain points

NEW FROM
BENSON AND HEDGES
LIGHTS &
ULTRA LIGHTS

TOBACCO SERIOUSLY DAMAGES HEALTH

TOBACCO SERIOUSLY DAMAGES HEALTH

TOBACCO SERIOUSLY DAMAGES HEALTH

SMOKING WHEN PREGNANT
HARMS YOUR BABY

Chief Medical Officers' Warning

BENSON AND HEDGES SPECIAL FILTER	BENSON AND HEDGES LIGHTS	BENSON AND HEDGES ULTRA LIGHTS
12 mg Tar 0.9 mg Nicotine	6 mg Tar 0.6 mg Nicotine	1 mg Tar 0.1 mg Nicotine

King in his own country again

Supported by thousands of his countrymen Severiano Ballesteros sent them home happy with victory in Madrid

'A very hard day's work. It has cost me five years of good health.' That was how Severiano Ballesteros described his first Peugeot Spanish Open win in ten years after he had held off last day challenges at Madrid's Club de Campo from compatriots Ignacio Garrido and José Rivero and Britain's Peter Baker.

In fact the victory took such a toll that Seve confessed to 'not having been able to breathe properly until my approach shot to the final green.' No doubt the great man was exaggerating slightly but this, his 54th win in Europe, was certainly a hard fought affair at a venue which, for once, basked beneath crystal clear blue skies and temperatures well into the eighties.

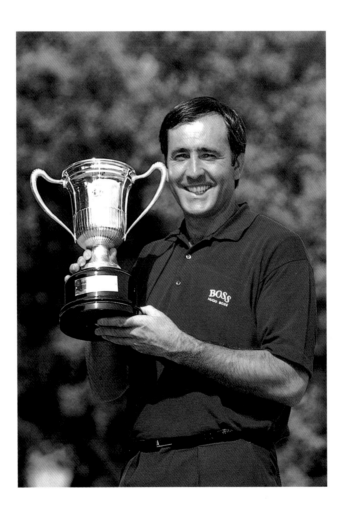

The 69th Spanish Open, the tenth to be held under the Peugeot banner, had a brand new logo and a new feel to it and Club de Campo was buzzing with excitement all week. The excellent weather together with a strong Spanish presence on the leaderboards brought the 'madrileños' out in droves and, for the first time ever in Spain, galleries surpassed the 30,000 mark. Spain's former Prime

Minister, Adolfo Suarez, a recent convert to golf put thousands on the gate by playing in the pro-am with José Maria Olazábal. Chema was then drawn in the same group as his friend Ballesteros for the first two rounds and the Spanish maestros were followed step by step by enormous galleries who enthusiastically applauded every shot, even the wayward ones. Olazábal, worried about a slow play warning on the tenth hole in Friday's second round later remarked that he had been far more interested in speeding up than in the shots he was supposed to be playing. He made the level par halfway cut by the skin of his teeth and then relaxed to play the last two rounds in a combined seven under.

Gordon Brand Junior looked the player most likely to spoil Seve's party but twenty minutes before the start of his second round he was in trouble having broken his pitching wedge. With no time for repairs Brand borrowed a replacement

from Tour official, José Maria 'Zorro' Zamora. Two rounds and fifteen birdies later he was in the lead. Zamora's wedge had changed hands permanently. In the third round Brand saved his seventh birdie of the day for the final green thus depriving Ballesteros of a share of the overnight lead. Seve's former caddie, Billy Foster, now carrying for Brand would, on Sunday, walk the course with his ex-boss for the first time since their split.

But Ballesteros wasn't about to let old liasions stand in his way and his closest rivals seemed incapable, anyway, of taking advantage of the Spaniard's

three bogey start to his final round. Peter Mitchell matched him error for error and Brand had two bogeys in his first five holes. Peter Baker posed a threat, his four early birdies giving him a share of the lead, and José Rivero was always in the

top three, but the main challenge came from young Ignacio Garrido whose father, former Ryder Cup player Antonio, had earlier missed the halfway cut. 'Nacho' as the 23-year old is affectionately known birdied the 12th to take the lead on 12

THE COURSE

Club de Campo is a testing championship course set on undulating terrain with very long holes, large bunkers, well-defined greens and with fairways bordered by stately trees. It was here that Manuel Piñero, José Maria Cañizares and Antonio Garrido attended the Club's famous caddie school.

Ignacio Garrido (left) led the
Spanish youth challenge.
Gordon Brand Junior (right)
and new caddie Billy Foster
weigh up a putt.

Local support for José Maria Olazábal (above). First round leader Peter Mitchell (below).

under but his third round 74 weighed heavily and a bogey at the 14th left him with too much to do.

Ballesteros had steadied himself and seemed oblivious to the capricious ebb and flow of names and numbers on the leaderboards. He too birdied the 12th and when he rolled in a putt for his third birdie of the day at the 15th Seve was not only back where he had started that morning in relation to par but, better still, he was in the lead. At the last, in a rare display of caution, Seve took a one iron off the tee and safely delivered his ball to the middle of the fairway. A glorious pitch soared to the left of the raised green and landed softly just four and a half feet from the pin to set up a birdie finish and Ballesteros stood motionless as a tide of wildly excited youngsters surged around him.

'It was great to see so many people here,' enthused Seve, 'and their support was vital especially after my appalling start.' I thought 'that's it, time to go home' but then I remembered all the other times I'd won without feeling confident so I told myself 'play with what you've' got. Be patient and it will work out,' that and the phenomenal support from the galleries was the key.'

Jeff Kelly

CLUB DE CAMPO, MADRID, MAY 18-21, 1995 · YARDAGE 6928 · PAR 72

Pos	Name	Country	Rnd 1	Rnd 2	Rnd 3	Rnd 4	Total	Prize Money £
1	Seve BALLESTEROS	(Sp)	70	67	66	71	274	91660
2	José RIVERO	(Sp)	68	69	71	68	276	47765
	Ignacio GARRIDO	(Sp)	67	66	74	69	276	47765
4	Peter BAKER	(Eng)	69	72	68	68	277	25400
	Gordon BRAND JNR.	(Scot)	71	66	65	75	277	25400
6	Eduardo ROMERO	(Arg)	70	69	69	70	278	17875
	Peter MITCHELL	(Eng)	66	67	73	72	278	17875
8	Russell CLAYDON	(Eng)	72	69	70	68	279	11785
	Derrick COOPER	(Eng)	70	72	70	67	279	11785
	Bernhard LANGER	(Ger)	71	70	69	69	279	11785
	Jay TOWNSEND	(USA)	69	67	71	72	279	11785
12	Anders SØRENSEN	(Den)	70	73	68	69	280	8906
	Jon ROBSON	(Eng)	69	70	74	67	280	8906
	Mark ROE	(Eng)	69	69	68	74	280	8906
15	Pedro LINHART	(Sp)	74	69	70	68	281	6954
	Frank NOBILO	(NZ)	73	70	69	69	281	6954
	Mark MOULAND	(Wal)	70	73	70	68	281	6954
	José Maria OLAZÁBAL	(Sp)	73	71	68	69	281	6954
	Jesper PARNEVIK	(Swe)	73	68	69	71	281	6954
	Colin MONTGOMERIE	(Scot)	70	71	70	70	281	6954
	Wayne RILEY	(Aus)	69	71	71	70	281	6954
	Howard CLARK	(Eng)	69	69	73	70	281	6954
	Costantino ROCCA	(It)	68	69	73	71	281	6954
24	Barry LANE	(Eng)	69	73	71	69	282	5775
	Mike MCLEAN	(Eng)	71	72	70	69	282	5775
	Ross MCFARLANE	(Eng)	72	68	71	71	282	5775
27	Michael JONZON	(Swe)	71	71	68	73	283	5032
	Greg TURNER	(NZ)	72	72	69	70	283	5032
	Peter O'MALLEY	(Aus)	73	68	70	72	283	5032
	Sam TORRANCE	(Scot)	70	69	71	73	283	5032
	Mike HARWOOD	(Aus)	69	70	77	67	283	5032
	David GILFORD	(Eng)	69	69	72	73	283	5032
33	Andrew SHERBORNE	(Eng)	72	71	68	73	284	4070
	Ross DRUMMOND	(Scot)	73	70	71	70	284	4070
	Jean VAN DE VELDE	(Fr)	71	73	73	67	284	4070
	Phillip PRICE	(Wal)	68	73	70	73	284	4070
	John BLAND	(SA)	71	69	74	70	284	4070
	Gavin LEVENSON	(SA)	69	71	72	72	284	4070
	Domingo HOSPITAL	(Sp)	71	68	70	75	284	4070
	Eamonn DARCY	(Ire)	69	69	76	70	284	4070
	David CARTER	(Eng)	70	68	75	71	284	4070
42	Jarmo SANDELIN	(Swe)	69	72	72	72	285	3410
	José COCERES	(Arg)	70	72	69	74	285	3410
	Paul BROADHURST	(Eng)	75	69	71	70	285	3410
45	Olle KARLSSON	(Swe)	72	70	76	68	286	2860
	Juan PIÑERO	(Sp)	72	71	72	71	286	2860
	Mats LANNER	(Swe)	71	73	66	76	286	2860
	Malcolm MACKENZIE	(Eng)	69	75	68	74	286	2860
	Steven RICHARDSON	(Eng)	71	70	73	72	286	2860
	Rodger DAVIS	(Aus)	70	71	74	71	286	2860
	Stuart CAGE	(Eng)	73	68	72	73	286	2860
52	Paolo QUIRICI	(Swi)	72	71	71	73	287	2255
	Roger CHAPMAN	(Eng)	74	70	71	72	287	2255
	Alberto BINAGHI	(It)	71	70	74	72	287	2255
	Manuel PIÑERO	(Sp)	73	68	70	76	287	2255
56	Paul EALES	(Eng)	72	71	73	72	288	1828
	Mark LITTON	(Wal)	72	71	74	71	288	1828
	Sven STRÜVER	(Ger)	71	73	72	72	288	1828
	Liam WHITE	(Eng)	72	72	74	70	288	1828
60	Raymond BURNS	(N.Ire)	72	72	75	70	289	1622
	Per-Ulrik JOHANSSON	(Swe)	73	68	75	73	289	1622
62	Mike CLAYTON	(Aus)	72	70	72	76	290	1485
	Phil GOLDING	(Eng)	74	70	75	71	290	1485
	Silvio GRAPPASONNI	(It)	70	68	78	74	290	1485
65	Fabrice TARNAUD	(Fr)	71	71	78	71	291	961
	Ignacio GERVAS	(Sp)	70	72	77	72	291	961
	Retief GOOSEN	(SA)	69	75	77	70	291	961
	Rolf MUNTZ	(Hol)	71	73	78	69	291	961
69	John BICKERTON	(Eng)	71	70	73	78	292	819
70	Richard BOXALL	(Eng)	73	70	78	72	293	817
71	Stephen MCALLISTER	(Scot)	69	67	80	80	296	815

SHOT OF THE WEEK

The first round double bogey disaster at the 15th loomed large in Seve Ballesteros' thoughts as he stepped onto the same tee on Sunday just one stroke off the lead. He steered the ball to the right to account for the sloping fairway and the almost perfectly executed drive landed high on the slope before kicking sharply left and coming to rest a sand wedge away from the green. Did his ball hit a spectator? No matter, the resulting birdie assured him of his first Spanish Open title in ten years.

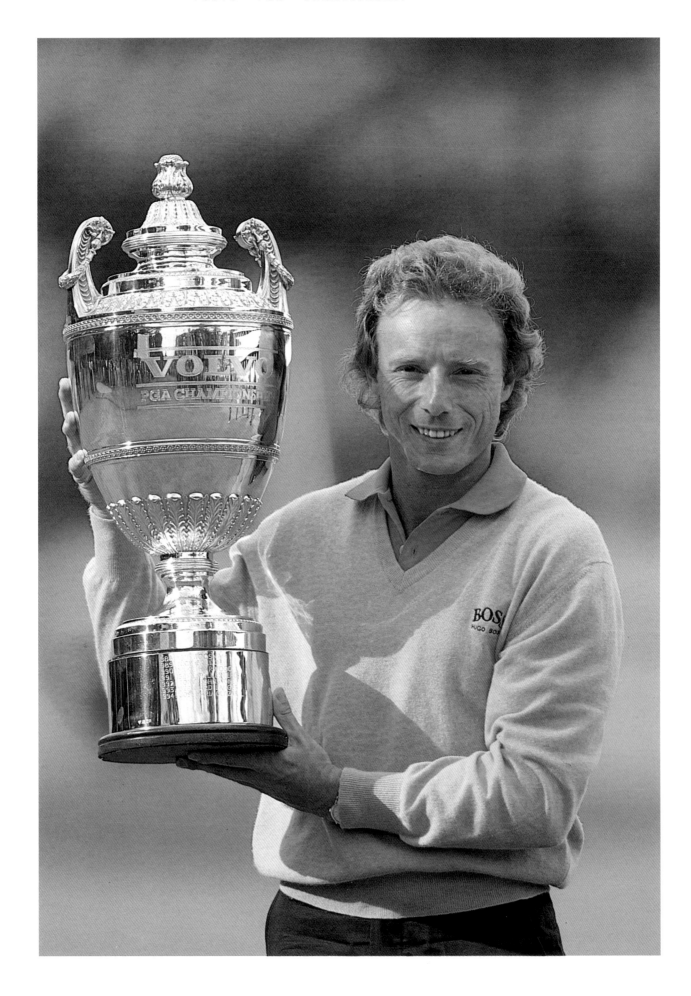

Records tumble to Langer

En route to his third PGA title

Bernhard Langer set two records

which will be hard to beat

Throughout its 71-year history the West course at Wentworth has witnessed many great players lay claim to the freedom of its verdant fairways. Gary Player and Severiano Ballesteros with five victories apiece in the World Match-Play Championship are two of the most notable who spring to mind.

To this pantheon can now be added the name of Bernhard Langer for when it comes to the Volvo PGA Championship there is little sign that his licence on Harry Colt's masterpiece is about to run out.

Two victories in this event in the past three years stack up handily alongside his first PGA Championship in 1987 when he

set a record aggregate of 270 and although this record remained, Langer notched up a few more during the Bank Holiday weekend. As soon as he completed opening rounds of 67 and 73 to make the cut, Langer set a new record for the most consecutive cuts, 57 in all, in a run which began in the 1991 PGA Championship.

Nick Faldo and José Maria Olazábal
(left) in silhouette. Neil Coles congratulates
Bernhard Langer (below) on new record.
Severiano Ballesteros (bottom),
still striking after all these years.

This edged him ahead of Neil Coles' mark
of 56 which began appropriately in the
1973 PGA and ended at the 1979 Open
Championship. 'Congratulations,' said
Coles, 'now go and double it.'

By winning by one stroke from New
Zealand's Michael Campbell and Sweden's
Per-Ulrik Johansson with a nine under par
score of 279, Langer also made it 17 years
in a row with a victory on the PGA
European Tour thereby equalling

97

Ballesteros' run which began in 1976 and ended with a winless 1993.

After collecting the Tour's largest first prize, £150,000, Langer commented: 'It's great to have won for the 17th year in a row. I have two records which are going to be hard to beat. This is always a special tournament to win; it's the players' own event, one of the biggest on Tour. It's always good to beat the best players on a good course.'

'Good' was a word very much in evidence during the week; good field, good course and, prior to the start, some very good news when it was announced that Volvo's partnership with the Tour would continue until 1999. The new deal, worth an estimated £20 million on top of the £30 million invested over the past eight years, means that Volvo will continue to sponsor the PGA Championship, with prize-money rising to £1 million in 1996, the Volvo Masters, the Volvo Scandinavian Masters, the Volvo German Open, the Order of Merit and the Bonus pool plus the courtesy car support programme and its comprehensive broadcast package of the Tour's European-wide telecasts. Volvo will remain the principal sponsor of the Tour but in future the Volvo name will disappear from the Tour's title and revert to the PGA European Tour.

It was a package which delighted everyone, not least Nick Faldo who was making his first European appearance of the year. 'I'm very happy with it,' said Faldo and as if to emphasis his pleasure set the early pace of the first day with a 67, highlighted by an eagle at the final hole following a two iron from 220 yards to ten feet. This score was matched by Langer with Frank Nobilo, Andrew Sherborne and Jesper Parnevik on 68. Defending champion José Maria Olazábal pitched in with a 69 but late in the day they all had

Jesper Parnevik (left) explodes, Robert Karlsson (right above) recovers and Bernhard Langer (right) dominates.

to give best to Peter Senior who regis-
tered six birdies in the last ten holes to
sneak in with a 66.

The eyes had it on the second day, or
to be more precise the eyes of Frank
Nobilo. Plagued by an eye complaint and
barely able to see, the gritty New
Zealander carved out a second 68 to take
a one stroke lead over Sherborne and
Gary Orr. Philip Walton and Sven Strüver
moved into contention on 138 with Faldo
and Senior a stroke behind them. Langer
lay four shots off the pace.

A blustery wind allied to some tricky
pin positions made scoring on the third
day difficult but the examination paper
threw up an unlikely successful candidate.
In contrast to Langer's 17-year run, Mark
Mouland had not won a tournament since

**Mark James (top)
on the skyline.
Mark Mouland
(above) is
sun-drenched.
Deep purple
shades surround
Per-Ulrik
Johansson (right).**

Frank Nobilo (above) explores some Wentworth flora. No repeat victory for José Maria Olazábal (left). Michael Campbell (opposite) earned his stripes.

1988 and was once noted mainly for being 'one of the lads' on Tour, good for a laugh and a drink and no stranger to post-midnight revelry. Now, ('if I'm in bed after ten it's a late night') he showed how talented he can be. A holed eight iron for an eagle at the eighth was followed by three birdies in succession from the 11th and two more at the 17th and 18th put him round in 65 with an eight under par total of 208.

Langer continued in his serene way and arrived at the 18th needing a par for a 67, a birdie for a 66. Following a perfect drive he then cut his three wood second into a bush, hacked out and took three more to get down for a six. That put him into a tie with Mouland and they lay a stoke ahead of Johansson and Sherborne. Faldo was two shots off the pace along with José Maria Cañizares and Colin Montgomerie moved into the reckoning at 211.

'Langer isn't the man you want to be chasing,' said Montgomerie after the third round and he was proved right. But victory was not achieved without a struggle.

THE COURSE

Following a prolonged absence of rain the West course was playing very fast and a capricious wind made scoring difficult. The greens were perfect and the overall condition of the course earned universal praise from the players.

Ahead of Langer, others were making a challenge. Peter O'Malley finished in a burst for a 67 but the real fireworks came from Campbell who, level par after 14 holes, erupted into action with a holed seven iron shot for an eagle at the 15th and then followed that with birdies on the final three holes. This put him round in 67 to set the target at eight under par.

Johansson failed to make a birdie at either of the last two holes so Langer arrived at the final hole needing a par five for victory. He took it quite carefully after a drive into the rough followed by two wedge shots to the green. His first putt from 15 feet ran on somewhat unnerv-

ingly to around a yard from the hole but, resolute as ever, he made no mistake with the return.

So it was a week of records for Langer and he himself was able to list the requirements for such consistency; fairly good technique, good short game, mental strength, good preparation, good course management, fitness and lots of family support.

These qualities can be found in varying amounts among many golfers but when they are gathered together in the rounded personality of Bernhard Langer they add up to one thing – champion.

Chris Plumridge

WEST COURSE, WENTWORTH CLUB, SURREY, MAY 26-29, 1995 · YARDAGE 6957 · PAR 72

Pos	Name	Country	Rnd 1	Rnd 2	Rnd 3	Rnd 4	Total	Prize Money £
1	Bernhard LANGER	(Ger)	67	73	68	71	279	150000
2	Michael CAMPBELL	(NZ)	69	73	71	67	280	78165
	Per-Ulrik JOHANSSON	(Swe)	71	69	69	71	280	78165
4	Jesper PARNEVIK	(Swe)	68	73	70	71	282	32828
	Andrew SHERBORNE	(Eng)	68	69	72	73	282	32828
	Peter SENIOR	(Aus)	66	73	73	70	282	32828
	Peter O'MALLEY	(Aus)	74	71	70	67	282	32828
	Thomas LEVET	(Fr)	72	68	71	71	282	32828
9	Mark MOULAND	(Wal)	72	71	65	75	283	18203
	Colin MONTGOMERIE	(Scot)	70	72	69	72	283	18203
	Silvio GRAPPASONNI	(It)	72	69	71	71	283	18203
12	José Maria CAÑIZARES	(Sp)	69	70	71	74	284	13928
	Nick FALDO	(Eng)	67	72	71	74	284	13928
	Richard BOXALL	(Eng)	72	71	70	71	284	13928
	Miguel Angel JIMÉNEZ	(Sp)	73	69	71	71	284	13928
	Gary ORR	(Scot)	70	67	75	72	284	13928
17	Jonathan LOMAS	(Eng)	74	68	74	69	285	10777
	Stephen AMES	(T&T)	74	69	72	70	285	10777
	Paul EALES	(Eng)	73	68	73	71	285	10777
	Mark JAMES	(Eng)	73	72	67	73	285	10777
	Sven STRÜVER	(Ger)	69	69	74	73	285	10777
	Phillip PRICE	(Wal)	72	73	71	69	285	10777
	Michel BESANCENEY	(Fr)	70	71	71	73	285	10777
	Sandy LYLE	(Scot)	74	71	71	69	285	10777
25	Santiago LUNA	(Sp)	72	73	70	71	286	8640
	José Maria OLAZÁBAL	(Sp)	69	72	72	73	286	8640
	Barry LANE	(Eng)	74	70	73	69	286	8640
	Joakim HAEGGMAN	(Swe)	73	72	72	69	286	8640
	Peter BAKER	(Eng)	70	72	74	70	286	8640
	Andrew OLDCORN	(Eng)	70	73	73	70	286	8640
	Lee WESTWOOD	(Eng)	73	68	73	72	286	8640
32	Gordon BRAND JNR.	(Scot)	73	69	71	74	287	7200
	Mike MCLEAN	(Eng)	73	70	70	74	287	7200
	Mike HARWOOD	(Aus)	75	70	75	67	287	7200
	Mark ROE	(Eng)	71	71	74	71	287	7200
	Philip WALTON	(Ire)	70	68	74	75	287	7200
37	Frank NOBILO	(NZ)	68	68	77	75	288	6120
	Costantino ROCCA	(It)	72	70	77	69	288	6120
	Eamonn DARCY	(Ire)	71	72	72	73	288	6120
	Seve BALLESTEROS	(Sp)	72	73	69	74	288	6120
	Retief GOOSEN	(SA)	72	67	74	75	288	6120
	Mike CLAYTON	(Aus)	74	69	73	72	288	6120
	Wayne RILEY	(Aus)	69	72	73	74	288	6120
44	Vicente FERNANDEZ	(Arg)	72	72	72	73	289	5040
	José RIVERO	(Sp)	74	66	75	74	289	5040
	Rodger DAVIS	(Aus)	70	73	71	75	289	5040
	Mats LANNER	(Swe)	73	72	70	74	289	5040
	Paul MCGINLEY	(Ire)	76	68	72	73	289	5040
49	Robert KARLSSON	(Swe)	72	72	70	76	290	3960
	Vijay SINGH	(Fij)	72	70	73	75	290	3960
	Greg TURNER	(NZ)	74	70	75	71	290	3960
	Paul CURRY	(Eng)	70	72	75	73	290	3960
	Darren CLARKE	(N.Ire)	71	70	82	67	290	3960
	Martin GATES	(Eng)	73	70	76	71	290	3960
	Jay TOWNSEND	(USA)	72	71	73	74	290	3960
56	Ignacio GARRIDO	(Sp)	72	70	74	75	291	2992
	Mark DAVIS	(Eng)	70	75	74	72	291	2992
	Peter MITCHELL	(Eng)	69	73	73	76	291	2992
	Kevin STABLES	(Scot)	74	71	71	75	291	2992
60	Derrick COOPER	(Eng)	72	72	75	73	292	2700
61	Russell CLAYDON	(Eng)	74	71	76	72	293	2610
62	Jean VAN DE VELDE	(Fr)	70	72	73	79	294	2475
	Scott WATSON	(Eng)	75	69	71	79	294	2475
64	Alexander CEJKA	(Ger)	72	72	77	74	295	2295
	Wayne WESTNER	(SA)	73	72	75	75	295	2295
66	Peter FOWLER	(Aus)	73	72	77	75	297	1350
67	ZHANG LIAN-WEI	(Chi)	70	72	78	80	300	1348

SHOT OF THE WEEK

In the final round, New Zealand's Michael Campbell had held his round together with some stalwart putting and was level par after 14 holes. After his drive at the 15th he had 194 yards to the flag and a perfectly struck seven iron flew into the hole to set up an inspirational finish of five under par for the last four holes.

Jonathan Lomas receives hole-in-one champagne from Marcus Westerby of Moët et Chandon flanked by Mitchell Platts of the PGA European Tour. Third PGA Championship for Bernhard Langer (opposite).

Walton downs a second title

Philip Walton captured his second
Tour title of the season with victory
at the Forest of Arden

To describe Philip Walton as a reluctant hero is something of an understatement. He is a complex character in many ways yet at the same time he is a man of simple tastes and modest disposition. On the course, he is an aggressive type of golfer, a player not given to backing off in tight situations, but off the course he is a person who prefers to avoid the limelight, particularly the inevitable interviews by press, radio and TV after winning a big tournament.

When Walton arrives on the podium to be quizzed by the various branches of the media, as he did in June after his famous play-off win against defending champion Colin Montgomerie in the Murphy's English Open, he dodges the issues with great humour and humility. He tries to give nothing away, but such is his Irish upbringing that he gives everything away.

On the first of four visits to the press tent that week, the questions were all to do with the Ryder Cup by Johnnie Walker. Had he not been quoted as saying, enquired one questioner, that he had no interest in the Ryder Cup and would not play even if selected? 'I was kidding,' he revealed after leading the field at Forest of Arden Hotel Golf and Country Club, Warwickshire, with a first round of seven under par 65. 'It's everybody's dream to play in the Ryder Cup.'

Walton's win at Forest of Arden earned him £108,330 and lifted him from 18th place in the Ryder Cup points table to seventh. It also earned him high praise from the man he had beaten at the second extra hole with a birdie four. 'Philip would be a good asset to any Ryder Cup team,' said European number one Montgomerie.

For the ever-modest Walton, 33, this was his second victory of the season on the Tour and his third big win in all, his first title coming in the 1990 Peugeot French Open and his next in the 1995 Open Catalonia Turespana Series in Girona. And it demonstrated he has a taste for the big time – his French Open win came in a play-off with Bernhard Langer and he proved to be undaunted by the prospect of taking on Montgomerie head-to-head.

To say Walton dominated the 1995 Murphy's English Open would be wrong, even though he was away to a flier with his opening 65 to share the lead with ami-

107

A forest of umbrellas.

able German Alexander Cejka. It would be wrong because Montgomerie, after a first round of 69, broke the Forest of Arden course record by a shot the next day with a nine-under-par 63, the fourth 63 of his career, and he was installed as the odds-on favourite to win after establishing a three stroke lead over Walton, his nearest challenger. Somewhat rashly, perhaps, Montgomerie made a comment to the press at the halfway stage that was

to return to haunt him: 'If I don't win from here, I will be very disappointed.'

The next day was miserable, weather-wise, and miserable also for Montgomerie, who stumbled to a level par 72 while Walton quietly went about his business to catch the favourite with a 69. Ever positive in gloomy situations, Montgomerie conceded he had played badly – he described

it as 'my worst round since whenever' – and then declared: 'But I turned a 75 into a 72, and I can win from here.'

Walton, meanwhile, was dosing himself with antibiotics after being diagnosed earlier in the week as being close to pneumonia and he, too, made a comment to the press that was to be remembered. 'Beware the wounded golfer,' said Walton as he left the press tent on Saturday evening for some self-prescribed medicinal

THE COURSE

Colin Montgomerie echoed the views of many competitors in praising the Forest of Arden Hotel Golf and Country Club course. 'It is one of the best, condition-wise, we have played this season,' he said. 'It's been set up for a tournament, and that's very nice to see.'

Colin Montgomerie's chip for victory stays out.

Craig Cassells (left) celebrates winning 13,750 pints of Murphy's for hole-in-one at the 18th. Philip Walton (below) and magic wand.

Murphy's and an early night.

Wounded he might have been, but afraid he was not. Paired with big Monty in the final round, and for the second successive day, Walton stuck to the task like a good 'un and although he was never ahead in the final nine holes, he was never far behind.

Many people thought the giant Scot would get the better of the chirpy Irishman as the closing holes loomed and that seemed to be the case when Montgomerie pitched quite brilliantly to 12 inches at the long 17th for a certain birdie. Walton, who had gambled with a driver second shot that almost caught the water guarding the green, did likewise and then the pair halved the 210-yard 18th in par to take the contest into extra holes.

They returned to the 18th tee to replay the finishing hole. Montgomerie, just off the back edge of the green but only 25 feet or so from the hole, hit the cup with his chip while Walton, a good 60 feet from the hole with his tee shot, putted seven feet short and then bravely sank the next with his broomhandle putter to stay alive.

And so to the long 17th again. This time it was Walton who applied the pressure with a superb third shot to within two feet of the hole and it was Montgomerie who succumbed with a sand-iron shot he later admitted was not one of his best. The resulting long putt was just too much to ask and Walton had deposed the champion.

It was Montgomerie's fourth play-off defeat in four attempts and he was asked in the press tent afterwards for his reflections on play-offs. 'I love them,' replied Montgomerie, before adding quickly: 'No, I hate them. But I didn't do anything wrong and there's nothing wrong with my game.'

Richard Dodd

FOREST OF ARDEN HOTEL & COUNTRY CLUB, JUNE 1-4, 1995 • YARDAGE 7102 • PAR 72

Pos	Name	Country	Rnd 1	Rnd 2	Rnd 3	Rnd 4	Total	Prize Money £
1	Philip WALTON	(Ire)	65	70	69	70	274	108330
2	Colin MONTGOMERIE	(Scot)	69	63	72	70	274	72210
3	Roger CHAPMAN	(Eng)	68	70	70	69	277	40690
4	Peter SENIOR	(Aus)	66	70	69	74	279	27593
	Darren CLARKE	(N.Ire)	72	67	69	71	279	27593
	Wayne WESTNER	(SA)	68	72	71	68	279	27593
7	Terry PRICE	(Aus)	68	71	73	68	280	17875
	Barry LANE	(Eng)	68	69	71	72	280	17875
9	Howard CLARK	(Eng)	68	73	71	69	281	14510
10	Dean ROBERTSON	(Scot)	70	72	74	66	282	12046
	Derrick COOPER	(Eng)	70	66	73	73	282	12046
	Jay TOWNSEND	(USA)	72	69	69	72	282	12046
13	José RIVERO	(Sp)	70	66	71	76	283	9983
	Malcolm MACKENZIE	(Eng)	74	68	68	73	283	9983
	Sandy LYLE	(Scot)	70	68	73	72	283	9983
16	Martin GATES	(Eng)	72	70	70	72	284	8051
	Ignacio GARRIDO	(Sp)	74	68	72	70	284	8051
	Gary EVANS	(Eng)	71	69	73	71	284	8051
	Greg TURNER	(NZ)	74	68	71	71	284	8051
	Mike CLAYTON	(Aus)	70	71	72	71	284	8051
	Paul MCGINLEY	(Ire)	72	68	72	72	284	8051
	Peter BAKER	(Eng)	69	68	74	73	284	8051
	Eamonn DARCY	(Ire)	70	69	74	71	284	8051
24	Michael CAMPBELL	(NZ)	67	71	74	73	285	6149
	Sam TORRANCE	(Scot)	70	72	75	68	285	6149
	Costantino ROCCA	(It)	69	71	71	74	285	6149
	Anders FORSBRAND	(Swe)	68	75	69	73	285	6149
	Paul AFFLECK	(Wal)	71	70	68	76	285	6149
	Jean Louis GUEPY	(Fr)	68	75	67	75	285	6149
	John MCHENRY	(Ire)	71	71	71	72	285	6149
	Joakim HAEGGMAN	(Swe)	71	72	69	73	285	6149
	Mark ROE	(Eng)	70	72	71	72	285	6149
	Mathias GRÖNBERG	(Swe)	68	71	77	69	285	6149
34	Mark MOULAND	(Wal)	71	66	73	76	286	4810
	Peter MITCHELL	(Eng)	72	68	70	76	286	4810
	Gary EMERSON	(Eng)	72	70	74	70	286	4810
	Juan QUIRÓS	(Sp)	70	71	75	70	286	4810
	Gary ORR	(Scot)	72	71	70	73	286	4810
	Øyvind ROJAHN	(Nor)	72	67	74	73	286	4810
	Mats HALLBERG	(Swe)	71	69	72	74	286	4810
41	Ross DRUMMOND	(Scot)	70	71	75	71	287	3900
	Niclas FASTH	(Swe)	71	71	72	73	287	3900
	Raymond BURNS	(N.Ire)	74	69	70	74	287	3900
	Wayne RILEY	(Aus)	68	74	75	70	287	3900
	José Maria CAÑIZARES	(Sp)	69	74	73	71	287	3900
	Paul BROADHURST	(Eng)	70	71	74	72	287	3900
	Craig CASSELLS	(Eng)	75	67	72	73	287	3900
48	Stephen AMES	(T&T)	70	73	73	72	288	3315
	Alexander CEJKA	(Ger)	65	72	75	76	288	3315
50	Andrew COLTART	(Scot)	69	68	79	73	289	3055
	Anders GILLNER	(Swe)	72	71	71	75	289	3055
52	Mark DAVIS	(Eng)	67	72	77	74	290	2795
	Rodger DAVIS	(Aus)	70	73	71	76	290	2795
54	Peter TERAVAINEN	(USA)	74	67	78	72	291	2285
	Mike HARWOOD	(Aus)	68	73	75	75	291	2285
	Peter HEDBLOM	(Swe)	70	72	74	75	291	2285
	Jon ROBSON	(Eng)	73	70	74	74	291	2285
	Paul CURRY	(Eng)	73	70	73	75	291	2285
	Russell CLAYDON	(Eng)	71	68	80	72	291	2285
60	David WILLIAMS	(Eng)	74	69	73	76	292	1885
	Fabrice TARNAUD	(Fr)	71	71	76	74	292	1885
	Ronan RAFFERTY	(N.Ire)	73	68	72	79	292	1885
63	Phillip PRICE	(Wal)	68	71	74	80	293	1690
	Jamie SPENCE	(Eng)	67	72	80	74	293	1690
	Jarmo SANDELIN	(Swe)	72	71	73	77	293	1690
66	Jean VAN DE VELDE	(Fr)	70	71	79	74	294	975
67	David FEHERTY	(N.Ire)	70	72	73	80	295	973

SHOT OF THE WEEK

It was a case of 'all hands to the boat' when Australian Rodger Davis hit his second shot onto an island in the lake at the long 17th in the first round. He was ferried to the island in a boat by his caddie and a course official, from where he delighted the crowds with a superb third shot onto the green to save par.

Langer leaves them all languishing

Bernhard Langer completed his second success in as many weeks with another dominant performance on his home soil

*I*t took Bernhard Langer only 13 days to complete a notable double on the 1995 Tour.

He had barely finished celebrating a record-sprinkled third Volvo PGA Championship at the Tour's Wentworth headquarters, before he was savouring the inclusion of the new Deutsche Bank Open-TPC of Europe at Hamburg's Gut Kaden club among his list of honours. Even an attack of influenza which afflicted him with a sore throat and headaches, failed to prevent the German adding to his aura of invincibility in his own country by sweeping to a ninth home victory by a margin of six strokes.

It was after all exactly what the Hamburg spectators had come to expect. Langer had shown his liking for the park-land course by winning the first Tour event there in 1992, and he again obliged, carrying the burden of expectation with his customary grace and good humour, despite finding it hard to talk and swallow because of the summer virus. But few onlookers were aware of this as he began with rounds of 67, 66 and 68, then slammed the door on his challengers led by Jamie Spence with a closing 69 for an 18 under par total of 270. 'It is always special to play in my own country because of the support I get,' said Langer. 'It makes

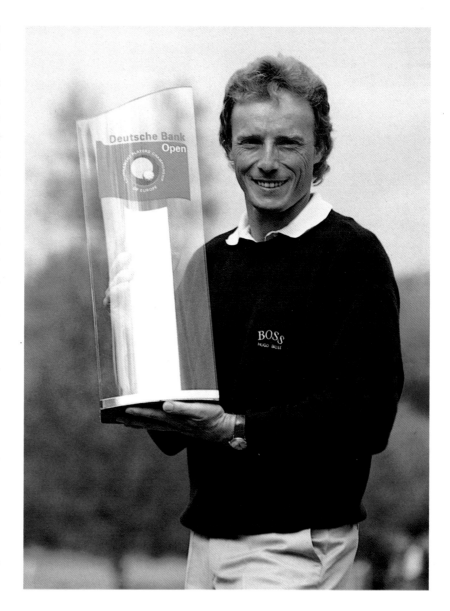

me feel very comfortable, but there are also disadvantages because some people expect me to win all the time. Not enough of my countrymen yet know how difficult that is.'

Largely due to Langer they are learning and when imported attractions like John Daly also conduct clinics for German teenagers, it helps to spread the gospel of golf to a wider audience. The American made an important contribution to a pilot scheme which featured 65 local children. After a month's instruction and practice the best ten juniors were offered free

membership of the Gut Kaden club and also free lessons and equipment. The project will continue to be funded by the Deutsche Bank.

On the course Daly's prodigious hitting was greeted with universal acclaim and although he was embarrassed at lasting only two rounds the American showed he was on the verge of regaining the form that made him the sensation of the 1991 US PGA Championship. He was unfortunate to see his drive at the par five third on the second day go over an internal out-of-bounds line. The resultant

double bogey put him two shots outside the qualifying mark after rounds of 72 and 77.

Langer had by then already acquired 12 birdies to take a four-stroke lead over Spence, with Sam Torrance, already a winner in Italy, and Costantino Rocca, already three times a runner-up, sharing third place at six under par.

Spence had become one of the select band to shoot 60 to win the Canon European Masters in Switzerland in 1992 and he went on to captain England to victory in the Alfred Dunhill Cup at St Andrews. But he failed to gain an expected Ryder Cup debut the following season because of illness and injury and fell from tenth to 50th in the rankings. He slid a further 42 places in the Volvo Order of Merit in 1994.

The Kent golfer had embarked on a programme of restoration with coach Dennis Sheehy and local hypnotist Fred Traexler. While the former had refashioned his swing over a period of five months, the latter had been working on mental stability 'He is able to take away the anxiety when you think you might duff a shot or miss a putt,' explained Spence. A top ten finish in the Portuguese Open had provided encouragement and when he opened with rounds of 68 and

THE COURSE

Gut Kaden is one of the most improved courses on the Tour, and very ecologically friendly following the burial of unsightly overhead power cables on four inward holes. A new first nine holes is now in play, but the 449-yards dog-leg 18th remains the key par four. The drive has to avoid bunkers and rough to find the fairway and correct line to the flag.

Jamie Spence was back on track.

69, scoring an eagle and nine birdies Spence felt his struggles might soon be coming to an end. Not that he was over-optimistic about overhauling Langer with whom he was paired for the last round, especially after the German had added a further shot to his halfway advantage after shooting a third day 68 to Spence's 69.

The most significant move had come from Anders Forsbrand, the Swede based at Valderrama, with a week's best 65 after qualifying on the exact cut off mark, 14 shots behind Langer. Forsbrand's last day 67 made him 12 under par for the final 36 holes and he was rewarded with fourth place, a stroke behind fellow countryman Mats Lanner.

But there was no stopping Langer's inexorable progress towards that ninth German victory after he had moved effort-lessly to an outward 33 and turned for home for the last time with an advantage of seven strokes. Spence birdied the 11th, 12th and 14th but they were no more than a gesture of defiance and for the second day in succession he ended a stroke fur-ther back than when he started. There were times when he thought he was see-ing double when he gazed at the leader-boards and spied his name between Langer and Lanner, the latter having an eagle and six birdies in his 66 to end only one shot behind.

Spence's valiant effort earned him more than £72,000 and quashed worries about his immediate future as a tourna-ment professional. 'I have given a lot of grief to my family because I have spent more time on the practice ground than at home,' he said. 'But this shows the sacri-fice was worth it.'

Langer, whose character, dedication, and resolution have earned the admiration of his fellow professionals, nodded appre-ciatively. Even with two Augusta green jackets and now a 33rd PGA European Tour victory to his name, he has never stopped working on his game.

Mike Britten

SHOT OF THE WEEK

A two iron from 220 yards by Mats Lanner that finished two feet from the third hole in the final round. The eagle three reminded him of the good times before he lost faith in his putter, and helped him to his best finish since he won in Madeira in 1994.

GUT KADEN, HAMBURG, JUNE 8-11, 1995 • YARDAGE 7029 • PAR 72

Pos	Name	Country	Rnd 1	Rnd 2	Rnd 3	Rnd 4	Total	Prize Money £
1	Bernhard LANGER	(Ger)	67	66	68	69	270	108330
2	Jamie SPENCE	(Eng)	68	69	69	70	276	72210
3	Mats LANNER	(Swe)	69	74	68	66	277	40690
4	Anders FORSBRAND	(Swe)	75	72	65	67	279	32500
5	Sam TORRANCE	(Scot)	71	67	71	71	280	25140
	Costantino ROCCA	(It)	68	70	71	71	280	25140
7	Roger WESSELS	(SA)	73	70	71	67	281	16753
	Michael CAMPBELL	(NZ)	71	68	74	68	281	16753
	Stephen MCALLISTER	(Scot)	73	68	69	71	281	16753
10	Jarmo SANDELIN	(Swe)	71	69	73	69	282	12480
	Gary ORR	(Scot)	70	74	71	67	282	12480
12	Mark LITTON	(Wal)	71	68	73	71	283	10058
	Jean Louis GUEPY	(Fr)	75	70	69	69	283	10058
	Peter BAKER	(Eng)	69	74	71	69	283	10058
	Santiago LUNA	(Sp)	71	74	69	69	283	10058
	Stephen AMES	(T&T)	70	69	71	73	283	10058
17	Darren CLARKE	(N.Ire)	73	68	75	68	284	8406
	Domingo HOSPITAL	(Sp)	73	73	67	71	284	8406
	Paul MCGINLEY	(Ire)	71	75	67	71	284	8406
20	Paul R SIMPSON	(Eng)	72	70	71	72	285	7215
	Michel BESANCENEY	(Fr)	71	74	67	73	285	7215
	Colin MONTGOMERIE	(Scot)	72	69	72	72	285	7215
	Malcolm MACKENZIE	(Eng)	73	68	74	70	285	7215
	Sandy LYLE	(Scot)	74	71	67	73	285	7215
	Michael ARCHER	(Eng)	74	70	69	72	285	7215
	Pierre FULKE	(Swe)	74	73	69	69	285	7215
27	Paul AFFLECK	(Wal)	75	69	72	70	286	5859
	Lee WESTWOOD	(Eng)	74	73	70	69	286	5859
	Russell CLAYDON	(Eng)	71	72	72	71	286	5859
	Stephen DODD	(Wal)	73	70	73	70	286	5859
	John BICKERTON	(Eng)	72	73	71	70	286	5859
	Ignacio GARRIDO	(Sp)	69	71	72	74	286	5859
	Emanuele CANONICA	(It)	69	77	69	71	286	5859
34	Jim PAYNE	(Eng)	73	74	68	72	287	4680
	Peter TERAVAINEN	(USA)	73	70	71	73	287	4680
	Antoine LEBOUC	(Fr)	71	73	75	68	287	4680
	Peter O'MALLEY	(Aus)	72	72	70	73	287	4680
	Olle KARLSSON	(Swe)	74	71	72	70	287	4680
	Ian WOOSNAM	(Wal)	74	72	74	67	287	4680
	Jean VAN DE VELDE	(Fr)	73	70	73	71	287	4680
	Wayne RILEY	(Aus)	73	70	73	71	287	4680
	Paul MOLONEY	(Aus)	71	71	73	72	287	4680
43	Ross DRUMMOND	(Scot)	71	71	71	75	288	3835
	David CARTER	(Eng)	77	69	73	69	288	3835
	Fredrik LINDGREN	(Swe)	71	71	78	68	288	3835
	Liam WHITE	(Eng)	71	75	71	71	288	3835
47	Gavin LEVENSON	(SA)	77	69	75	68	289	3055
	Mark JAMES	(Eng)	71	74	72	72	289	3055
	Peter MITCHELL	(Eng)	71	72	74	72	289	3055
	Mark MOULAND	(Wal)	74	67	77	71	289	3055
	Andrew SHERBORNE	(Eng)	71	73	69	76	289	3055
	José Manuel CARRILES	(Sp)	73	73	75	68	289	3055
	Alberto BINAGHI	(It)	72	75	69	73	289	3055
	Craig CASSELLS	(Eng)	72	73	74	70	289	3055
55	Roger CHAPMAN	(Eng)	73	71	74	72	290	2340
	Sven STRÜVER	(Ger)	70	69	77	74	290	2340
	Andrew COLTART	(Scot)	76	71	70	73	290	2340
58	Fredrik ANDERSSON	(Swe)	76	71	71	73	291	1950
	Mike MCLEAN	(Eng)	70	71	76	74	291	1950
	Paul LAWRIE	(Scot)	76	71	72	72	291	1950
	Scott WATSON	(Eng)	75	71	71	74	291	1950
	Ian SPENCER	(Eng)	73	69	77	72	291	1950
63	Jonathan LOMAS	(Eng)	73	74	74	71	292	1511
	Paul WAY	(Eng)	74	73	70	75	292	1511
	Niclas FASTH	(Swe)	75	72	76	69	292	1511
	David J RUSSELL	(Eng)	71	73	76	72	292	1511
67	Paul MAYO	(Wal)	75	71	75	72	293	973
68	Carl MASON	(Eng)	74	73	72	75	294	971
69	Ove SELLBERG	(Swe)	71	72	77	75	295	968
	Gary EMERSON	(Eng)	73	74	75	73	295	968
71	George RYALL	(Eng)	74	73	77	72	296	965
72	Neal BRIGGS	(Eng)	72	73	79	75	299	963

Contemplative pose from Ian Woosnam.

All in the mind for Oldcorn

After working with a psychologist
Andrew Oldcorn had a relaxing
and rewarding time in Jersey

Andrew Oldcorn might well be the last person you'd expect to find on the psychologist's couch. The career of the Bolton-born, Edinburgh-based Englishman with the rich Scottish accent, has long been characterised by such a determination to succeed, that, one supposed, the intricacies of the mind game had been solved long ago.

It was Oldcorn, you will remember, who, when his career was being ravaged by the debilitating mystery virus ME – Myalgic Encephalomyelitis – confounded everyone by taking the halfway lead in the 1991 Open Championship. 'I want to be an example that if you fight you can win against this,' he said at Royal Birkdale.

It was also Oldcorn who, two years later, having emerged from almost four years of battling the illness, surprised everyone yet again by notching up his first Tour victory at the Turespana Masters-Open Andalucia. 'I am absolutely ecstatic,' he said. 'I knew I had a title in me.'

And it was Oldcorn who popped up

to add an epilogue to the fairytale that seemed to have ended in Cadiz. The 35-year old's victory in the DHL Jersey Open at La Moye, however, was as assured as Oldcorn has proved himself single-minded.

It came as something of a surprise, therefore, that the man who has shown so many inner reserves in his professional career, should admit he had been working with a psychologist. 'I've been working

with Dr Richard Cox from Edinburgh,' said Oldcorn, after securing his three-shot victory. 'I felt so in control out there. Despite the pressure I felt perfectly relaxed.'

The good Doctor Cox works with the Scottish rugby team, and it was its former captain and rugby legend, Gavin Hastings, who recommended Oldcorn should give him a try. Whatever else Cox taught Oldcorn, discretion he already has in abundance. 'I'd like to keep what was said between him and me to myself, otherwise I will be giving stuff away to the other guys.'

Geoff Boycott couldn't have been more succinct. Nor indeed, could the great English opener have given less away than Oldcorn, who, over the course of the weekend, was as parsimonious with his dropped shots as he was precise with his irons.

Once Oldcorn had nosed himself into a three-shot lead going into the final round – thanks to a third round 66, six under par – he was never again caught, and rarely threatened.

Having proved that he has an aptitude for links golf at Royal Birkdale in 1991, he reaffirmed the fact over Jersey's historic La Moye links with a near-faultless closing 69. To four birdies was added a solitary bogey – at the 172-yard, par three 12th, where he missed the green with a five iron. And to his solitary Andalucian crown was added a Jersey title.

Along with the kudos, a £50,000 winner's cheque, and bragging rights, victory also brought with it a place in the prestigious Gene Sarazen World Open later in the year. The tournament, which aims to bring together all the national champions from around the world, had recognised little Jersey and the Channel Isles sovereign rights, and rewarded the Jersey Open champion accordingly. Reward for Oldcorn, then, a trip to Atlanta in November. Reward for runner-up Dean Robertson from Scotland, however, meant he could stay at home in November if he wanted.

The £33,330 the former Walker Cup man from Paisley, Glasgow, picked up for his week's work, ensured that the former Scottish Amateur champion, avoided a quick return to the PGA European Tour Qualifying School. The year before he had been one of 14 players involved in a sudden-death play-off for two cards. 'I wasn't nervous,' remembered the Scot. 'How could I be? There were 14 of us for two cards. I had nothing to lose.' At Montpellier Robertson chipped in at the first extra hole for his Tour card. Careers have been made and destroyed by less.

Having obtained his Volvo Tour passport in such fashion, the 24-year old quickly learned the importance to making the most of one's chances. In Jersey, having played his way to 12 under par after 71 holes – two behind the leader – Robertson went in search of the closing birdie that might just catch Oldcorn.

On the Friday, Robertson had driven the 397-yard closing hole from the tee – missing out on an albatross hole-in-one by inches. Come Sunday he leaked his

Olle Karlsson in flowery setting.

drive right into the rough, leaving him a tricky recovery. 'I wasn't trying to hit it hard. I had missed the fairway by a couple of yards. I didn't have much chance of controlling it, so I just wanted to get on the green.'

The resulting recovery did just that – floating over the flagstick to some 20 feet – setting up a closing par for a round of 68, and second spot. 'The last is a birdie hole. If I had come off it with a bogey, that would have been disappointing.' he said.

Playing behind, Oldcorn, who had just birdied the 482-yard 16th to move to 15 under (where he reached the green in two) just needed to par in. 'From the moment I won in Cadiz, the next thing I wanted to do was to win again, to prove to other people – not to myself – that it wasn't just a one-off,' said Oldcorn. 'Now I want to get into contention again. That, after all, is what we're all out here for. I feel that I can go on from this.'

Having been through so much already, who knows what, or where, Oldcorn will go next?

Matthew Chancellor

THE COURSE

Jersey's La Moye Golf Club on the south-western corner of the island, near the famous Corbiere lighthouse, is perched high, 250 feet above sea level, offering breathtaking views of St Ouen's Bay out towards Guernsey and beyond. As traditional a links as you could find anywhere, with dry, close-cropped, undulating, sandy fairways; quite untypically it begins with a par three, which, at 165 yards offers a gentle start to a round. However, the front nine is some 150 yards longer than the second loop, and consequently many of La Moye's members prefer to begin their challenge at the tenth.

LA MOYE GOLF CLUB, ST BRELADE, JERSEY, JUNE 15-18, 1995 • YARDAGE 6813 • PAR 72

Pos	Name	Country	Rnd 1	Rnd 2	Rnd 3	Rnd 4	Total	Prize Money £
1	Andrew OLDCORN	(Eng)	70	68	66	69	273	50000
2	Dean ROBERTSON	(Scot)	66	70	72	68	276	33330
3	Paul MOLONEY	(Aus)	68	71	70	68	277	16890
	Olle KARLSSON	(Swe)	69	69	70	69	277	16890
5	Brian DAVIS	(Eng)	68	70	75	65	278	10733
	Mark JAMES	(Eng)	71	69	70	68	278	10733
	Roger WESSELS	(SA)	69	68	74	67	278	10733
8	Malcolm MACKENZIE	(Eng)	64	72	72	71	279	6427
	David WILLIAMS	(Eng)	68	70	72	69	279	6427
	Martin GATES	(Eng)	70	72	71	66	279	6427
	Wayne STEPHENS	(Eng)	70	68	69	72	279	6427
12	Philip WALTON	(Ire)	73	69	71	67	280	4995
	David CARTER	(Eng)	68	77	69	66	280	4995
14	Glenn RALPH	(Eng)	70	71	71	69	281	4145
	Richard BOXALL	(Eng)	69	68	75	69	281	4145
	Paul AFFLECK	(Wal)	69	70	72	70	281	4145
	Derrick COOPER	(Eng)	70	71	71	69	281	4145
	Lee WESTWOOD	(Eng)	67	70	78	66	281	4145
	Peter MITCHELL	(Eng)	73	69	70	69	281	4145
20	Carl MASON	(Eng)	70	72	71	69	282	3465
	Paul CURRY	(Eng)	64	74	70	74	282	3465
	Peter BAKER	(Eng)	71	70	72	69	282	3465
	Des SMYTH	(Ire)	72	69	73	68	282	3465
24	Ronan RAFFERTY	(N.Ire)	66	69	78	70	283	3105
	John BICKERTON	(Eng)	71	70	69	73	283	3105
	Eamonn DARCY	(Ire)	68	72	74	69	283	3105
	Paul BROADHURST	(Eng)	70	73	69	71	283	3105
28	Howard CLARK	(Eng)	68	71	72	73	284	2835
	Greg TURNER	(NZ)	70	74	72	68	284	2835
30	John MELLOR	(Eng)	72	71	72	70	285	2610
	John MCHENRY	(Ire)	69	70	73	73	285	2610
	Stuart CAGE	(Eng)	71	70	74	70	285	2610
33	Gavin LEVENSON	(SA)	68	70	74	74	286	2340
	Jim PAYNE	(Eng)	69	71	76	70	286	2340
	Gary EMERSON	(Eng)	74	71	69	72	286	2340
	Heinz P THÜL	(Ger)	72	69	74	71	286	2340
	Fabrice TARNAUD	(Fr)	72	68	73	73	286	2340
38	Joakim GRONHAGEN	(Swe)	69	76	69	73	287	1980
	Ian PALMER	(SA)	70	70	77	70	287	1980
	Robert LEE	(Eng)	75	70	71	71	287	1980
	Ross DRUMMOND	(Scot)	70	70	78	69	287	1980
	Paul MCGINLEY	(Ire)	75	66	73	73	287	1980
	David J RUSSELL	(Eng)	74	70	74	69	287	1980
	George RYALL	(Eng)	75	70	73	69	287	1980
45	Liam WHITE	(Eng)	73	71	74	70	288	1680
	Philip TALBOT	(Eng)	73	72	75	68	288	1680
	Jeremy ROBINSON	(Eng)	71	70	75	72	288	1680
48	David RAY	(Eng)	64	77	74	74	289	1500
	Steven RICHARDSON	(Eng)	70	72	72	75	289	1500
	Keith WATERS	(Eng)	73	72	74	70	289	1500
51	Mike MILLER	(Scot)	73	71	73	73	290	1290
	Christy O'CONNOR JNR	(Ire)	71	72	76	71	290	1290
	John HAWKSWORTH	(Eng)	71	69	77	73	290	1290
	Craig CASSELLS	(Eng)	70	72	75	73	290	1290
55	Jonathan WILSHIRE	(Eng)	72	73	74	72	291	1080
	Mark LITTON	(Wal)	72	66	82	71	291	1080
	Gabriel HJERTSTEDT	(Swe)	70	70	78	73	291	1080
58	Ricky WILLISON	(Eng)	71	73	80	68	292	930
	Martyn ROBERTS	(Wal)	74	68	72	78	292	930
	Ian SPENCER	(Eng)	74	70	74	74	292	930
61	Bill LONGMUIR	(Scot)	72	71	77	75	295	855
	Andrew SHERBORNE	(Eng)	71	73	78	73	295	855
63	Mark NICHOLS	(Eng)	68	75	75	78	296	795
	Carlos LARRAIN	(Ven)	73	71	78	74	296	795
65	Ross MCFARLANE	(Eng)	69	73	82	77	301	750

SHOT OF THE WEEK

Sometimes it takes one moment of magic to turn a week around. The 80-yard sand-wedge shot that flew into the hole at the 370-yard, par four tenth, on a thoroughly wet and miserable Saturday afternoon, began the momentum that carried Andrew Oldcorn to a third-round 66, and ultimately to victory at La Moye. Oldcorn's ball pitched some ten feet beyond the flag before skidding back over the wet, slippery green, into the cup for an unlikely eagle two. And the magic continued at the following hole, with yet another eagle, at the par five 11th. 'I've never had two eagles before in a row,' he said, 'which, in the conditions, was quite something.'

Brilliant Broadhurst draws away

A final round of 63 gave Paul Broadhurst

an eight-stroke winning margin at one

of the toughest venues on the Tour

*L*eading amateur in the Open Championship in 1988, a winner on Tour in only his eighth event, the 1989 Rookie of the Year, a record-equalling 63 in the 1990 Open at St Andrews, unbeaten on his Ryder Cup debut the following year.

It all started so well for Paul Broadhurst. And then it all started to go wrong. So wrong that by the end of 1994 the man who seemed to have the world at his feet instead had it crashing around him. From the dizzy heights of Kiawah Island the 29-year old from Warwickshire had plunged to 131st on the Volvo Order of Merit. Had it not been for his victory in the Benson and Hedges International Open the previous season he would have fallen off the Tour altogether. 'At one point I pulled out of a tournament when I couldn't even hit a wedge on the practice range,' he recalled. 'My swing was all over the place, my mind was gone, I wasn't well and I took three weeks off to

try to get my act together.'

It took much longer than that, but after linking up again with his old coach Frank Miller the form that he feared he might have lost for good finally returned.

Le Golf National, staging the Peugeot

French Open for the fifth successive year, is not a place for the faint-hearted. Not even on a still day and certainly not in the strong winds (gusting up to 30mph) which greeted the players on the first two days.

Several players had come straight from the US Open, including a limping José Maria Olazábal with worrying news that a small tumour had developed on the same right foot which was operated on in January – further surgery would be needed in due course – and defending champion Mark Roe, a commendable 13th in his first-ever major championship in America. Seve Ballesteros had been due to play too, but withdrew because of back problems.

Broadhurst served notice of his comeback with an opening 67 which contained eight birdies and two trips to the water, first at the long ninth and then at the 15th, a hole laying claim to the title 'toughest on Tour'. Not excessively long at 421 yards, it was, however,

123

Greg Turner (left) took
the halfway lead and
Neal Briggs (opposite)
had his best finish.

directly into the wind and with a lake
both down the right and virtually encir-
cling the green the 147-strong field were a
collective 142 over par there in the first
round. One ahead of Denmark's Anders
Sorensen at the end of the day, the
Midlander stretched that to three the following afternoon, but then came to the
long 18th. Stretching as it does down the

opposite side of the same lake, it is the
15th's partner-in-crime and, having safely
negotiated one, Broadhurst came to grief
at the other. Hooking his drive and seeing
it suffer a splash landing was bad enough,
but when he chipped from left of the
green back into the water a quadruple
bogey nine had to go on his card. The
only comfort was that Keith Waters,

Michel Besanceney, Peter Fowler and
Joakim Gronhagen all had tens on theirs
and Emmanuel Dussart an 11.

As a result, the halfway leader was
New Zealander Greg Turner, who got the
closing stretch of holes exactly right when
he said; 'It's like walking through a minefield with hobnail boots on.' Twelve players did not even make it to halfway, a

knee injury forcing Roe to quit after 27 holes.

The Saturday belonged to Italian Costantino Rocca, winner of the title in 1993. His 66 in the easier – let's make that 'less difficult' – conditions took him to nine under par, three in front of Challenge Tour graduate Neal Briggs and four ahead of Turner and Broadhurst.

That advantage, though, was gone in one hole on the final afternoon. In the bushes at the back of the first green Rocca opened with a six against Brigg's birdie three and when he double-bogeyed the short second as well Rocca was on his way to a round where just about everything that could go wrong did go wrong.

In total contrast, everything for Broadhurst up ahead was going right at long last. A hat-trick of

birdies from the second and another at the sixth swept him two clear of Briggs and then, after chipping in to save par at the 12th, he simply became inspired. With putts of only 12 inches, three feet, six feet and four feet he birdied the next four holes – yes, including the 15th – and, in perfect coup de grace, made a 15-footer on the last for a course record 63 and an astonishing eight stroke victory.

It was the biggest winning margin on the Volvo Tour since Vijay Singh took the 1992 Volvo German Open by 11. And it made Broadhurst the 43rd member of the PGA European Tour's Millionaires' Club. The door to the club had been opened in readiness for him a long time before and how relieved he was to arrive there in the style of old.

Mark Garrod

THE COURSE

Close to Versailles in the south-west corner of Paris, Le Golf National has rightly been heralded as one of the best new golf designs in Europe. Opened in 1990, it has staged the Peugeot French Open each year since and will do so until 1998 at least. The recently-published Peugeot Golf Guide says of the Albatros championship course: 'Only those with handicap under 24 can hope to tackle it without despair. American-style holes alternate with those typically found at the coast in a panorama of large, artificial dunes. The smallest error can prove to be costly.' They are not wrong.

NATIONAL G.C., PARIS, FRANCE, JUNE 22-25, 1995 · YARDAGE 7120 · PAR 72

Pos	Name	Country	Rnd 1	Rnd 2	Rnd 3	Rnd 4	Total	Prize Money £
1	Paul BROADHURST	(Eng)	67	75	69	63	274	91660
2	Neal BRIGGS	(Eng)	73	69	68	72	282	61100
3	Pierre FULKE	(Swe)	69	76	71	68	284	34430
4	Greg TURNER	(NZ)	70	70	71	74	285	23350
	Sandy LYLE	(Scot)	75	69	70	71	285	23350
	Costantino ROCCA	(It)	69	72	66	78	285	23350
7	Anders SØRENSEN	(Den)	68	76	73	69	286	14176
	Peter O'MALLEY	(Aus)	72	73	69	72	286	14176
	José RIVERO	(Sp)	72	71	74	69	286	14176
10	Jamie SPENCE	(Eng)	71	71	76	69	287	11000
11	Paul AFFLECK	(Wal)	72	71	72	74	289	9471
	José Maria OLAZÁBAL	(Sp)	69	79	71	70	289	9471
	Peter BAKER	(Eng)	74	75	73	67	289	9471
14	Adam HUNTER	(Scot)	69	73	76	72	290	7755
	Frank NOBILO	(NZ)	72	73	73	72	290	7755
	Paul MOLONEY	(Aus)	77	70	74	69	290	7755
	Olle KARLSSON	(Swe)	74	71	72	73	290	7755
	Eamonn DARCY	(Ire)	74	74	69	73	290	7755
19	Phil GOLDING	(Eng)	71	73	77	70	291	6618
	Ronan RAFFERTY	(N.Ire)	72	74	70	75	291	6618
	Wayne RILEY	(Aus)	72	72	73	74	291	6618
22	Liam WHITE	(Eng)	69	76	73	74	292	5692
	David WILLIAMS	(Eng)	73	72	74	73	292	5692
	Jonathan LOMAS	(Eng)	71	73	74	74	292	5692
	Jean VAN DE VELDE	(Fr)	76	71	74	71	292	5692
	Barry LANE	(Eng)	75	75	72	70	292	5692
	Eoghan O'CONNELL	(Ire)	73	76	72	71	292	5692
	Ross MCFARLANE	(Eng)	72	72	73	75	292	5692
	Sven STRÜVER	(Ger)	74	73	73	72	292	5692
30	John HAWKSWORTH	(Eng)	70	80	73	70	293	4716
	Marc FARRY	(Fr)	70	77	72	74	293	4716
	José COCERES	(Arg)	74	76	72	71	293	4716
	Mark DAVIS	(Eng)	75	73	72	73	293	4716
34	Michael JONZON	(Swe)	72	76	74	72	294	4180
	Terry PRICE	(Aus)	72	78	75	69	294	4180
	Des SMYTH	(Ire)	71	77	74	72	294	4180
	David CARTER	(Eng)	72	75	78	69	294	4180
	Paul LAWRIE	(Scot)	77	72	74	71	294	4180
39	Silvio GRAPPASONNI	(It)	73	77	75	70	295	3520
	Stephen DODD	(Wal)	70	78	73	74	295	3520
	Michael ARCHER	(Eng)	70	78	73	74	295	3520
	Gordon BRAND JNR.	(Scot)	74	76	75	70	295	3520
	Steven RICHARDSON	(Eng)	75	75	71	74	295	3520
	Paul EALES	(Eng)	73	73	71	78	295	3520
	Mark MOULAND	(Wal)	75	73	76	71	295	3520
46	Jean Louis GUEPY	(Fr)	77	71	73	75	296	3025
	Peter MITCHELL	(Eng)	77	71	74	74	296	3025
48	Christian CEVAER	(Fr)	78	71	77	71	297	2695
	Paul MAYO	(Wal)	71	77	78	71	297	2695
	Ignacio GARRIDO	(Sp)	75	74	76	72	297	2695
	Fredrik ANDERSSON	(Swe)	73	75	76	73	297	2695
52	David J RUSSELL	(Eng)	73	71	78	76	298	2310
	Roger CHAPMAN	(Eng)	74	72	77	75	298	2310
	Tim PLANCHIN	(Fr)	72	73	81	72	298	2310
55	Stuart CAGE	(Eng)	74	75	72	78	299	1881
	Retief GOOSEN	(SA)	78	72	75	74	299	1881
	Lee WESTWOOD	(Eng)	76	73	77	73	299	1881
	Peter TERAVAINEN	(USA)	73	76	74	76	299	1881
	Tony JOHNSTONE	(Zim)	76	73	74	76	299	1881
60	Martin GATES	(Eng)	71	78	77	74	300	1540
	Juan QUIRÓS	(Sp)	73	77	78	72	300	1540
	Mike CLAYTON	(Aus)	79	71	80	70	300	1540
	Santiago LUNA	(Sp)	76	73	78	73	300	1540
	Raymond BURNS	(N.Ire)	76	72	82	70	300	1540
65	Joakim HAEGGMAN	(Swe)	72	78	79	72	301	932
	Roger WESSELS	(SA)	75	73	76	77	301	932
	Antoine LEBOUC	(Fr)	73	75	79	74	301	932
	Paul CURRY	(Eng)	77	71	79	74	301	932
	Stephen MCALLISTER	(Scot)	76	73	75	77	301	932
70	Malcolm MACKENZIE	(Eng)	75	75	78	74	302	816
	Frédéric REGARD	(Fr)	78	72	76	76	302	816
72	Per HAUGSRUD	(Nor)	73	71	78	81	303	813
73	Russell CLAYDON	(Eng)	75	75	80	74	304	811
74	David CURRY	(Eng)	72	75	78	80	305	809
75	Paul R SIMPSON	(Eng)	74	76	83	80	313	807

SHOT OF THE WEEK

He may have finished only 72nd of the 75 to survive the halfway cut, but 30-year old Norwegian Per Haugsrud takes pride of place here for one moment of sheer delight in a season of toil. While others were running into double figures elsewhere Haugsrud hit a 224-yard four iron on the 530-yard third hole in round two and achieved only the second albatross two of the year. An albatross on the Albatros course. Perfection.

INSPIRATION BY TIFFANY.

For more than 150 years Tiffany & Co. has inspired some of the world's most celebrated achievements ✦ People the world over have come to expect something special when they open a Tiffany blue box ✦ Whether you are commissioning a custom design trophy, planning a Corporate Sports Sponsorship, or sending a business gift, Tiffany's Corporate Division will help you make a uniquely memorable impression ✦ To learn more about the benefits of a Tiffany Corporate Account call 0171 408-2271.

TIFFANY & CO.

SINCE 1837

25 OLD BOND STREET LONDON W1.

Nobilo focuses on victory

Recovered from a troublesome eye problem,
Frank Nobilo was looking good in Germany

N obody put the evil eye on Frank Nobilo before he played in the BMW International at St Eurach on the cusp of June and July. Somebody had already done that more than a month before. It was not enough, anyway, to stop the stylish New Zealander keeping his gaze fixed steadily on his target and hitting the bullseye dead centre with his first European victory for two years.

Nobilo had been troubled by a malaise of the eyeballs when he competed in the Volvo PGA Championship at Wentworth at the end of May. He could see nothing clearly; everything had a blurred halo around it, and he was seriously worried. Nobody ever won a golf tournament without his eyes wide open and functioning properly, and Nobilo's were not. And then some.

In desperation, he went to an eye specialist who told him that he was suffering from a condition known as keratits. The correct medicinal compound was pro-

duced, Nobilo slapped it on, and in a matter of days a couple of weeks of worry were blessedly over.

Relieved, Nobilo took himself off to St Eurach, where he encountered, among others, Bernhard Langer with a bad back, Sandy Lyle with a malfunctioning calculator and Jarmo Sandelin with a disintegrating game plan. Nobilo did not back into the BMW title, he played too well for that, but there is no doubting that some of his rivals did rather ease his path to victory, which he achieved with a total of 272, 16 under par.

It was Nobilo's first win since he took the Turespana Open Meditarrania in 1993, and only his fourth in eight years as a Tour player. Something of a mystery that, Nobilo exudes class with every shot, and as very probably the best player to emerge from New Zealand since the great left-hander, Bob Charles, he has the game and the temperament to have done much, much better.

Nobilo probably knew as he travelled from Munich airport to the stylish St

Eurach course in the last few days of flaming June that if he beat one particular man in the field, he would probably do pretty well. The man's name was Bernhard Langer, a heck of a job to dislodge once he got his teeth stuck into a tournament, and nigh-on invincible in his own country.

Langer was going for his tenth victory on German soil. He was the people's favourite, and those who might just have brought a touch more expertise to the prediction game, the players, would not have demurred. To add fuel to the argument, Langer came to the tournament with the mother of all pains in the neck; and Langer is almost beyond argument the best injured player in the game.

In his time the German, who hides his greatness as a golfer with unparalleled modesty and innate good manners, has produced some of his finest hours when indisposed by flu, or an aching back, or something similarly unpleasant.

The problem had been caused, it emerged, by probably nothing much more serious than a night spent sleeping awkwardly. A momentary frisson of concern might have shivered its way down the back of Bernard Gallacher, the European Ryder Cup captain, when he heard of Langer's indisposition – events later in the week would have eased his fears. Langer looked out of it after a first-round 73, eight shots off the pace. By Sunday he had hauled himself back up into a share of second place alongside Jarmo Sandelin, the third-round leader, only a couple of shots outside a play-off. Beware the injured golfer, so the weathered maxim goes. It could have been coined with Herr Langer in mind.

So, what of the winner? Nobilo came into the tournament following a distinguished tenth place in the US Open at Shinnecock Hills. He felt pretty pleased with himself for that, as he deserved to be. 'Somebody worked out that I had the third or fourth best stroke average in the Majors in the 1990s,' he said. 'I reckon that's something to be proud about.'

Indeed it was, but it was nothing compared with the way he felt at the end of four days in the sweltering heat of St Eurach. He opened with a 67 to be two shots behind Irish Tour rookie Raymond Burns and Mats Hallberg, of Sweden, who were prevented from claiming course records by the fact that in the first two days the field was playing preferred lies.

Not quite in the van, but not far from it, either.

On day two Nobilo had a 69, but was put somewhat in the shade by two notable stories, one of success, one of sadness. Success went to Marc Farry, the tall Frenchman, who had his second 67 of the tournament and led by two from Nobilo with Eoghan O'Connell, Sandelin and

Burns a further stroke behind. The first prize at St Eurach was £91,660, £60,000 more than Farry had ever made in an entire season before. No wonder the grey-haired Frenchman looked a trifle haggard that night. He was to finish 71, 72 to finish five shots astern of the winner in joint seventh place.

Meanwhile, for one Alexander Walter Barr Lyle there was absolutely nothing to be glad about. Sandy, who had had a first round of 76, then burnt his way round the course in 64 to put himself into contention before he learnt that, although he knew he had had a 76 in round one and signed for that score, the individual hole scores on his card had added up to only 75.

Anders Forsbrand, who had been his marker, had put him down for a four at the 14th, when he had had a five. 'I knew I'd taken five, but I didn't spot it in Anders' scoring,' he wailed. 'It's my fault, I know it, but I still feel pretty angry about it all.' He then proved it by taking an uncharacteristic flying kick at his unwitting golf bag and wandered off, distraught, dismayed and disqualified for signing for a

lower score than he had taken. The general feeling was that Lyle had been cruelly unlucky. Rule 6-6, implemented by Tournament Director Mike Stewart, does not take a lack of luck into account. Rules are rules, and Lyle had to take an early flight home.

The third round was utterly dominated by Sandelin, the extrovert Finnish-born Swede, who produced the round of the day, a nine-birdie 63 that this time did break the course record, preferred lies having been dispensed with. While Sandelin was up to his deeds of derring-do, Nobilo had his second 69 in succession, but was still five behind the big-hitting Swede with the 52-inch driver as they pegged up

for the final round.

Sandelin was undone on the final day by his inexperience. He had got into position to win by playing the way he knows best, aggressively, but on a steamy Sunday afternoon he abandoned his usual free-hitting style and tried instead to defend his lead. He should never have done it. Attacking golf is what he is good at, and he would almost certainly been better off playing the game that had put him up there in the first place. A closing 74 was poor reward for what had been up to then a spectacular week for the flamboyant Swede.

Nobilo, on the other hand, was attempting to produce fireworks and succeeding. He eagled the first, having to hole only a putt of four feet, and although he bogeyed the second he then had five birdies in eight holes from the fifth and had caught Sandelin by the turn, which he reached in 33 to the Swede's 38.

Sandelin committed another gaffe when his long driver put him in all sorts of bother on the 16th. By this time the smooth-swinging Nobilo was in a three-stroke lead, and the second bogey of his round at the last was an irrelevance that took almost no gloss off a closing 67.

Langer, meantime, had reached the turn in 32, five under par, and looked dangerous, but a muted inward nine meant that he concluded the tournament with his third consecutive 67. 'If somebody had offered me second place after 73 on Thursday I'd have said he was crazy,' he said. He had fought the good fight, but had been outvoted. Frank Nobilo, on the other hand, had offered himself as a candidate, campaigned brilliantly for four days and got elected. It was a week, you might say, when the eyes had it.

Mel Webb

THE COURSE

St Eurach is a modern, testing lay-out that rolls it way through hills and valleys in the foothills of the mountains that come winter are the playground of the world's wealthiest skiers and the snowy playing fields of the world's best skiers – Germisch Partenkirchen is a mere 20 minute drive up the road. It was being used for the second time for the tournament, and with its subtly contoured greens and winding fairway it was a fitting venue for the £550,000 tournament.

St Eurach Land und Golfclub, Munich, June 29-July 2, 1995 · Yardage 7090 · Par 72

Pos	Name	Country	Rnd 1	Rnd 2	Rnd 3	Rnd 4	Total	Prize Money £
1	Frank NOBILO	(NZ)	67	69	69	67	272	91660
2	Bernhard LANGER	(Ger)	73	67	67	67	274	47765
	Jarmo SANDELIN	(Swe)	68	69	63	74	274	47765
4	Mike CLAYTON	(Aus)	73	67	67	68	275	25400
	Jean Louis GUEPY	(Fr)	70	72	65	68	275	25400
6	Fredrik LINDGREN	(Swe)	72	67	68	69	276	19250
7	Philip TALBOT	(Eng)	70	68	72	67	277	11706
	David GILFORD	(Eng)	70	69	69	69	277	11706
	Silvio GRAPPASONNI	(It)	72	70	66	69	277	11706
	Raymond BURNS	(N.Ire)	65	72	69	71	277	11706
	Peter BAKER	(Eng)	72	67	67	71	277	11706
	Martin GATES	(Eng)	72	67	67	71	277	11706
	Marc FARRY	(Fr)	67	67	71	72	277	11706
14	Derrick COOPER	(Eng)	73	69	70	66	278	8250
	Mark MCNULTY	(Zim)	69	72	69	68	278	8250
16	Peter MITCHELL	(Eng)	70	69	71	69	279	7425
	Peter HEDBLOM	(Swe)	74	67	68	70	279	7425
	Eoghan O'CONNELL	(Ire)	72	65	70	72	279	7425
19	Mark JAMES	(Eng)	68	70	74	68	280	6446
	Emanuele CANONICA	(It)	73	69	72	66	280	6446
	Jamie SPENCE	(Eng)	70	72	69	69	280	6446
	Thomas GÖGELE	(Ger)	70	73	68	69	280	6446
	David CARTER	(Eng)	70	68	70	72	280	6446
24	Klas ERIKSSON	(Swe)	71	71	69	70	281	5692
	Jay TOWNSEND	(USA)	75	67	69	70	281	5692
	Mats HALLBERG	(Swe)	65	74	71	71	281	5692
	Mark ROE	(Eng)	70	68	71	72	281	5692
28	Russell CLAYDON	(Eng)	72	73	68	69	282	4876
	Joakim GRÖNHAGEN	(Swe)	71	70	71	70	282	4876
	Mathias GRÖNBERG	(Swe)	72	70	70	70	282	4876
	John BICKERTON	(Eng)	70	71	70	71	282	4876
	Christian CEVAER	(Fr)	71	72	68	71	282	4876
	Gary EVANS	(Eng)	71	73	64	74	282	4876
34	Jonathan LOMAS	(Eng)	72	71	70	70	283	4235
	José RIVERO	(Sp)	71	69	73	70	283	4235
	Peter FOWLER	(Aus)	71	69	71	72	283	4235
	Mark MOULAND	(Wal)	71	69	71	72	283	4235
38	Terry PRICE	(Aus)	67	71	76	70	284	3850
	Costantino ROCCA	(It)	71	71	69	73	284	3850
	Fredrik JACOBSON	(Swe)	71	72	67	74	284	3850
41	John MELLOR	(Eng)	72	72	70	71	285	3575
	Retief GOOSEN	(SA)	71	72	72	70	285	3575
43	Paul MAYO	(Wal)	71	72	72	71	286	3355
	Jeff CRANFORD	(USA)	72	70	73	71	286	3355
45	Stephen DODD	(Wal)	73	72	68	74	287	2860
	Steven BOTTOMLEY	(Eng)	74	68	72	73	287	2860
	David FEHERTY	(N.Ire)	71	72	72	72	287	2860
	Andrew SHERBORNE	(Eng)	69	73	73	72	287	2860
	Jean VAN DE VELDE	(Fr)	72	71	73	71	287	2860
	Craig CASSELLS	(Eng)	70	73	74	70	287	2860
	Roger WESSELS	(SA)	70	73	67	77	287	2860
52	Dean ROBERTSON	(Scot)	73	70	70	75	288	2200
	Mark NICHOLS	(Eng)	71	72	71	74	288	2200
	Paul MOLONEY	(Aus)	74	69	71	74	288	2200
	Juan QUIRÓS	(Sp)	70	70	74	74	288	2200
	Darren CLARKE	(N.Ire)	71	73	73	71	288	2200
57	Scott WATSON	(Eng)	74	71	68	76	289	1716
	Gabriel HJERTSTEDT	(Swe)	72	71	70	76	289	1716
	Peter O'MALLEY	(Aus)	73	72	69	75	289	1716
	Phillip PRICE	(Wal)	71	74	74	70	289	1716
	John BLAND	(SA)	75	70	76	68	289	1716
62	David CURRY	(Eng)	71	71	73	75	290	1540
63	Ronan RAFFERTY	(N.Ire)	71	73	70	77	291	1430
	Richard BOXALL	(Eng)	72	73	70	76	291	1430
	Sven STRÜVER	(Ger)	74	68	74	75	291	1430
	Florian BRUHNS	(Ger)	73	71	74	74	292	(Am)
66	Gary ORR	(Scot)	75	69	74	75	293	825

SHOT OF THE WEEK

Nobilo was five shots behind Jarmo Sandelin when he embarked on the final lap of the tournament. His round was still in its infancy when he produced a supreme four iron second shot on the par five first to give himself a short putt for an eagle, which he duly holed with a minimum of fuss. He had been on the course for less than ten minutes and already he had reduced Sandelin's lead by two. It was a killing blow; he never looked back from that moment on.

Torrance turns back the clock

Sam Torrance's first victory

in the Irish Open occurred in 1981

and 14 years later he was victorious again

S am Torrance slipped into a reflective mood while pondering his position at the halfway stage. A second successive 68 had him level with fellow Scot, Colin Montgomerie, and a stroke behind the surprise leader, Germany's Sven Strüver. 'By winning this title in 1981, I made the Ryder Cup for the first time,' he mused. 'Wouldn't it be marvellous to secure an eighth appearance by winning it again, on Sunday.'

Those sceptics among us were more than happy to indulge a player who had always held a rather special place in Irish hearts. By Sunday evening, however, Torrance had brought a seemingly wild dream to glorious reality by sinking an eagle putt to capture the Murphy's Irish Open title in a play-off with Howard Clark and Stuart Cage. And when David Feherty embraced him in his moment of triumph, the Ulsterman was effectively representing an adoptive nation.

There were many spectators old enough to remember his victory at Portmarnock 14 years previously. And they roared their approval. 'What crowds!' exclaimed the newly-crowned champion.

'And do they love the Scots!'

It had been a splendid climax to a golfing festival in delightful sunshine at Mount Juliet, where attendances over the four days reached a cumulative record of 111,000. Greg Norman, the world's number one, was among the overseas challengers; so was the 1982 US Masters champion Craig Stadler, making a competitive debut in Ireland. But after some remarkable fluctuations, the Europeans reigned supreme.

Strüver, who had made an ill-fated visit to Ireland as an amateur in 1988 when he damaged a knee in a bunker at Royal Portrush, had a more positive impact this time around. Indeed his opening round of 65 for a two-stoke lead, matched the tournament record for the course, established by Nick Faldo in 1993 and equalled by John Daly on the final day in 1994.

Not only had he the effrontery to upstage the Great White Shark, but he

THE COURSE

The condition of Mount Juliet was described by Greg Norman as: 'By far the best I've ever seen in Europe.' Bernhard Langer said: 'I've never seen the course in such good shape.' Meanwhile, tournament director Andy McFee rated the greens (Stimpmeter speed of 11.0) as: 'The best we have played on this year.'

Greg Norman (above) drew the crowds but was upstaged by Sven Strüver (right) in the first round.

SHOT OF THE WEEK

From his drive at the second play-off hole, the long, 518-yard 17th, Sam Torrance had 240 yards to the pin. He made glorious contact with a three-wood, hitting 'as good a shot as I've ever played,' to leave the ball nine feet beyond the hole. It set up the eagle chance which secured him the title.

Stuart Cage (below) was early play-off victim.

was seven strokes clear of distinguished compatriot, Bernhard Langer, the defending champion. As it happened, Strüver's fine play for the remainder of the tournament owed much to daily, telephone contact with Langer, who acted in the role of mentor to the gifted 27-year old from Hamburg.

Meanwhile, speculation as to which Scot would edge clear on 'moving day' was resolved when a third round 69 lifted Montgomerie to the top of the leaderboard. But the most significant move was made by Norman – 26th to joint second – with a thrilling 65 which included seven birdies and an eagle. 'I reckoned I needed two good rounds to win the championship and I've played really well to get one of them,' he said.

So Norman was right up there in contention, joint second with David Gilford and Torrance, a stroke behind Montgomerie on 205, 11 under par. The feeling that it would take 13 or 14 under to win, seemed to be confirmed for Torrance when, on his arrival at the course on Sunday, he learned that Langer had surged from the pack to be joint leader on 11 under, with six holes left.

But in attempting to extend his birdie blitz, the holder found water at the 13th for a wretched, double-bogey six.

Unaware of what would develop later in the day, he said pragmatically: 'I knew 11 under wouldn't be enough; I was aiming to get to 13 which would give the leaders something to think about.'

For once, Langer was wrong. As fortunes swung crazily during a hectic afternoon, there were actually six players – Torrance, Montgomerie, Clark, Cage, Derrick Cooper and Strüver – tied on 11 under when the field had gone through the 15th. And one by one they fell away. Montgomerie bogeyed the 17th; Strüver and Cooper bogeyed the last; so did Torrance and Clark, except that they had got to 12 under with birdies on the 17th.

Eventually, they were joined by Cage in a three-way play-off at the treacherous,

476-yard 18th, with water down the left side. Cage found the water and was first to fall, leaving Torrance and Clark to continue the fight down the long 17th. There, Clark scrambled brilliantly to sink a putt of 15 feet for a birdie four but Torrance, with a three wood to nine feet, sank the putt for an eagle three and the title.

It was his 20th European victory, his second of the season and his 29th internationally. 'Up to now, the Australian PGA of 1980 had always stood apart, but to win in a field of this class, this way, makes this the finest win of my career,' he said afterwards. And in keeping with his grand plan, Ryder Cup selection was virtually secured.

Dermot Gilleece

Mount Juliet CC, Thomastown, Co.Kilkenny, July 6-9, 1995 • Yardage 7143 • Par 72

Pos	Name	Country	Rnd 1	Rnd 2	Rnd 3	Rnd 4	Total	Prize Money £
1	Sam TORRANCE	(Scot)	68	68	70	71	277	111107
2	Stuart CAGE	(Eng)	70	69	69	69	277	57897
	Howard CLARK	(Eng)	71	68	68	70	277	57897
4	Robert ALLENBY	(Aus)	67	72	70	69	278	21397
	Derrick COOPER	(Eng)	74	69	66	69	278	21397
	David GILFORD	(Eng)	70	69	67	72	278	21397
	Sven STRÜVER	(Ger)	65	70	73	70	278	21397
	Peter BAKER	(Eng)	72	69	67	70	278	21397
	Craig STADLER	(USA)	69	73	70	66	278	21397
	Colin MONTGOMERIE	(Scot)	68	68	69	73	278	21397
11	Greg NORMAN	(Aus)	70	71	65	73	279	12266
12	Roger WESSELS	(SA)	70	68	71	71	280	10546
	Ian WOOSNAM	(Wal)	73	67	71	69	280	10546
	Wayne RILEY	(Aus)	68	71	68	73	280	10546
	Michael CAMPBELL	(NZ)	68	69	70	73	280	10546
16	Miguel Angel JIMÉNEZ	(Sp)	68	73	67	73	281	8815
	Wayne WESTNER	(SA)	70	67	73	71	281	8815
	Domingo HOSPITAL	(Sp)	68	71	70	72	281	8815
	Jean VAN DE VELDE	(Fr)	71	73	66	71	281	8815
20	Gary ORR	(Scot)	70	68	73	71	282	7700
	John MELLOR	(Eng)	74	69	71	68	282	7700
	Bernhard LANGER	(Ger)	72	72	69	69	282	7700
	Sandy LYLE	(Scot)	68	71	72	71	282	7700
24	Martin GATES	(Eng)	68	74	69	72	283	6900
	Andrew COLTART	(Scot)	71	71	68	73	283	6900
	Ross MCFARLANE	(Eng)	73	71	67	72	283	6900
	Des SMYTH	(Ire)	71	71	72	69	283	6900
28	Rodger DAVIS	(Aus)	74	70	69	71	284	6000
	Frank NOBILO	(NZ)	71	70	70	73	284	6000
	Ronan RAFFERTY	(N.Ire)	71	71	70	72	284	6000
	Paul MCGINLEY	(Ire)	73	66	71	74	284	6000
	Eamonn DARCY	(Ire)	71	68	73	72	284	6000
33	Olle KARLSSON	(Swe)	70	74	66	75	285	4933
	Barry LANE	(Eng)	73	71	73	68	285	4933
	David CARTER	(Eng)	72	72	74	67	285	4933
	Terry PRICE	(Aus)	69	69	72	75	285	4933
	Dean ROBERTSON	(Scot)	74	68	68	75	285	4933
	Jonathan LOMAS	(Eng)	72	68	72	73	285	4933
	Jarmo SANDELIN	(Swe)	72	72	68	73	285	4933
	Philip WALTON	(Ire)	69	69	71	76	285	4933
	Michael JONZON	(Swe)	72	71	72	70	285	4933
42	Anders FORSBRAND	(Swe)	70	68	72	76	286	4066
	Steven RICHARDSON	(Eng)	71	71	70	74	286	4066
	Phil GOLDING	(Eng)	70	69	73	74	286	4066
	Retief GOOSEN	(SA)	74	70	67	75	286	4066
46	Christian CEVAER	(Fr)	68	74	71	74	287	3533
	Liam WHITE	(Eng)	72	67	73	75	287	3533
	Michel BESANCENEY	(Fr)	72	72	70	73	287	3533
	Miguel Angel MARTIN	(Sp)	72	69	70	76	287	3533
50	Silvio GRAPPASONNI	(It)	71	73	71	73	288	2800
	Adam HUNTER	(Scot)	73	69	73	73	288	2800
	Darren CLARKE	(N.Ire)	73	71	76	68	288	2800
	Martyn ROBERTS	(Wal)	71	71	72	74	288	2800
	Andrew SHERBORNE	(Eng)	73	68	73	74	288	2800
	Richard BOXALL	(Eng)	72	70	75	71	288	2800
	John MCHENRY	(Ire)	73	71	71	73	288	2800
57	Per-Ulrik JOHANSSON	(Swe)	72	72	73	72	289	2116
	Marc FARRY	(Fr)	71	70	74	74	289	2116
	Paul WAY	(Eng)	68	74	73	74	289	2116
	Lucas PARSONS	(Aus)	70	71	73	75	289	2116
61	Mike CLAYTON	(Aus)	69	75	72	74	290	1833
	Paolo QUIRICI	(Swi)	69	75	69	77	290	1833
	Rolf MUNTZ	(Hol)	72	72	73	73	290	1833
	Ove SELLBERG	(Swe)	72	71	71	76	290	1833
65	Andrew OLDCORN	(Eng)	70	73	74	74	291	1333
	Mats LANNER	(Swe)	72	72	72	75	291	1333
67	John BICKERTON	(Eng)	72	71	74	75	292	994
	Stephen HAMILL	(N.Ire)	73	70	75	74	292	994
	John HAWKSWORTH	(Eng)	71	68	76	77	292	994
	Paul R SIMPSON	(Eng)	68	74	77	73	292	994
	Joakim GRÖNHAGEN	(Swe)	69	74	70	79	292	994
72	Roger CHAPMAN	(Eng)	67	73	79	74	293	986
	Michael ARCHER	(Eng)	74	69	73	77	293	986
	David J RUSSELL	(Eng)	70	74	73	76	293	986
75	Jay TOWNSEND	(USA)	75	68	82	70	295	982
76	Peter HEDBLOM	(Swe)	76	67	74	81	298	980
77	Mats HALLBERG	(Swe)	72	72	83	72	299	978

Craig Stadler nearly hits his hat.

Riley homes in at last

After 11 years of competing in Europe

Wayne Riley chose Carnoustie

to make his breakthrough

Wayne Riley, without a win in 11 seasons in Europe, put his name alongside Tommy Armour, Henry Cotton, Ben Hogan, Gary Player and Tom Watson in the records. The Australian showed admirable resolve as he rebuffed a sustained challenge from Nick Faldo, to win the Scottish Open at Carnoustie and in the process join a select band who have won championships on this venerable Angus links.

Riley won with a measured performance which belied the fact that he was also a relative newcomer to the art of leading from the front. He went into the final round with a five-shot cushion over Faldo and for most of the time seemed almost as serene as the Scottish weather as he compiled a closing round of level par 72 to finish two shots ahead of Faldo and four shots in front of Colin Montgomerie in the race for the £108,330 first prize.

'This is a great moment for me,' said the 1991 Australian Open Champion who has inherited the nickname of Radar on Tour after the Radar O'Reilly character in the MASH television series. 'I feel as if a

huge burden has just been lifted from my shoulders. I'm over the moon. I always believed I was good enough to win on the PGA European Tour but after all this time you do start to have some doubts.' The Australian might have been labouring under a mental burden but it didn't seem to cause him too much trouble as he celebrated Carnoustie's return to big time golf with six under par 66 in the opening round.

In most instances a 66 would have been more than enough to lead at Carnoustie but the gods were in a welcoming mood and the world's finest golfers took advantage of their largesse with a bout of scoring seldom seen at such a treacherous course.

The first round started and finished shrouded in a North See 'haar' but in between the sun shone in cloudless skies and the wind barely ruffled the flags. It represented ideal weather and the competitors weren't slow to take advantage of such benign conditions and none more so than Colin Montgomerie who romped round in a course record 64 which included eight birdies and no blemishes on his card.

'It was an almost perfect round,' Montgomerie said before berating himself for missing two further short putts which would have inflicted further damage to Carnoustie's reputation as Britain's toughest course. At the end of the round Montgomerie's 64 put him two shots

THE · SCOTTISH · OPEN

The venerable Carnoustie course made a welcome return to big-time professional golf when it played host to the Scottish Open. The Angus course has staged five Open Championships and a host of other national events but it had been two decades since it had been under the international spotlight when Tom Watson had beaten Australian Jack Newton in an 18-hole play-off to win the first of his five Open titles.

Watson joined the select band of

international superstars who have won The Open at Carnoustie. Tommy Armour made a sentimental journey back to Scotland from his adopted home in America to win the first Open held there in 1931 and he was later joined by Henry Cotton (1937), Ben Hogan (1953), Gary Player (1968) and Watson (1975). Hogan's triumph in 1953 was all the more remarkable because it was the one and only time he competed in the Championship.

ahead of a chasing pack comprising Michael Campbell, Ian Woosnam and Craig Parry but the Scot was to lose the outright lead 24 hours later when Riley added a 69 to his opening 66 to tie him at nine under par.

Parry's progress during the opening two rounds had been imperial but it wasn't until the end of the penultimate round that the assembled multitude started to see him as a serious threat to the bigger names surrounding him on the leaderboard. At the end of the second round Colin Montgomerie and Nick Faldo were still locked together as favourites although the biggest headlines were reserved for Seve Ballesteros who added a second round 80 to his opening 81 to miss the cut by no less than 17 shots. It was the Spaniard's fourth successive missed cut and as if that wasn't enough to depress his legion of Scottish fans he would have finished dead last had Scotland's Mike Miller not come in late in the day with an 86 to save the Spaniard from that particular fate.

Carnoustie's fearsome reputation took a bit of a battering in the opening two rounds with no less than 69 competitors registering scores under the par of 72 but it was an altogether sterner test in the third round when the wind started to blow and squalls drifted across the course.

Nick Faldo made a strong bid for the title.

Gordon Sherry (right) gave amateur golf a giant boost. Third round 75 scuppered Colin Montgomerie (below).

The arrival of the wind signalled the end of a number of challenges and the biggest casualty of all was local favourite, Colin Montgomerie, who drifted out of contention with a three over par 75. Montgomerie was almost inconsolable at the end of his round, blaming his putting for his demise. 'It was horrendous,' he said. 'The third round is always important and I've blown it again. It's the most frustrating day I've ever had on a golf course. I two-putted every green. Every … green,' he added, carefully avoiding using the expletive which would have given us a more graphic indication of how he felt.

Montgomerie's 75 put paid to his chances altogether, and with Nick Faldo little more than marking time with a 71 as austere as the conditions he battled under, it enabled Riley to open up a five-shot lead with his second successive three under par 69.

Riley's 69 tied the best round of the day and it set the diminutive Australian

up with a chance to make amends for losing a three-shot lead going into final round of the Open V33 last season and also to turn the tables on Faldo, who in 1988 had overtaken the Australian down the stretch to win the French Open at Chantilly.

The clubhouse leader could have been excused for being concerned about Faldo's

presence behind him on the leaderboard but, if he was, he didn't let it show. He's a confident individual and a character too.

'If I can't win from here I would be just as well selling ice cream in Sydney,' he said on the eve of the final round.

He did and so Sydney's street vendors can rest easy for a while.

Colin Callander   141

CARNOUSTIE, ANGUS, SCOTLAND, JULY 12-15, 1995 • YARDAGE 7187 • PAR 72

Pos	Name	Country	Rnd 1	Rnd 2	Rnd 3	Rnd 4	Total	Prize Money £
1	Wayne RILEY	(Aus)	66	69	69	72	276	108330
2	Nick FALDO	(Eng)	70	68	71	69	278	72210
3	Colin MONTGOMERIE	(Scot)	64	71	75	70	280	40690
4	Craig PARRY	(Aus)	67	73	72	71	283	32500
	Gordon SHERRY	(Scot)	73	70	71	69	283	(Am)
5	Ronan RAFFERTY	(N.Ire)	74	68	70	72	284	21507
	Peter O'MALLEY	(Aus)	71	73	72	68	284	21507
	Martin GATES	(Eng)	74	69	74	67	284	21507
	David DUVAL	(USA)	72	69	75	68	284	21507
9	Katsuyoshi TOMORI	(Jap)	70	66	77	72	285	14510
10	Olle KARLSSON	(Swe)	69	71	73	73	286	10750
	Anders FORSBRAND	(Swe)	72	71	73	70	286	10750
	Sam TORRANCE	(Scot)	69	72	75	70	286	10750
	Domingo HOSPITAL	(Sp)	67	77	69	73	286	10750
	Mark DAVIS	(Eng)	72	68	71	75	286	10750
	José RIVERO	(Sp)	69	73	74	70	286	10750
	Mark MCNULTY	(Zim)	75	71	71	69	286	10750
17	Michael CAMPBELL	(NZ)	66	77	72	72	287	8580
	Greg TURNER	(NZ)	71	71	73	72	287	8580
19	Peter MITCHELL	(Eng)	72	72	74	70	288	7518
	Robert KARLSSON	(Swe)	73	72	75	68	288	7518
	Steve STRICKER	(USA)	74	70	76	68	288	7518
	Sandy LYLE	(Scot)	74	70	72	72	288	7518
	Roger CHAPMAN	(Eng)	69	75	72	72	288	7518
	Lee WESTWOOD	(Eng)	73	71	75	69	288	7518
25	Des SMYTH	(Ire)	72	72	75	70	289	6337
	Mark JAMES	(Eng)	74	71	74	70	289	6337
	Costantino ROCCA	(It)	73	71	73	72	289	6337
	Andrew COLTART	(Scot)	74	72	69	74	289	6337
	Jean Louis GUEPY	(Fr)	69	73	76	71	289	6337
	Jay DELSING	(USA)	73	70	74	72	289	6337
31	David GILFORD	(Eng)	72	71	74	73	290	5411.25
	Ian WOOSNAM	(Wal)	66	74	78	72	290	5411.25
	Vicente FERNANDEZ	(Arg)	71	74	77	68	290	5411.25
	José COCERES	(Arg)	71	73	71	75	290	5411.25
35	Brian MARCHBANK	(Scot)	70	75	74	72	291	4615
	Robert ALLENBY	(Aus)	73	72	73	73	291	4615
	David FEHERTY	(N.Ire)	71	68	74	78	291	4615
	Santiago LUNA	(Sp)	71	75	73	72	291	4615
	Jay TOWNSEND	(USA)	73	71	74	73	291	4615
	Jamie SPENCE	(Eng)	69	72	76	74	291	4615
	Barry LANE	(Eng)	68	74	76	73	291	4615
	Mike HARWOOD	(Aus)	71	71	77	72	291	4615
43	Iain PYMAN	(Eng)	72	73	75	72	292	3835
	Retief GOOSEN	(SA)	75	71	73	73	292	3835
	Ignacio GARRIDO	(Sp)	74	71	73	74	292	3835
	Philip WALTON	(Ire)	70	75	74	73	292	3835
47	Terry PRICE	(Aus)	69	73	79	72	293	3445
	Scott WATSON	(Eng)	69	71	79	74	293	3445
	Tiger WOODS	(USA)	69	71	75	78	293	(Am)
49	Paul LAWRIE	(Scot)	70	69	77	78	294	2795
	Russell CLAYDON	(Eng)	73	73	74	74	294	2795
	Manuel PIÑERO	(Sp)	74	71	78	71	294	2795
	David FROST	(SA)	72	73	75	74	294	2795
	Vijay SINGH	(Fij)	67	75	73	79	294	2795
	Mark ROE	(Eng)	70	75	79	70	294	2795
	Peter HEDBLOM	(Swe)	72	73	76	73	294	2795
	Eamonn DARCY	(Ire)	74	70	74	76	294	2795
57	Raymond BURNS	(N.Ire)	70	74	80	71	295	2101
	André BOSSERT	(Swi)	72	73	78	72	295	2101
	Stephen AMES	(T&T)	72	72	76	75	295	2101
60	Tony JOHNSTONE	(Zim)	71	75	72	78	296	1852
	Stephen MCALLISTER	(Scot)	73	73	75	75	296	1852
	Steven RICHARDSON	(Eng)	73	72	74	77	296	1852
	Jim PAYNE	(Eng)	71	74	76	75	296	1852
64	Steen TINNING	(Den)	71	73	77	76	297	1315
	Gary ORR	(Scot)	71	75	75	76	297	1315
	Andrew OLDCORN	(Eng)	72	73	73	79	297	1315
	Jean VAN DE VELDE	(Fr)	72	73	77	75	297	1315
68	Klas ERIKSSON	(Swe)	69	72	79	78	298	971
69	Colin GILLIES	(Scot)	72	74	73	80	299	968
	Ross DRUMMOND	(Scot)	73	71	75	80	299	968
71	Peter FOWLER	(Aus)	74	72	74	80	300	963
	Gordon BRAND JNR.	(Scot)	70	74	80	76	300	963
	John MORSE	(USA)	71	74	78	77	300	963
74	Craig RONALD	(Scot)	73	73	76	79	301	959
75	Donnie HAMMOND	(USA)	72	74	82	74	302	957
76	Gary EVANS	(Eng)	69	77	77	81	304	955

SHOT OF THE WEEK

There comes a time when all potential champions must stand up and be counted and that's just what Wayne Riley did on the penultimate hole in the final round at Carnoustie. The Australian had hit his second shot to about 20 feet from the flag and was left with a treacherous putt to consolidate his lead and determine the outcome of the tournament. 'That was the one,' Riley said later. 'I was under the gun right there.' Riley had two things in mind as he studied the line. He wanted to hole it as a single putt would give him an insurmountable lead going down the last but he couldn't afford to be too aggressive in case he charged the first putt past and then missed the return. 'It was a feel putt,' he said. 'I knew that if I hit it hard it would come about six feet from the left but I didn't want to do that so I aimed about nine feet to the left and tried to get it to die at the hole. It was the perfect putt,' he added, 'when it dropped in I knew I had won.'

The competition wasn't up to the competition.

ProQuip are the first and only weatherwear manufacturer to receive the PGA European Tour's most prestigious accolade, the Tournament Quality Award.

This is because more professionals choose to wear ProQuip on Tour than any other rainsuit. Which leaves other weatherwear manufacturers out in the cold.

All ProQuip 'Tournament Quality' rainsuits feature Gore-Tex® drop liners, the world's most breathable waterproof fabric.

ProQuip International Ltd., Wisloe Road, Cambridge, Gloucestershire GL2 7AF. Tel: (0453) 890707. Fax: (0453) 890826.

PROQUIP

IF YOU'RE PRO QUALITY YOU'RE PROQUIP

A walk on the wild side

John Daly defied gale force winds
at St Andrews to win the second
major championship of his career

T wo years ago John Daly made his first trip to golf's holy of holies and liked what he saw. Admittedly it was in October and the weather was in the sub-zero bracket but in helping the United States win the Alfred Dunhill Cup, Daly provided ample forewarning that the 1995 Open Championship at St Andrews would place him firmly in the limelight again.

Daly's brand of golf, titanic hitting coupled with a silky short game, appeared to be tailor-made for the Old Course but his erratic form and previous history of personal problems placed him among the also-rans with a bookmakers' price of 80-1. This price was also based on Daly's modest Open record which had seen him finish dead last in 1992 and 1994 alongside a 14th place in 1993.

Other players with longer pedigree were favoured on a course that had been prepared to pristine perfection and with the weather proving benign prior to the off, there were fears that the armoury of modern equipment carried by the competitors would render the test inadequate.

Such misgivings were, as it turned out, ill-founded as the Old Course's chief defence, the wind, came bustling in to make this one of the wildest Opens for many a year.

Even on the first day there was

enough wind to make matters interesting and it signalled the emergence of that consummate links player, Tom Watson. Through the green, Watson is still majestic, on the greens less so. He actually started by holing from 70 feet from the back of the first green but nothing else fell on the first nine. Coming home his putter began to behave and four birdies and an eagle at the 14th added up to 31 back and a 67. This was matched by Ben Crenshaw, a man who putts beautifully but finds the longer shots are less consistent. Both departments were working splendidly and six birdies with just one dropped shot was evidence of this.

Daly notched seven birdies in his opening 67 and the leading quartet was completed by Mark McNulty, runner-up to Nick Faldo at St Andrews in 1990.

Four players, David Feherty, Vijay Singh, Bill Glasson and Mats Hallberg lay on 68 and among those on 69 were US Open champion Corey Pavin. Defending champion Nick Price had a 70 which included the only birdie of the day at the 17th, Greg Norman, who nearly pulled out with a back injury, was on 71, but Nick Faldo had a dispiriting 74.

As is always the case at the Open, there were a number of cameos enacted away from the leaders. The most memorable of these occurred at the 14th and involved none other than Jack Nicklaus. Moving along at three over par after 13 holes, he put his second shot at the 14th into the notorious Hell bunker. Attempting a rather ambitious recovery, his ball hit the face and stayed in. It stayed in after the next effort and also the next and the one after that. He eventually emerged, put his next shot on the green and then three-putted for a ten. There was no truth in the rumour that the bunker would be re-named the Bear Trap.

The wind increased in pace on the second day and three players, Brad Faxon, Japan's Katsuyoshi Tomori and Daly ended it tied for the lead at six under par. They led by one stroke from six others including Costantino Rocca and Ernie Els. Faldo pulled himself up into contention with a 67 to lead the British challenge alongside David Gilford, Sam Torrance and the remarkable amateur Gordon Sherry who outscored his two illustrious playing companions, Norman and

Watson. The cut fell at 148 and because of the ten stroke rule, 99 players survived thereby costing the R&A an extra £120,000 in prize money.

These are the bare facts concerning that day because it really belonged to one man. After 23 Opens and 80 rounds, Arnold Palmer made his final emotional approach up the 18th fairway and for a moment we were transported back to 1960 when he made his very first appearance on the crumpled links. It mattered not that he would miss the cut by a considerable margin, what did matter was that he was here to receive due acknowledgement for his contribution not only to the Open but to the game as a whole. The fact that there were another 158 competitors, many of whom were watching that last nostalgic walk, playing for £1.25 million was attributable to Palmer for it was he who brought the game into the living room with panache, zest and flair and gave impetus to a Championship that was searching for credibility. Now it was time to say goodbye but even though he had promised himself there would be no sentimental breakdown, the voice was breaking and the tears were gathering as he gave his farewell press conference. The memories may be sepia tinted but there was no lack of colour in Arnold Palmer's exit.

Then it was the turn of the new generation and as if to prove the cosmopolitan nature of the Open it came in the shape of a New Zealand Maori with Scottish ancestry. As the wind snapped the flagsticks back, 26-year old Michael Campbell put together the round of the Championship, a 65 that was immaculate in its precision. A former graduate of the PGA European Challenge Tour, Campbell had put in some solid performances on the 1995 Volvo Tour but was without a victory. His round put him in a position to change all that as he collected four birdies on the first nine and then birdied three in a row from the 12th. The crisis came, inevitably, at the 17th when his second shot with a nine iron finished up against the face of the Road Bunker. He

Nick Faldo (left) takes the first in his stride.
Fond farewell from Arnold Palmer (above).

THE COURSE

Although drought was spreading across the country, just enough rain had fallen on the Old Course to present it in perfect condition for its 24th Open Championship. If it had been any faster in the high winds which prevailed it would have been almost unplayable. As it was, it provided a searching but fair examination and stood as a tribute to Walter Woods, who retired as head greenkeeper after the Championship.

had nowhere to go but vertically. He opened the face of his sand-wedge to the maximum and the ball rose, clipping the top of the bunker and rolling down to a couple of feet. The crisis was over and the Championship lead was secure.

Two shots behind Campbell came Rocca after another solid display, with Steve Elkington a further stoke back after

Steven Bottomley (above) finished in style. Michael Campbell (right) saw his hopes vanish in the final round.

a 69. Pavin, Els, Daly and Tomori were four shots shy and it looked as though a new name would go on the trophy since the only previous winner in contention, Tom Watson, lay six shots off the pace.

Of all the contenders, the one who seemed the most unlikely to come through was Daly. The long swing and the towering tee shot would surely be blown awry in the 50mph gusts which swept across the course on that final day. But Daly gave lie to these expectations with a three birdie burst to the turn to take over the lead. Campbell had staggered at the fifth and sixth to turn in 39

and had lost six shots to Daly. Rocca was out in 38 to lie three behind and as they turned for home the main challenge came from a most unlikely quarter.

After seven appearances at the PGA European Tour Qualifying School and two seasons on the Challenge Tour, 30-year old Steven Bottomley had just retained his card for the 1995 Volvo Tour. Now he was in the thick of the action on the last day of the Open and revelling in it. While others were blown off course, Borromley held his game together wonderfully well, finishing with the flourish of a birdie three at the last for a 69 and a five under par total of 283.

Who could catch him? American Mark Brooks was the first but he was rueing the six he took at the 16th after a visit to the Principal's Nose bunker and then along came Daly. Two fives at the 16th and 17th meant he needed a par at the last to finish at six under, a birdie to put him out of reach. His drive was too far left and a par resulted so now only Rocca had an outside chance of joining him. The Italian needed a par and a birdie over the last two holes to tie and when his second to the 17th finished on the road, that seemed to be that. Taking his putter, Rocca hit an extraordinary shot in which the ball leapt almost vertically off the face and loaded with top-spin, bounded up the bank to finish four feet away. Down went the putt, so it was three to tie. His drive to the last was long and slightly left of the

Costantino Rocca (left) was buried in the play-off. Last hurrah from Jack Nicklaus (above)?

green leaving a tricky chip to the pin.

With only the wind providing any background noise, Rocca settled over his chip shot. He opened the blade of his sand-wedge and took a long backswing but halfway down it was as if he suddenly realised he could thin the ball over the green and out of bounds. He decelerated with disastrous consequences. The ball flopped forward and ran into the Valley of

Sin. While Daly's wife, Paulette hugged her husband in anticipation of victory, Rocca faced a putt of over 60 feet to tie. He struck it firmly up the hill and it ran unerringly into the cup. Pandemonium followed and Rocca sank first to knees and they lay prostrate as the enormity of what he had done swept over him.

Campbell too had a lengthy putt to tie but it was too much to ask and so the Open was set for its second four hole play-off in six years.

After what had gone before it was an anti-climax. Rocca was emotionally drained, Daly who had been boosted by some countrymen prior to the play-off, came out blazing. Rocca three-putted the first to fall one behind, Daly holed from 30 feet at the second to move two ahead. On the 17th, the third extra hole, Rocca found the Road Bunker, took three to get out and was trailing Daly by five shots as they played the 18th. It was all over as Daly played the last almost on the run to capture his second major championship following the 1991 US PGA.

It had been a long road back for Daly whose alcohol problems and subsequent brushes with authority had received the full glare of the media spotlight. Now all he could do was gaze in wonder at the name engraved on the old claret jug. D A L Y it spelled, not for the first time (see 1947) and quite possibly not for the last.

Chris Plumridge

SHOT OF THE WEEK

Whether Costantino Rocca ever stood over a short putt and fantasised that it was for the Open is not known. What is known that he faced a putt of 65 feet to tie the Open on the 72nd hole and holed it. In the history of the Championship there has never been a more dramatic final stroke than that, one that will live long in the memory of all who witnessed it.

OLD COURSE, ST ANDREWS, FIFE, SCOTLAND, JULY 20-23, 1995 · PAR 72 · YARDS 6933

Pos	Name	Country	Rnd 1	Rnd 2	Rnd 3	Rnd 4	Total	Prize Money £
1	John DALY	(USA)	67	71	73	71	282	125000
2	Costantino ROCCA	(It)	69	70	70	73	282	100000
3	Michael CAMPBELL	(NZ)	71	71	65	76	283	65666
	Mark BROOKS	(USA)	70	69	73	71	283	65666
	Steven BOTTOMLEY	(Eng)	70	72	72	69	283	65666
6	Vijay SINGH	(Fij)	68	72	73	71	284	40500
	Steve ELKINGTON	(Aus)	72	69	69	74	284	40500
8	Corey PAVIN	(USA)	69	70	72	74	285	33333
	Mark JAMES	(Eng)	72	75	68	70	285	33333
	Bob ESTES	(USA)	72	70	71	72	285	33333
11	Brett OGLE	(Aus)	73	69	71	73	286	26000
	Sam TORRANCE	(Scot)	71	70	71	74	286	26000
	Payne STEWART	(USA)	72	68	75	71	286	26000
	Ernie ELS	(SA)	71	68	72	75	286	26000
15	Greg NORMAN	(Aus)	71	74	72	70	287	18200
	Brad FAXON	(USA)	71	67	75	74	287	18200
	Ben CRENSHAW	(USA)	67	72	76	72	287	18200
	Robert ALLENBY	(Aus)	71	74	71	71	287	18200
	Per-Ulrik JOHANSSON	(Swe)	69	78	68	72	287	18200
20	David DUVAL	(USA)	71	75	70	72	288	13500
	Barry LANE	(Eng)	72	73	68	75	288	13500
	Peter MITCHELL	(Eng)	73	74	71	70	288	13500
	Andrew COLTART	(Scot)	70	74	71	73	288	13500
24	Bernhard LANGER	(Ger)	72	71	73	73	289	10316
	Mark CALCAVECCHIA	(USA)	71	72	72	74	289	10316
	Jesper PARNEVIK	(Swe)	75	71	70	73	289	10316
	Lee JANZEN	(USA)	73	73	71	72	289	10316
	Katsuyoshi TOMORI	(Jap)	70	68	73	78	289	10316
	Bill GLASSON	(USA)	68	74	72	75	289	10316
	Steve WEBSTER	(Eng)	70	72	74	73	289	(Am)
30	David FROST	(SA)	72	72	74	72	290	8122
	David FEHERTY	(N.Ire)	68	75	71	76	290	8122
	Tom WATSON	(USA)	67	76	70	77	290	8122
	Darren CLARKE	(N.Ire)	69	77	70	74	290	8122
	Ross DRUMMOND	(Scot)	74	68	77	71	290	8122
	José Maria OLAZABAL	(Sp)	72	72	74	72	290	8122
	Hisayuki SASAKI	(Jap)	74	71	72	73	290	8122
	John HUSTON	(USA)	71	74	72	73	290	8122
	Peter JACOBSEN	(USA)	71	76	70	73	290	8122
39	Nick PRICE	(Zim)	70	74	70	77	291	7050
	Mark MCNULTY	(Zim)	67	76	74	74	291	7050
	Nick FALDO	(Eng)	74	67	75	75	291	7050
	Seve BALLESTEROS	(Sp)	75	69	76	71	291	7050
	Brian WATTS	(USA)	72	71	73	75	291	7050
	John COOK	(USA)	69	70	75	77	291	7050
	Phil MICKELSON	(USA)	70	71	77	73	291	7050
	Warren BENNETT	(Eng)	72	74	73	72	291	7050
	Gordon SHERRY	(Scot)	70	71	74	76	291	(Am)
47	Mark O'MEARA	(USA)	72	72	75	73	292	6350
	Ian WOOSNAM	(Wal)	71	74	76	71	292	6350
	Brian CLAAR	(USA)	71	75	71	75	292	6350
	Tommy NAKAJIMA	(Jap)	73	72	72	75	292	6350
	Ken GREEN	(USA)	71	72	73	76	292	6350
	Anders FORSBRAND	(Swe)	70	74	75	73	292	6350
53	Russell CLAYDON	(Eng)	70	74	71	78	293	5900
	Jim GALLAGHER JNR	(USA)	69	76	75	73	293	5900
	Peter O'MALLEY	(Aus)	71	73	74	75	293	5900
56	Raymond FLOYD	(USA)	72	74	72	76	294	5475
	Tom KITE	(USA)	72	76	71	75	294	5475
	Peter SENIOR	(Aus)	71	75	78	70	294	5475
	Paul BROADHURST	(Eng)	73	72	76	73	294	5475
	Paul LAWRIE	(Scot)	73	71	74	76	294	5475
	David GILFORD	(Eng)	69	72	75	78	294	5475
	Justin LEONARD	(USA)	73	67	77	77	294	5475
	Martin GATES	(Eng)	73	73	72	76	294	5475
	Eduardo HERRERA	(Col)	74	72	73	75	294	5475
	Derrick COOPER	(Eng)	71	76	74	73	294	5475
66	Jonathan LOMAS	(Eng)	74	73	75	73	295	4975
	Olle KARLSSON	(Swe)	71	76	73	75	295	4975
	Gary HALLBERG	(USA)	72	74	72	77	295	4975
	Gary PLAYER	(SA)	71	73	77	74	295	4975
	Peter BAKER	(Eng)	70	74	81	70	295	4975
	Scott HOCH	(USA)	74	72	73	76	295	4975
	José RIVERO	(Sp)	70	72	75	78	295	4975
	Jeff MAGGERT	(USA)	75	70	78	72	295	4975
	Frank NOBILO	(NZ)	70	71	80	74	295	4975
	Mats HALLBERG	(Swe)	68	76	75	76	295	4975
	Tiger WOODS	(USA)	74	71	72	78	295	(Am)
76	Patrick BURKE	(Aus)	75	72	78	71	296	4500
	Jay HAAS	(USA)	76	72	70	78	296	4500
	Ricky KAWAGISHI	(Jap)	72	76	80	68	296	4500
	Steve LOWERY	(USA)	69	74	76	77	296	4500
	Bob LOHR	(USA)	76	68	79	73	296	4500
	Sandy LYLE	(Scot)	71	71	79	75	296	4500
	Jack NICKLAUS	(USA)	78	70	77	71	296	4500
	Jarmo SANDELIN	(Swe)	75	71	77	73	296	4500
	Dean ROBERTSON	(Scot)	71	73	74	78	296	4500
85	Miguel Angel JIMÉNEZ	(Sp)	75	73	76	73	297	4125
	Mark DAVIS	(Eng)	74	71	76	76	297	4125
	Eduardo ROMERO	(Arg)	74	74	72	77	297	4125
	Jay DELSING	(USA)	72	75	73	77	297	4125
	Gene SAUERS	(USA)	69	73	75	80	297	4125
	Wayne RILEY	(Aus)	70	72	75	80	297	4125
91	John HAWKSWORTH	(Eng)	73	74	75	76	298	4000
	Bill LONGMUIR	(Scot)	72	76	72	78	298	4000
93	Lee WESTWOOD	(Eng)	71	72	82	74	299	4000
	José COCERES	(Arg)	71	76	78	74	299	4000
95	Simon BURNELL	(Eng)	72	76	75	77	300	4000
	Davis LOVE III	(USA)	70	78	74	78	300	4000
	Gary CLARK	(Eng)	71	76	80	74	301	(Am)
97	Mark NICHOLS	(Eng)	75	68	78	81	302	4000
	Don POOLEY	(USA)	76	71	80	75	302	4000
99	Pedro LINHART	(Sp)	72	75	77	79	303	4000

George and Barbara Bush were keen spectators.

Unisys and The PGA European Tour

Unisys is a major information management company applying information services and technology expertise worldwide. As part of our sports

marketing programme we are delighted to be the Official Provider of Information Services to the PGA European Tour for the next three years.

THE INFORMATION MANAGEMENT COMPANY

Hoch grabs the headlines

With all the attention on newly-crowned Open champion John Daly, his countryman Scott Hoch took the honours in Holland

The arrival in Hilversum of big-hitting Open champion John Daly for the Heineken Dutch Open was front-page news, but eight days later it was fellow American Scott Hoch who claimed the headlines with a last round of 65 that gave him a two-stroke win over Scotland's Sam Torrance and rookie Swede Michael Jonzon.

There was huge interest in the tournament after all the excitement in St Andrews the week before and the press, radio and TV people had plenty to go at, even before a ball was struck in earnest.

Daly, larger than life, was in great demand from all quarters and his endless patience and courteous treatment of all and sundry was simply magnificent after all that had happened to him in his often tempestuous life. He never seemed to tire of answering the same questions over and over again... about his eating, his drinking, his hell-raising days. And, of course, his big-hitting.

Then there was Costantino Rocca to talk to, the man whose fluffed chip shot beside the 72nd green at St Andrews followed by that incredible putt through the Valley of Sin, set the Open Championship alight.

Rocca lost the resulting play-off, decisively it has to be said, but here he was in Holland a couple of days later, and he was still smiling. Of course he was disappointed, he said, but this was another week, another tournament. Rocca ate alone each evening at the Auberge de Hoefstag, though he was not entirely without company. Diners stopped by to commiserate and wish him well. He greeted them all with that sincere flashing Italian smile of his.

And what about Steven Bottomley, the man made famous overnight by TV for his brilliant showing in the Open by finishing joint third, just one shot behind Daly and Rocca? He, too, received star treatment in Hilversum with players, caddies and spectators all anxious to shake his hand and warmly congratulate him on a fantastic effort.

There was one delightful little cameo in the entrance to the clubhouse on the Tuesday before the tournament when fellow Yorkshireman Stuart Cage, who just three weeks earlier had been in a play-off for the Murphy's Irish Open, wrapped a congratulatory arm around Bottomley's broad shoulders and said: 'Steven, you're my hero.' Replied Bottomley: 'Thanks Stuart, but there's one thing that's really bugging me.' 'Yes,' said

THE COURSE

Almost to a man, the players enjoyed the tree-lined Hilversum course with its winding fairways and its magnificent colours. Everybody likened it to the lovely English courses of Berkshire and Surrey and after the wide open spaces of St Andrews the week before, it certainly demanded a new discipline.

Cage, 'it's because I'm still ahead of you in the Volvo Order of Merit.' And they fell about laughing.

Such is the camaraderie of European professional golf, and it is something which Daly would like to be a part of. 'The players here (in Europe) all stick together and have a lot of friendships, and are really good to each other,' he said in Holland. 'In the US, we have other things to do and we're all going our different ways. We all have our friends, but it's not like Europe. We are all going different ways too much.'

Scott Hoch was going in only one direction in Holland, though between rounds one and four nobody really noticed. Hoch, in the same management stable as the Open champion, admitted he was there 'on Daly's coat tails' and also because his wife wanted to visit Amsterdam. He was joint leader with Ireland's Philip Walton after the first round on six under par 65.

Torrance surged into the lead on day two with a 64, just one shot outside the eight-year-old course record, and his 132 halfway total put him two clear of Walton and Paul Eales, who was round in 65. The normally down-to-earth Torrance took on a proverbial air in talking about the difficulties of bidding for an eighth Ryder Cup cap by declaring: 'Worry is the interest you pay on the inevitable.' And he quickly added: 'My wife Suzanne told me that.

I've drawn a lot of strength from her over the years through her philosophy on life.'

Torrance was still at the head of the field after three rounds, scoring a 69 to share the lead with New Zealander Frank Nobilo on 12 under par. 'I'm not disappointed at being caught because today is not pay day,' he said. 'The third round is always horrific. You can't win tournaments in the third round, but you can lose them.'

The final afternoon, played on yet another day of brilliant sunshine and just enough wind swirling through the trees to make the bid for the £108,330 first prize a

Tree trouble for Colin Montgomerie (below), Michael Jonzon (right) burst into the reckoning.

searching test, the lead changed hands several times, though Torrance and Nobilo, paired together in the last match, looked set to dominate the proceedings until, that is, Michael Jonzon burst on the scene with four birdies in the first nine holes to close the gap on the leaders.

The powerfully-built, blond-haired Jonzon, a graduate of the 1994 PGA European Tour Qualifying School, dropped a shot at the tenth but three consecutive birdies from the 12th took him to the top of the leaderboard on 14 under par. 'When I saw my name at the top of the leaderboards I just tried to keep playing and stay as calm as possible, but then I dropped two shots,' he said.

Hoch, who lost a US Masters play-off to Nick Faldo in 1989, was playing in the match behind Jonzon, and he came charging through the field to match his first round of 65 and set a target of 15 under par. Torrance, who had struggled after the turn, needed to finish birdie, eagle to force a play-off. He chipped in at the 17th for the birdie but his seven wood shot to the 493-yard 18th drifted into a greenside bunker and in the event he took five to give Jonzon a cash bonus and a place in the top 40 of the Volvo Order of Merit.

Torrance at least took the satisfaction of going ahead of Bernhard Langer to take up the top position on the Volvo Order of Merit.

Richard Dodd

HILVERSUMSCHE GC, HILVERSUM, JULY 27-30, 1995 • PAR 71 • YARDS 6636

Pos	Name	Country	Rnd 1	Rnd 2	Rnd 3	Rnd 4	Total	Prize Money £
1	Scott HOCH	(USA)	65	70	69	65	269	108330
2	Sam TORRANCE	(Scot)	68	64	69	70	271	56450
	Michael JONZON	(Swe)	70	65	70	66	271	56450
4	Derrick COOPER	(Eng)	68	69	66	69	272	32500
5	Terry PRICE	(Aus)	66	70	67	71	274	25140
	Frank NOBILO	(NZ)	68	68	65	73	274	25140
7	Richard BOXALL	(Eng)	68	72	64	71	275	15815
	Colin MONTGOMERIE	(Scot)	67	70	67	71	275	15815
	Peter MITCHELL	(Eng)	68	69	69	69	275	15815
	Darren CLARKE	(N.Ire)	68	69	73	65	275	15815
11	Paul EALES	(Eng)	69	65	71	71	276	11570
	Philip WALTON	(Ire)	65	69	73	69	276	11570
13	Costantino ROCCA	(It)	70	71	68	68	277	9983
	Ross MCFARLANE	(Eng)	67	69	73	68	277	9983
	Phil GOLDING	(Eng)	71	68	69	69	277	9983
16	Thomas LEVET	(Fr)	66	73	70	69	278	7936
	Mark JAMES	(Eng)	70	65	71	72	278	7936
	Rodger DAVIS	(Aus)	70	71	67	70	278	7936
	John HUSTON	(USA)	70	69	75	64	278	7936
	Russell CLAYDON	(Eng)	69	71	70	68	278	7936
	Christy O'CONNOR JNR	(Ire)	72	68	69	69	278	7936
	Silvio GRAPPASONNI	(It)	73	66	69	70	278	7936
	Ian WOOSNAM	(Wal)	70	66	71	71	278	7936
	Mark MOULAND	(Wal)	73	65	67	73	278	7936
25	Oyvind ROJAHN	(Nor)	67	71	72	69	279	6435
	John HAWKSWORTH	(Eng)	73	67	70	69	279	6435
	Greg TURNER	(NZ)	75	65	68	71	279	6435
	Peter O'MALLEY	(Aus)	69	70	70	70	279	6435
	David WILLIAMS	(Eng)	72	68	64	75	279	6435
30	Domingo HOSPITAL	(Sp)	69	68	73	70	280	5499
	Howard CLARK	(Eng)	69	72	75	64	280	5499
	Miguel Angel JIMÉNEZ	(Sp)	71	70	69	70	280	5499
	Vicente FERNANDEZ	(Arg)	73	67	70	70	280	5499
	Niclas FASTH	(Swe)	68	70	72	70	280	5499
35	Christian CEVAER	(Fr)	71	69	69	72	281	4290
	Jim PAYNE	(Eng)	71	69	70	71	281	4290
	Paul BROADHURST	(Eng)	69	72	68	72	281	4290
	Andrew SHERBORNE	(Eng)	69	70	72	70	281	4290
	Paul AFFLECK	(Wal)	70	70	66	75	281	4290
	Rolf MUNTZ	(Hol)	71	66	76	68	281	4290
	Mike MCLEAN	(Eng)	70	68	72	71	281	4290
	Peter HEDBLOM	(Swe)	69	70	70	72	281	4290
	Stuart CAGE	(Eng)	70	70	66	75	281	4290
	José COCERES	(Arg)	72	64	70	75	281	4290
	Gary EMERSON	(Eng)	74	67	69	71	281	4290
	Bernhard LANGER	(Ger)	72	69	71	69	281	4290
	Lee WESTWOOD	(Eng)	70	71	69	71	281	4290
48	Jonas SAXTON	(USA)	67	73	71	71	282	3315
	Roger CHAPMAN	(Eng)	70	68	74	70	282	3315
50	Jonathan LOMAS	(Eng)	70	70	69	74	283	2925
	John DALY	(USA)	72	66	73	72	283	2925
	Pierre FULKE	(Swe)	71	68	72	72	283	2925
	Dean ROBERTSON	(Scot)	71	70	73	69	283	2925
54	Manuel PIÑERO	(Sp)	70	67	75	72	284	2285
	Paul WAY	(Eng)	70	69	74	71	284	2285
	Mats LANNER	(Swe)	69	71	71	73	284	2285
	Ignacio GARRIDO	(Sp)	71	70	71	72	284	2285
	Tony JOHNSTONE	(Zim)	71	70	74	69	284	2285
	Vijay SINGH	(Fij)	66	70	76	72	284	2285
60	Alexander CEJKA	(Ger)	66	70	73	76	285	1885
	Steven BOTTOMLEY	(Eng)	72	69	71	73	285	1885
	Paul MOLONEY	(Aus)	68	73	76	68	285	1885
63	Emanuele CANONICA	(It)	69	70	75	72	286	1690
	Joakim GRONHAGEN	(Swe)	72	67	74	73	286	1690
	Jean Louis GUEPY	(Fr)	68	71	76	71	286	1690
66	Hendrick BUHRMANN	(SA)	68	70	75	74	287	975
67	Daniel WESTERMARK	(Swe)	69	71	71	78	289	973

SHOT OF THE WEEK

At the 16th hole in the second round, Sam Torrance pulled his tee shot into the trees but hit a hooking five iron second shot through the top of a bush and under overhanging tree branches to reach the green and save his par. 'It was a very dangerous shot,' he said. 'If it had been the fourth round, I would have chipped it out.'

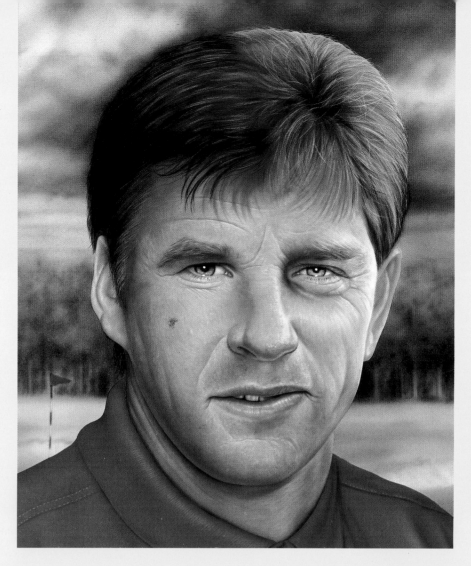

If you want to know which Bridgestone ball you should play, ask Nick.

Nick Faldo or Nick Price, we hear you ask. They both require very different types of ball, but like our picture they are united in their preference for Bridgestone.

Nick Faldo's choice is the Bridgestone Rextar Promodel. A three-piece wound balata ball developed jointly by Nick and Bridgestone, with superior trajectory for out-standing distance and greater stability in all types of weather conditions.

A new compound balata cover and rubber thread work together to provide the optimum spin rate and control. We were even able to limit excessive back spin giving Nick the consistency and pinpoint control that is so critical.

For the ultimate in feel and control pick the ball played by the world's greatest technician, the Bridgestone Rextar Promodel. For a more durable surlyn cover choose the Rextar SS90.

Nick Price on the other hand plays the Bridgestone Precept EV Extra Spin.

A unique two-piece ball of exceptional performance well suited to Nick's energetic swing, giving him extra yards on every drive.

Yet when hit with an iron the high velocity core and Super Spin cover combine to give consistent stop on the greens. (An ordinary ball would just keep on rolling.)

The result is unprecedented distance, superior control and back-to-back 'Major' wins for Nick Price.

But you don't have to be a top-ranking pro to play a Precept ball.

The range is available in Extra Spin, Extra Distance, Senior, and Lady. Whatever your style of play, whatever your handicap, there's a Bridgestone ball that will make your game.

For details contact Bridgestone Sports Division on: 0121-511 1488.

BRIDGESTONE

It's the ball that makes your game

Parnevik makes history at home

Jesper Parnevik became the first

Swedish golfer to win a PGA European Tour

title on home ground

The Scandinavian Masters official was all smiles as huge crowds swamped the Barseback course just outside Malmo to watch Jesper Parnevik become the first Swede to win a PGA European Tour event on Swedish soil.

There had been 18 Scandinavian Enterprise Opens, five PLM Opens and four previous Scandinavian Masters, the event that was born out of a merger of the other two, before Parnevik made his impressive breakthrough and, at the time, strengthened his bid to make the Johnnie Walker Ryder Cup team.

In Malmo that week he was in his most impressive form since narrowly losing the 1994 Open to Zimbabwe's Nick Price at Turnberry. Parnevik not only teamed up successfully with Per-Ulrik Johansson in the Canon Shoot-Out, he also fired a 65 in the pro-am and 67, 67, 69, 67 in the tournament to win by five from the always consistent Colin Montgomerie and by seven from the defending champion, the much-travelled Vijay Singh.

Parnevik's performance, in a country where golf has grown dramatically in the past 15 years, where the well-organised official coaching scheme is producing more and more talented young players, was a tour de force. He strode the fairways

of the impressive and by no means easy Barseback course with supreme confidence and the Swedes reacted with justifiable nationalistic pride. They cheered Parnevik, now competing regularly on the US Tour where he is gaining extensively in experience, to the echo. He had magnificent support from one of the most rumbustious crowds of the season but one of the fairest.

When he walked down the dog-leg tree-lined last hole on the third day it was as if he had won the title there and then.

In fact he had moved three clear of the always impressive Montgomerie, still chasing his first win of the 1995 Volvo Tour season, and the talented 26-year old Maori Michael Campbell from Wellington. There was still a pressure-packed round to go, but try telling the Swedes that important detail on that Saturday afternoon.

Happily Parnevik did not let them down the next day. Despite the pressure of trying to win in front of his own folk, something runner-up Montgomerie admitted he has always found difficult to do in his home country of Scotland, the 30-year old Swede from Daneryd, Stockholm, came through majestically, producing many excellent shots and holing out well at crucial times. He was reminding us of how close he came to being the 1994 Open champion.

Some players cannot handle pressure, others such as Nick Faldo or Seve Ballesteros or Montgomerie are inspired by fans lining every fairway sometimes three deep. Parnevik can handle that situation too. It helps him lift his game and in Malmo on that final day when, as Montgomerie put it 'he never missed a fairway, never missed a makeable putt and remained cool with the whole of Sweden on his back', he moved to a higher level of personal achievement. The fans at

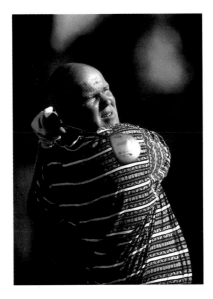

Barseback loved what he did but not as much as he did himself.

That sunny Sunday afternoon there was pride not only in the winner's eyes but also in those of his father Bo, Sweden's best-known comedian and impersonator, and of his wife Mia heavily pregnant with their first child. A few weeks later she presented Jesper with a far greater prize than the £108,330 winner's cheque at Barseback, a daughter, Josephine.

The atmosphere at the Scandinavian Masters was electric for four days, but although Parnevik became the focus of attention over the weekend, the golfer

who drew huge crowds, even as early as 8.00 in the morning on the third day, was the Open champion, John Daly.

The 'grip it and rip it' exponent had made the papers even before the event started when he turned up bald as a coot having decided a few days earlier, not hastily but deliberately after playing the Heineken Dutch Open in Amsterdam, that the only way to silence those who were making comments about his short-at-the-front, long-at-the-back haircut was to take all his hair off for the second time in his career and let it grow back to US marine standard length all over.

Daly's reputation came before him.

Two weeks earlier he had confounded the pundits by winning his second major at the home of golf. In windy weather he had tamed the Old Course to beat the gallant Italian Costantino Rocca in their play-off for the title. That was with hair. Now he had the Kojak look but if his appearance had changed dramatically his golf had not. He impressed mightily on the course even if still 'getting over' the significance of what he had achieved at St. Andrews. That had taken almost two weeks to sink in.

Daly has had a chequered career. The former US PGA champion has not always seen eye-to-eye with the authorities and,

THE COURSE

Barseback is unusual in that the course is played mainly through pine trees on high ground overlooking the Oresund but there are three superb links-style holes down by the sea on land normally protected from development by the planners. It is these three holes, the ninth, tenth and 11th where wind is such a factor that give Barseback's championship course its added character. The championship course, much admired by the professionals, is in fact a mixture of holes from the Old course designed by Swede Ture Bruce and the New designed by Donald Steel. From the elevated tee at the short eighth you can see Copenhagen in Denmark. Tony Johnstone of Zimbabwe set the course record of 65 in 1992 and this was matched in the final round in 1995 by defending champion Vijay Singh.

New look John Daly helped swell the crowds (opposite).

Jamie Spence (left) pitches while Colin Montgomerie and Vijay Singh (below) share consolation prizes.

in the past, has made the wrong kind of headlines on the sports pages but, drinking nothing stronger than Diet Coke these days, he came proudly to Sweden for the first time and insisted he would keep coming back because he liked the country so much.

Unlike some Americans, Daly loves to travel. Coming as he does from tiny Dardanelle in Arkansas where there is only a nine-hole course it is maybe not surprising that he wants to see as many countries in the world as he can sooner rather than later. At Bareseback he finished ninth, 11 shots behind winner Parnevik but made a great many new friends with his at times adventurous play. The fans love it when Daly pulls out the driver and 'has a go' but then nobody hits it further more consistently in top-line world golf today.

Golf has boomed in Scandinavia over the past 20 years. Since Olympic ice-hockey and soccer star Sven Tumba first introduced big-name golf to Sweden by bringing Jack Nicklaus and Lee Trevino among others to play in invitational events in the early 1970s, golf has blossomed in a way that even Tumba could never have imagined. The statistics tell the story. In 1980 there were 150 clubs and 85,000 licensed players. In 1995 there are 370 clubs and 375,000 licensed golfers. In a country where the season is, because of the climate, necessarily short, the game is being played today with almost religious-style Japanese fervour.

Recent Swedish team wins in the Eisenhower Trophy, the World Amateur Team Championship in New Zealand and in the Alfred Dunhill Cup at St. Andrews and the World Cup in Rome gave the game a further boost, but what the home fans really wanted was a Swede to win at home, a Swede they could cheer to the echo the way the Spaniards do for Severiano Ballesteros, the Germans for Bernhard Langer, the Scots for Colin Montgomerie and the Welsh for Ian Woosnam.

It might have been Anders Forsbrand, Per-Ulrik Johansson, Mats Lanner, Robert Karlsson or Jarmo Sandelin who made the home win breakthrough but it was the always entertaining Parnevik who deservedly made Tour history. He may now spend more time in America than in Europe but, he insists, he will always come back to play in the Scandinavian Masters, now one of the biggest and most successful Championships in Europe.

Winning at home was reward enough for the golfer whose preference for wearing the brim of his baseball cap turned up in the fashion of one of the characters in the old Bowery Boy films, may have distracted us somewhat in the past from recognising him as a serious performer with great natural talent. It is the same syndrome as that which surrounds the American Payne Stewart, a double major title winner remembered much more by the fans as the US Tour player who wears bizarre knickerbocker style outfits advertising teams playing on the National Football League. Make no mistake, however, Stewart and Parnevik are serious players on golf's world stage.

Parnevik with homes in Florida, not far from where Jack Nicklaus has his base and, significantly enough, if he realises his ambition to become a full-blown international star, Monte Carlo, had had only one previous victory in Europe before Barseback. In 1993 he had impressively beaten a top-quality field to win the Scottish Open over the King's course at Gleneagles Hotel, another event which attracts huge crowds.

Renton Laidlaw   163

BARSEBÄCK, SWEDEN, AUGUST 3-6, 1995 • PAR 72 • YARDS 7301

Pos	Name	Country	Rnd 1	Rnd 2	Rnd 3	Rnd 4	Total	Prize Money £
1	Jesper PARNEVIK	(Swe)	67	67	69	67	270	108330
2	Colin MONTGOMERIE	(Scot)	70	69	67	69	275	72210
3	Vijay SINGH	(Fij)	72	70	70	65	277	40690
4	Robert ALLENBY	(Aus)	67	72	70	69	278	30015
	Eamonn DARCY	(Ire)	72	70	69	67	278	30015
6	Miguel Angel JIMÉNEZ	(Sp)	67	73	70	69	279	22750
7	Ross MCFARLANE	(Eng)	66	76	67	71	280	17875
	Paul BROADHURST	(Eng)	66	74	72	68	280	17875
9	John DALY	(USA)	71	74	67	69	281	14510
10	Ian WOOSNAM	(Wal)	67	71	70	74	282	11650
	Michael JONZON	(Swe)	70	72	68	72	282	11650
	Michael CAMPBELL	(NZ)	69	67	70	76	282	11650
	Paul WAY	(Eng)	71	71	67	73	282	11650
14	André BOSSERT	(Swi)	70	72	71	70	283	9162
	Emanuele CANONICA	(It)	71	71	69	72	283	9162
	Paul MCGINLEY	(Ire)	72	69	72	70	283	9162
	Barry LANE	(Eng)	68	68	74	73	283	9162
	Jamie SPENCE	(Eng)	70	67	74	72	283	9162
19	Lee WESTWOOD	(Eng)	70	71	71	72	284	8060
20	Paolo QUIRICI	(Swi)	71	71	70	73	285	7410
	Gary ORR	(Scot)	69	74	69	73	285	7410
	Mats LANNER	(Swe)	71	73	68	73	285	7410
	Richard BOXALL	(Eng)	72	72	69	72	285	7410
	Frank NOBILO	(NZ)	66	73	74	72	285	7410
25	Des SMYTH	(Ire)	71	72	74	69	286	5967
	Thomas LEVET	(Fr)	69	69	76	72	286	5967
	Gary EMERSON	(Eng)	70	74	69	73	286	5967
	Peter O'MALLEY	(Aus)	72	72	72	70	286	5967
	Mathias GRÖNBERG	(Swe)	72	71	71	72	286	5967
	Anders FORSBRAND	(Swe)	68	70	75	73	286	5967
	Roger CHAPMAN	(Eng)	73	69	66	78	286	5967
	Ronan RAFFERTY	(N.Ire)	71	73	75	67	286	5967
	Carl MASON	(Eng)	69	73	71	73	286	5967
	Joakim GRONHAGEN	(Swe)	73	72	71	70	286	5967
35	Ignacio GARRIDO	(Sp)	72	71	73	71	287	4745
	Juan QUIROS	(Sp)	73	70	69	75	287	4745
	David CARTER	(Eng)	70	68	76	73	287	4745
	Mike MCLEAN	(Eng)	66	72	75	74	287	4745
	Philip TALBOT	(Eng)	75	70	69	73	287	4745
	Paul AFFLECK	(Wal)	70	69	75	73	287	4745
41	Stephen AMES	(T&T)	74	71	71	72	288	4030
	Klas ERIKSSON	(Swe)	74	70	75	69	288	4030
	Retief GOOSEN	(SA)	68	75	73	72	288	4030
	Silvio GRAPPASONNI	(It)	71	71	73	73	288	4030
	Adam HUNTER	(Scot)	71	68	72	77	288	4030
46	Sven STRÜVER	(Ger)	74	70	73	72	289	3445
	Paul EALES	(Eng)	70	72	73	74	289	3445
	Niclas FASTH	(Swe)	69	75	73	72	289	3445
	Rolf MUNTZ	(Hol)	69	74	74	72	289	3445
50	Jean VAN DE VELDE	(Fr)	73	71	76	70	290	2795
	Santiago LUNA	(Sp)	73	71	72	74	290	2795
	Michel BESANCENEY	(Fr)	73	72	71	74	290	2795
	Jarmo SANDELIN	(Swe)	69	76	75	70	290	2795
	Ian PALMER	(SA)	71	73	73	73	290	2795
	Pedro LINHART	(Sp)	74	71	71	74	290	2795
56	John MELLOR	(Eng)	73	71	74	73	291	2080
	Fredrik ANDERSSON	(Swe)	71	71	72	77	291	2080
	Steen TINNING	(Den)	72	72	76	71	291	2080
	Phillip PRICE	(Wal)	71	73	75	72	291	2080
	Fredrik LINDGREN	(Swe)	69	76	72	74	291	2080
	Stuart CAGE	(Eng)	67	72	78	74	291	2080
62	Martyn ROBERTS	(Wal)	72	73	76	71	292	1401
	Fredrik JACOBSON	(Swe)	71	74	75	72	292	1401
	Keith WATERS	(Eng)	72	71	75	74	292	1401
	Mike HARWOOD	(Aus)	69	71	79	73	292	1401
	Adam MEDNICK	(Swe)	73	71	73	75	292	1401
	Greg TURNER	(NZ)	73	72	72	75	292	1401
	Mark LITTON	(Wal)	70	73	75	74	292	1401
69	Jeremy ROBINSON	(Eng)	72	73	77	72	294	967
	Steven BOTTOMLEY	(Eng)	68	75	73	78	294	967
	Olle NORDBERG	(Swe)	70	73	79	72	294	967
72	Fabrice TARNAUD	(Fr)	71	72	75	77	295	963
73	Raymond BURNS	(N.Ire)	77	68	75	76	296	961
	Johan SELBERG	(Swe)	75	70	75	76	296	(Am)
74	Gabriel HJERTSTEDT	(Swe)	72	70	77	78	297	959
75	Rodger DAVIS	(Aus)	69	72	78	79	298	957
76	Mark ROE	(Eng)	71	72	75	DISQ		955

SHOT OF THE WEEK

Tournament winner Jesper Parnevik hit his tee shot into the trees at the 17th on the third day and was faced with an awkward three iron recovery shot which he knew he would have to draw to make the green. The pin was at the back and the margin for error into the wind off the sea was slight but so effectively did Parnevik execute the shot that he hit the ball to eight feet and made a birdie.

PUT MORE EXCITEMENT INTO YOUR DRIVING!

ScanPartner

Best Buy, Car of the Year… the Volvo 850 has inspired the praise of enthusiastic drivers the world over. Some will tell you about the blend of power and complete control, about how they rediscovered the excitement of driving without compromising on comfort or safety. Others will talk of an attractive range of options that allow you to personalise your car to suit the challenges of your own life-style. So why not judge for your-self? Perhaps by exploring the excitement of the 225 bhp Volvo 850 T-5? The Volvo 850 Saloon or Estate. Ready to drive at your Volvo dealer.

VOLVO

It's Cejka the record-breaker

Alexander Cejka broke all sorts of records

in winning his second title of the year

Alexander Cejka, Czech-born but now a German citizen, had a week to remember, breaking four 1995 PGA European Tour records as he romped to victory in the Hohe Brücke Open at Litschau, Austria. Hohe Brücke, the National State Lottery company, were sponsoring the event for the third time at Waldviertel Golf Club.

Starting with a course record 61, 11 under par, Cejka went on to win by four shots from Ronan Rafferty, Ignacio Garrido and Rolf Muntz with a four round aggregate of 267 and then declared that, like Open champion John Daly, he would shave his head.

'I made a bet with my friend and coach, Peter Karz, in Munich that we would both shave off our hair if I won another Tour event,' said 24-year old Cejka, who had gained his first win in the Turespana Open de Andalucia.

Yet whatever his hair style, there was no close shave about Cekja's Austrian success. He led by four shots after the first and second days, by five at the end of the third round and was never headed as he took the first prize of £41,660.

His first round of 61 broke the previous course record, set by Mark Davis in this event last year, by three shots and was the lowest round on the Tour for 1995, beating Wayne Westner's 62 in the Lexington SA PGA in February.

Cejka's 129 for two rounds also beat the previous best for the year of 131 by Colin Montgomerie in the Dubai Desert Classic; his 197 for three rounds bettered Jarmo Sandelin's 200 in the BMW International Open and his final total of 267 was one better than the previous 1995 best of Fred Couples in winning the Dubai tournament.

Though many of the leading Europeans were in America, competing in the US PGA championship, and conditions in Austria were near perfect, Cejka's victory should not be undervalued because he played superb golf on a course measuring 6,937 yards.

Cejka, whose passion is driving fast cars as well as golf balls, looked as if he might break 60 on the opening day when, after early morning mist had held up play for 100 minutes, he quickly made up for lost time with birdies at each of the first six holes. He also birdied the ninth to turn in 29 and when he had further birdies at the tenth and 11th holes to go to nine under even Cejka admitted he had visions of a 59.

Not surprisingly, he could not keep up the pace but Cejka had other birdies at the 16th and 18th for his 61. His 11 birdies for the round was also one less than the European record set in previous years by

Four rounds under 70 for Ignacio Garrido.

Shooting a second round 68, Cejka stayed four ahead at the halfway mark but it was Muntz who, with an eight-birdie 65, became his closest challenger on 133. Paul McGinley, a last-minute entry, shot 67 to move into joint third place on 134 with McGovern (69) while Rafferty was on 135. Raffery's 66 included seven birdies in his first 15 holes, which gave him a run of 13 birdies in 22 holes from the tenth hole on the opening day.

Cejka had another 68 in the third round but dropped shots for the first time in the tournament, having bogeys at the short ninth, where he found sand, and the 12th, where he three-putted.

Though Rafferty shot a 67 to go into second place on 202 he was still five behind while Stephen Dodd, with a 64, Muntz (70), McGinley (69) and Garrido (68) were one shot further back.

On the last day Garrido provided the most excitement for, starting six shots off the lead, he went out in 33 to 36 by Cejka and then birdied the tenth and 11th holes to be only one behind. Rafferty, at this point, was two off the pace. But Rafferty could make no further progress and Garrido dropped a shot at the short 13th. Cejka also bogeyed that hole but he had birdies at the 12th, 14th and 15th to pull away again, and he finished with a 70 to go to 21 under par overall.

John Oakley

Fred Couples and Ernie Els and there was one further sting in his 61. Davis saw his course record broken at close quarters because he played with Cejka for the first two days.

Cejka ended his first day four shots clear of Steven Richardson and Brendan McGovern with Garrido and Muntz back on 68 while Rafferty, the 1993 winner, did well to finish on 69. Three over after nine holes, Rafferty birdied six of his last seven holes.

SHOT OF THE WEEK

John Bickerton, the 25-year old Worcester golfer, played the shot of the week at the 545-yard fifth hole. Just short in two of a green which rose sharply and then fell to a pin tucked on the downslope, he hit a low 25-yard pitch with his lob-wedge which landed on the upslope, checked, and then rolled over the top, took a sharp swing from left to right and went straight into the hole for an eagle three.

GC WALDVIERTEL, LITSCHAU, AUSTRIA, AUGUST 10-13, 1995 · YARDAGE 6937 · PAR 72

Pos	Name	Country	Rnd 1	Rnd 2	Rnd 3	Rnd 4	Total	Prize Money £
1	Alexander CEJKA	(Ger)	61	68	68	70	267	41660
2	Rolf MUNTZ	(Hol)	68	65	70	68	271	18640
	Ronan RAFFERTY	(N.Ire)	69	66	67	69	271	18640
	Ignacio GARRIDO	(Sp)	68	67	68	68	271	18640
5	Pedro LINHART	(Sp)	68	67	71	68	274	8950
	Paul MCGINLEY	(Ire)	67	67	69	71	274	8950
	Michel BESANCENEY	(Fr)	67	68	71	68	274	8950
8	Heinz P THÜL	(Ger)	67	69	71	68	275	5362
	Phil GOLDING	(Eng)	68	73	67	67	275	5362
	Nic HENNING	(SA)	69	71	69	66	275	5362
	Andrew CLAPP	(Eng)	70	69	70	66	275	5362
12	Philip TALBOT	(Eng)	72	66	69	69	276	4043
	Warren BENNETT	(Eng)	68	70	67	71	276	4043
	Gavin LEVENSON	(SA)	68	68	73	67	276	4043
15	Stephen DODD	(Wal)	72	67	64	74	277	3521
	Mathias GRÖNBERG	(Swe)	69	72	70	66	277	3521
	John BICKERTON	(Eng)	69	67	72	69	277	3521
18	Ricky WILLISON	(Eng)	69	68	71	70	278	3020
	Craig RONALD	(Scot)	66	70	70	72	278	3020
	Mark MOULAND	(Wal)	75	66	69	68	278	3020
	Stephen MCALLISTER	(Scot)	72	68	71	67	278	3020
	Stephen PULLAN	(Eng)	70	71	68	69	278	3020
23	Steven RICHARDSON	(Eng)	65	71	71	72	279	2625
	Jean VAN DE VELDE	(Fr)	69	71	72	67	279	2625
	Magnus PERSSON	(Swe)	72	69	69	69	279	2625
	Brendan MCGOVERN	(Ire)	65	69	70	75	279	2625
	Massimo SCARPA	(It)	67	70	71	71	279	2625
28	Per HAUGSRUD	(Nor)	72	70	71	67	280	2325
	Joakim GRONHAGEN	(Swe)	69	70	68	73	280	2325
	David CARTER	(Eng)	67	71	73	69	280	2325
31	Jonathan HODGSON	(Eng)	73	68	72	68	281	2137
	Tierri CORTE	(It)	71	66	73	71	281	2137
	Markus BRIER	(Aut)	70	72	69	70	281	(Am)
33	Miguel Angel MARTIN	(Sp)	69	72	69	72	282	1875
	Chris DAVISON	(Eng)	67	74	70	71	282	1875
	Marc FARRY	(Fr)	68	68	71	75	282	1875
	Brian MARCHBANK	(Scot)	69	70	72	71	282	1875
	Raymond BURNS	(N.Ire)	73	70	69	70	282	1875
	Roger CHAPMAN	(Eng)	70	67	68	77	282	1875
	Fabrice TARNAUD	(Fr)	71	71	68	72	282	1875
	Antoine LEBOUC	(Fr)	69	69	73	71	282	1875
41	Ian PALMER	(SA)	68	71	74	70	283	1600
	Marc PENDARIES	(Fr)	71	71	72	69	283	1600
	Mike MILLER	(Scot)	71	70	73	69	283	1600
44	Vanslow PHILLIPS	(Eng)	71	70	72	71	284	1400
	Paul PAGE	(Eng)	71	71	72	70	284	1400
	Matthias DEBOVE	(Fr)	70	73	69	72	284	1400
	Keith WATERS	(Eng)	70	73	72	69	284	1400
	Daniel CHOPRA	(Swe)	76	65	77	66	284	1400
49	Kalle VAINOLA	(Fin)	71	72	73	69	285	1175
	Robert EDWARDS	(Eng)	68	75	77	65	285	1175
	Klas ERIKSSON	(Swe)	73	70	73	69	285	1175
	Mats HALLBERG	(Swe)	71	69	74	71	285	1175
53	Paul R SIMPSON	(Eng)	70	73	71	72	286	1025
	Fredrik JACOBSON	(Swe)	74	69	71	72	286	1025
55	Robert LEE	(Eng)	69	71	71	76	287	925
	Tim PLANCHIN	(Fr)	70	72	73	72	287	925
57	Mark LITTON	(Wal)	68	73	72	75	288	808
	Claude GRENIER	(Can)	68	73	74	73	288	808
	Daniel WESTERMARK	(Swe)	70	73	71	74	288	808
60	Matthew HAZELDEN	(Eng)	71	72	72	74	289	737
	Adam HUNTER	(Scot)	73	69	74	73	289	737
62	Carl Magnus STRÖMBERG	(Swe)	74	68	70	78	290	675
	Mikael KRANTZ	(Swe)	72	68	75	75	290	675
	Mark STEVENSON	(Eng)	70	73	70	77	290	675
65	Patrick PLATZ	(Ger)	73	70	77	71	291	625
66	Peter TERAVAINEN	(USA)	67	74	77	74	292	400
	Nikolaus ZITNY	(Aut)	71	71	73	77	292	(Am)
67	Marco DURANTE	(It)	71	71	76	75	293	398
68	Thomas NIELSEN	(Nor)	67	75	77	75	294	396
69	Gianluca PIETROBONO	(It)	72	70	80	73	295	394
70	Craig CASSELLS	(Eng)	71	72	83	77	303	392
71	John MCHENRY	(Ire)	73	70	DISQ			

THE COURSE

Waldviertel Golf Club, situated in the picturesque countryside of Lower Austria, has many elevated tees which give an excellent view of the course, which was lengthened this year to 6,937 yards. Water comes into play at the fourth, fifth, eighth and 11th holes, out-of-bounds is on the right at the first, fifth, tenth and 18th and trees and thick rough are behind many of the greens.

Teravainen turns his dream into reality

Plagued by health problems,

Peter Teravainen finally broke through

for his maiden Tour victory

Who said golf was never meant to be a fair game? Not Peter Teravainen, that's for sure.

The studious American, a Yale University graduate, was the archetypal journeyman professional until he had a dream that he could win on the PGA European Tour. The dream came true after nearly 14 years of toil which had earned him a modest career total of £445,559, a quarter of which came in his best season (1991) when he headed for home with £112,500.

By and large, he was not exactly making big money out of professional golf. But he was a stayer, and a believer. And eventually the dream came true with a surprise win in the Chemapol Trophy Czech Open. A PGA European Tour title at last. And a prize beyond even his wildest dreams – £125,000.

Teravainen had kept going through nearly 14 years of adversity and ailments, playing several weeks at a stretch and then

returning home to his wife Veronica and daughter, Taina Siying in Singapore. But after his one good season in 1991, he missed much of the 1993 action after knee surgery and struggled through 1994 with tendinitis in the shoulder.

Even worse problems hit him in 1995 when mysterious pains in both shins almost ground him to a halt. He could barely walk 18 holes and could not practise at all because of the pain. Various treatments failed and the Tour physiotherapists told him his condition was similar to that experienced by long-distance runners. Sympathy, but no cure. He had to pack ice on his shins after every round and although he stopped playing for three weeks in March, he returned to the fray because, he said, he felt he had to keep playing. 'I hadn't made any money,' he remarked. With more than half the 1995 season gone, he had missed 16 halfway cuts and had earned less than £9,000, languishing in the lower regions of the Volvo Order of Merit.

Then real help arrived. His wife came to Europe for a visit and brought with her a supply of Chinese medicated bandages, which are similar in appearance to nicotine patches. The effects were dramatic.

171

He wore a patch on each shin and also on his left knee, which was still troubling him, and the pain slowly began to ebb. He could start practising again and he no longer had to pack ice round his shins at the end of a round. He was still missing cuts, though—five in a row going into the Hohe Brücke Open, where he finished 62nd—but he could see the way ahead. He had his dream.

Teravainen arrived in the magnificent spa town of Marianske Lanze, about two hours north-east of Prague and close to the German border, for the Chemapol Trophy Czech Open full of hope but with no inkling of what was about to happen. He opened his sensational week with a 67, which attracted little attention because there were six players ahead of him on the leaderboard. But a 66 the next day took him into the joint lead with Ronan

Masonic-style recovery (above) from Darren Clarke. Sam Torrance (below) stayed on top of the Volvo Order of Merit.

Rafferty and it was then that he told his remarkable and, as it turned out, prophetic story.

'I've had a bad season all right but I still have dreams of winning a tournament,' said the bespectacled American. 'This year I'd had to pray for good health, and my prayers have been answered in the last two months, and more so in the last three weeks. This has been my worst year in nearly 14 years here but I'm not dreaming of making cuts any more. I'm dreaming of winning tournaments. People I've played with will say: 'What a laugh.' I guess it's hard to be confident when you've been shooting 77s all the time but in the back of my mind I thought that if my legs got better I was not going to play to make cuts, I was going to dream of winning. I've never won a tournament, but I want to very much.'

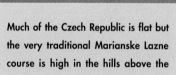

Howard Clark virtually clinched Ryder Cup place.

Teravainen was halfway to seeing his dream come true and by tea-time on the Saturday he had taken one further important step with a third round of 68 to be placed one stroke behind joint leaders Rafferty and Howard Clark, who was making a late charge for a Ryder Cup berth. 'I've really got some good swings going and Ronan commented on it,' said Teravainen.

The quiet American was paired in the penultimate group on the final day with Sweden's Niklas Fasth, who had his own dream, as well as some special memories of Marianske Lanze. It was here in a wintry October of 1994 that Fasth arrived for the inaugural Chemapol Trophy Czech Open needing to make the cut to retain his card for 1995. He finished 52nd and gained the very last card.

Now here he was in Marianske Lanze

THE COURSE

Much of the Czech Republic is flat but the very traditional Marianske Lazne course is high in the hills above the famous spa town of that name and winds its way through beautiful pine forests. Founded in 1905, it is the oldest course in the Czech Republic.

again, but this time playing a starring role. He went on to finish joint fifth, earning £24,817 and for the second year running he retained his playing rights.

The last-round battle was always between Rafferty, Clark and Teravainen, with Rafferty looking a sure-fire winner when he raced to the turn in 31, giving him a three-stroke margin over his two main challengers. But as he faltered with three fives in the closing five holes, Clark and Teravainen were neck and neck over the finishing stretch. Both birdied the long 17th to go to the final hole comfort-

ably ahead of the field on 16 under par and Teravainen set the target with a good second putt on the 72nd green for a par four. Clark, though, pulled his tee shot into trees, bunkered his second and was faced with a putt of five feet to force a play-off. He left the putt short.

While all this was happening, Teravainen was sitting quietly in the Recorder's area. Shocked gasps from the big crowd around the 18th green as Clark missed told him he was the champion. His dream had come true.

Richard Dodd

173

Mariánské Lázne GC, Czech Republic, August 17-20, 1995 • Par 71 • Yards 6753

Pos	Name	Country	Rnd 1	Rnd 2	Rnd 3	Rnd 4	Total	Prize Money £
1	Peter TERAVAINEN	(USA)	67	66	68	67	268	125000
2	Howard CLARK	(Eng)	66	68	66	69	269	83320
3	Peter HEDBLOM	(Swe)	68	66	68	69	271	42220
	Ronan RAFFERTY	(N.Ire)	65	68	67	71	271	42220
5	Darren CLARKE	(N.Ire)	67	72	65	69	273	24817
	Santiago LUNA	(Sp)	69	67	68	69	273	24817
	Jean Louis GUEPY	(Fr)	68	68	69	68	273	24817
	Niclas FASTH	(Swe)	66	69	66	72	273	24817
9	Lee WESTWOOD	(Eng)	69	71	69	66	275	14610
	Klas ERIKSSON	(Swe)	71	67	69	68	275	14610
	Gary ORR	(Scot)	68	69	69	69	275	14610
	Greg TURNER	(NZ)	69	70	69	67	275	14610
13	Sven STRÜVER	(Ger)	71	68	68	69	276	11282
	Barry LANE	(Eng)	67	67	70	72	276	11282
	José RIVERO	(Sp)	70	68	66	72	276	11282
	Sam TORRANCE	(Scot)	66	71	69	70	276	11282
17	Paul MOLONEY	(Aus)	71	68	69	69	277	9900
	Roger CHAPMAN	(Eng)	69	66	71	71	277	9900
19	Domingo HOSPITAL	(Sp)	69	66	71	72	278	8675
	Costantino ROCCA	(It)	69	71	70	68	278	8675
	Gary EMERSON	(Eng)	70	70	69	69	278	8675
	Alexander CEJKA	(Ger)	68	68	73	69	278	8675
	Des SMYTH	(Ire)	70	69	69	70	278	8675
	Marc FARRY	(Fr)	73	67	70	68	278	8675
25	Mark DAVIS	(Eng)	69	67	73	70	279	6885
	Richard BOXALL	(Eng)	70	70	67	72	279	6885
	Christian CEVAER	(Fr)	71	70	69	69	279	6885
	Derrick COOPER	(Eng)	72	69	70	68	279	6885
	David GILFORD	(Eng)	68	71	71	69	279	6885
	Rodger DAVIS	(Aus)	70	69	68	72	279	6885
	Mark JAMES	(Eng)	67	73	74	65	279	6885
	André BOSSERT	(Swi)	70	70	71	68	279	6885
	Paul EALES	(Eng)	72	68	69	70	279	6885
	Joakim HAEGGMAN	(Swe)	69	71	67	72	279	6885
35	Jim PAYNE	(Eng)	69	72	70	69	280	5175
	Dean ROBERTSON	(Scot)	66	73	74	67	280	5175
	Paul WAY	(Eng)	69	71	71	69	280	5175
	Sandy LYLE	(Scot)	68	72	73	67	280	5175
	Mark LITTON	(Wal)	73	64	72	71	280	5175
	Fredrik LINDGREN	(Swe)	68	70	72	70	280	5175
	Olle KARLSSON	(Swe)	71	70	69	70	280	5175
	Malcolm MACKENZIE	(Eng)	71	70	70	69	280	5175
	Raymond BURNS	(N.Ire)	67	74	65	74	280	5175
	Philip WALTON	(Ire)	71	67	72	70	280	5175
45	Phil GOLDING	(Eng)	69	72	67	73	281	4275
	Peter MITCHELL	(Eng)	66	72	74	69	281	4275
47	Silvio GRAPPASONNI	(It)	74	67	71	70	282	4050
48	Joakim GRONHAGEN	(Swe)	67	70	76	70	283	3525
	Nic HENNING	(SA)	69	70	73	71	283	3525
	Ross DRUMMOND	(Scot)	69	71	69	74	283	3525
	Peter FOWLER	(Aus)	74	67	69	73	283	3525
	Jon ROBSON	(Eng)	75	66	67	75	283	3525
	Oyvind ROJAHN	(Nor)	69	71	70	73	283	3525
54	John BLAND	(SA)	70	70	72	72	284	2775
	David WILLIAMS	(Eng)	71	69	73	71	284	2775
	Stephen DODD	(Wal)	67	71	75	71	284	2775
	Jarmo SANDELIN	(Swe)	70	71	72	71	284	2775
58	Robert KARLSSON	(Swe)	69	69	74	73	285	2287
	Vicente FERNANDEZ	(Arg)	71	69	75	70	285	2287
	Daniel WESTERMARK	(Swe)	73	68	71	73	285	2287
	John BICKERTON	(Eng)	71	70	70	74	285	2287
62	José Maria CAÑIZARES	(Sp)	70	69	73	74	286	2062
	Neal BRIGGS	(Eng)	71	70	71	74	286	2062
64	Paul LAWRIE	(Scot)	70	69	74	74	287	1650
	Ross MCFARLANE	(Eng)	68	70	78	71	287	1650
	Gordon J BRAND	(Eng)	72	69	77	69	287	1650
67	Steven BOTTOMLEY	(Eng)	72	69	75	75	291	1123

SHOT OF THE WEEK

Mark Davis made any early impression on the opening day with a spectacular birdie at the 414-yard first hole. He drove into the trees, chipped out sideways and then holed a 188-yard four iron for his birdie. He went on to score 69.

Montgomerie changes his luck

After nearly a year without a victory
Colin Montgomerie found fortune
smiling on him again

Recognise the sweater? Colin Montgomerie did as he decided what to wear for the last round of the Volvo German Open at Schloss Nippenburg near Stuttgart. It was the same one he had worn for the final round at Hubbelrath a year earlier, a round which had seen him prevent Bernhard Langer from winning the famous championship for a record sixth time.

Montgomerie is not known for being superstitious or a creature of habit. But he was prepared to try anything. Another 12 months of superlative golf was coming to an end, yet if he did not successfully defend the title it would be 12 months without a victory. So on went the sweater.

The 32-year old Scot had arrived for this, the final qualifying event for the Johnnie Walker-sponsered European Ryder Cup team, top of the points table and assured of a third cap. But, like those fretting over their places, he was also short on sleep. In his case it was the US PGA championship a fortnight earlier which was causing him to wake up in the early hours. With three closing birdies, the last of them from 20 feet, he had equalled the lowest total ever recorded in any of the four majors. Unfortunately, however, Steve Elkington equalled it too and when the Australian made a birdie putt from 25 feet on the first play-off hole, Montgomerie remained the world's highest-ranked player without a major to his name.

'I keep going over every putt I missed that week,' he said. 'I felt I played the best golf—in fact, I don't think it was close—but I didn't capitalise on all my good shots.' Seventeen under par for the four rounds at the Riviera Club in Los Angeles, Montgomerie, jumper now there for all to see even if they didn't know its significance, began the last 18 holes at Schloss Nippenburg on 12 under par, but still only in third place. Australian Paul Moloney was one in front of him and Sam Torrance two ahead.

Before their battle was resolved, though, the Ryder Cup issue had to be sorted out and with seventh-placed Howard Clark and ninth-placed Per-Ulrik

**A problematic week
for Ian Woosnam.**

Johansson both missing the halfway cut the weekend was more about sweating than sweaters.

Inevitably, it was Ian Woosnam who attracted most of the attention. He, like Swede Jesper Parnevik, had been asked to go to Germany by European captain Bernard Gallacher, who already had Nick Faldo and José Maria Olazábal in need of wild cards. To climb into the top ten – he was currently 13th – Woosnam had to finish fifth and with a day to go he was joint 11th, even after a brief flirtation with a broomhandle putter during a bizarre second round when he took to the course with two putters in his bag and used both. When the final push was needed, however, Woosnam could not come up with what was required. Instead of the 66 which would have automatically put him into the side he managed only 74, his chances effectively over once he had double bogeyed the 396-yard ninth.

Tenth-placed Philip Walton was not to know this as he strived to keep his berth on the side. The Irishman required 'only' 65th place to climb above Johansson, but after earning over 250,000 points trying to get another 1,400 was to prove as painful as having teeth pulled with pliers.

For 63 holes he seemed to be coping well, but for the last nine the pressure was there for all to see as he dropped seven shots in as many holes. His 77 dropped him to 69th place and it could have been heart-breaking. Could have been, but

wasn't, the failure of Woosnam, Parnevik and the 12 others who had a chance to make the team with a week to go meant that Johansson and Walton survived to become the two new caps at Oak Hill and Clark, David Gilford and Mark James secured their places as well.

Torrance and Montgomerie, meanwhile, were being joined in the race for the title by Yorkshire's Stuart Cage and Swede Niclas Fasth. With only three holes to play it was Torrance 16 under, Cage and Fasth 15 under and Montgomerie 14 under.

Fasth, whose fifth place in the Chemapol Trophy Czech Open the previous week had been his best finish on Tour, bogeyed the 16th, but birdied the 522-yard last to set the target of 269, 15 under par. Cage needed a birdie to beat it, but instead found water and bogeyed.

Volvo Order of Merit leader Torrance drove into heavy rough on the 16th and bogeyed that. It opened the door and Montgomerie stepped right in. On the

THE COURSE

Schloss Nippenburg, 20 miles from the centre of Stuttgart, became the first PGA European Tour course to be used on the Volvo Tour. Laid out by Bernhard Langer in association with European Golf Design's Ross McMurray, over 700,000 cubic metres of earth were moved and over 200,000 new bushes and trees planted. The two nine-hole loops were completed in October 1993, opened for play in August 1994 and officially opened by Mark McCormack on April 29, less than four months before the championship.

No home win this time for Bernhard Langer (above).
Rough times for Barry Lane (below).

short 17th he stood over a putt of 30 feet and told himself, as he had with good effect on the 70th, 71st and 72nd holes at Riviera, that: 'this one has to go in.' It worked again.

Now level with Torrance and Fasth, Montgomerie knew another birdie was still probably needed at the last. He very nearly went one better, his chip for an eagle stopping only inches from the cup.

It left Torrance having to make a birdie himself to force a play-off, that dreaded word for Montgomerie, whose record after the US PGA was played five, lost five. Torrance could not manage it and at long last Montgomerie was back in the winner's enclosure and back at the top of the money list.

Mark Garrod   179

Golf Club Schloss Nippenburg, Stuttgart, August 24-27, 1995 • Par 71 • Yards 6705

Pos	Name	Country	Rnd 1	Rnd 2	Rnd 3	Rnd 4	Total	Prize Money £
1	Colin MONTGOMERIE	(Scot)	69	64	68	67	268	108330
2	Sam TORRANCE	(Scot)	68	65	66	70	269	56450
	Niclas FASTH	(Swe)	68	67	68	66	269	56450
4	Stuart CAGE	(Eng)	70	64	68	68	270	27593
	Pedro LINHART	(Sp)	68	66	68	68	270	27593
	Paul MOLONEY	(Aus)	67	65	68	70	270	27593
7	Mark JAMES	(Eng)	67	67	70	67	271	17875
	Jay TOWNSEND	(USA)	72	66	67	66	271	17875
9	José COCERES	(Arg)	67	67	70	68	272	13755
	Joakim HAEGGMAN	(Swe)	70	69	66	67	272	13755
11	Paul EALES	(Eng)	66	67	70	70	273	11570
	Des SMYTH	(Ire)	69	66	69	69	273	11570
13	Gary ORR	(Scot)	69	63	71	71	274	9577
	Gordon BRAND JNR.	(Scot)	67	66	69	72	274	9577
	Andrew OLDCORN	(Eng)	67	71	67	69	274	9577
	Eduardo ROMERO	(Arg)	69	69	69	67	274	9577
	Paul MCGINLEY	(Ire)	68	68	67	71	274	9577
18	Darren CLARKE	(N.Ire)	66	73	68	68	275	8385
19	Ronan RAFFERTY	(N.Ire)	67	70	69	70	276	7821
	David GILFORD	(Eng)	68	67	71	70	276	7821
	Oyvind ROJAHN	(Nor)	67	71	68	70	276	7821
22	Mike MCLEAN	(Eng)	66	71	70	70	277	6435
	Andrew MURRAY	(Eng)	71	69	71	66	277	6435
	Thomas LEVET	(Fr)	67	71	69	70	277	6435
	Jesper PARNEVIK	(Swe)	66	70	72	69	277	6435
	Barry LANE	(Eng)	69	69	70	69	277	6435
	Heinz P THÜL	(Ger)	68	68	71	70	277	6435
	Sven STRÜVER	(Ger)	67	71	66	73	277	6435
	Miguel Angel MARTIN	(Sp)	70	70	71	66	277	6435
	Eamonn DARCY	(Ire)	69	70	68	70	277	6435
	Roger WESSELS	(SA)	69	68	67	73	277	6435
	Paul AFFLECK	(Wal)	64	68	73	72	277	6435
33	Mats LANNER	(Swe)	70	68	73	67	278	5135
	Ian WOOSNAM	(Wal)	69	69	66	74	278	5135
	Paul LAWRIE	(Scot)	65	71	73	69	278	5135
	Mark LITTON	(Wal)	69	69	70	70	278	5135
37	Ian PALMER	(SA)	68	70	73	68	279	4485
	Paul WAY	(Eng)	69	65	73	72	279	4485
	Bernhard LANGER	(Ger)	70	69	70	70	279	4485
	Peter O'MALLEY	(Aus)	68	72	72	67	279	4485
	David J RUSSELL	(Eng)	67	67	73	72	279	4485
	Jonathan LOMAS	(Eng)	70	67	72	70	279	4485
43	Daniel WESTERMARK	(Swe)	70	70	72	68	280	3770
	Marc FARRY	(Fr)	70	68	74	68	280	3770
	Malcolm MACKENZIE	(Eng)	67	72	73	68	280	3770
	Paolo QUIRICI	(Swi)	67	72	73	68	280	3770
	John HAWKSWORTH	(Eng)	71	68	70	71	280	3770
48	Steven RICHARDSON	(Eng)	69	69	68	75	281	2925
	Fredrik LINDGREN	(Swe)	67	73	68	73	281	2925
	Santiago LUNA	(Sp)	69	71	70	71	281	2925
	Mike MILLER	(Scot)	70	66	75	70	281	2925
	Adam HUNTER	(Scot)	72	68	68	73	281	2925
	David CARTER	(Eng)	67	67	74	73	281	2925
	Olle KARLSSON	(Swe)	68	68	74	71	281	2925
	Fabrice TARNAUD	(Fr)	70	66	70	75	281	2925
56	Peter MITCHELL	(Eng)	72	67	74	69	282	2080
	José RIVERO	(Sp)	66	73	70	73	282	2080
	Nic HENNING	(SA)	69	71	70	72	282	2080
	Christian CEVAER	(Fr)	67	70	74	71	282	2080
	Anders SORENSEN	(Den)	67	71	73	71	282	2080
	Michael ARCHER	(Eng)	69	71	72	70	282	2080
62	Juan QUIROS	(Sp)	71	67	72	73	283	1573
	John BICKERTON	(Eng)	70	70	76	67	283	1573
	Jon ROBSON	(Eng)	72	68	69	74	283	1573
	Alberto BINAGHI	(It)	69	69	73	72	283	1573
	André BOSSERT	(Swi)	70	66	72	75	283	1573
67	Paul BROADHURST	(Eng)	71	68	70	75	284	972
	José Maria CAÑIZARES	(Sp)	71	68	75	70	284	972
69	Philip WALTON	(Ire)	68	69	71	77	285	968
	Scott WATSON	(Eng)	69	67	73	76	285	968
71	Stephen AMES	(T&T)	69	69	71	77	286	965
72	Peter TERAVAINEN	(USA)	69	71	71	76	287	963
73	Gary EMERSON	(Eng)	70	69	76	73	288	961
74	Mark DAVIS	(Eng)	69	70	72	78	289	959
75	Erol SIMSEK	(Ger)	67	73	77	73	290	957
76	John MELLOR	(Eng)	71	69	75	78	293	955
77	Stephen MCALLISTER	(Scot)	72	68	76	80	296	953

SHOT OF THE WEEK

'I don't come to tournaments to finish second,' said Colin Montgomerie. Between his Volvo German Open win in 1994 and his retaining of the title a year later he had been second no fewer than five times. In the circumstances 'Shot of the Week' at Schloss Nippenburg was a tie – between Montgomerie and Montgomerie. First the birdie putt of 30 feet on the 17th hole of the last round, then the perfectly weighted chip at the final hole which left him a tap-in for another birdie. The winning birdie.

WHY DO PEOPLE WHO CAN AFFORD TO BUY THEIR OWN PLANES CHOOSE TO FLY ON OURS?

The Robb Report is a magazine read almost exclusively by American millionaires.

Every year, it asks its gilded subscribers to vote in a "Best of the Best" survey. And every year since the survey started, Delta Air Lines have been chosen "Best Airline."

Apparently, the average American plutocrat thinks the standard of service in First and Business Class impeccable. And they love the punctuality of our flights and the convenience of our routes.

Of course, all this would be mere fiddle-faddle if Robb Report readers were the type of people who hardly ever leave their own back yards.

But, they're the type of people who take at least five trips abroad a year and spend over two weeks in foreign hotels.

The type of people in fact, who expect and enjoy the highest of standards and the best of everything when they fly. Then again, you don't have to be a millionaire for that.

Just someone who flies Delta.

You'll love the way we fly

Grönberg scales new heights

Mathias Grönberg secured his maiden
Volvo Tour victory in the scenic setting
of the Swiss Alps

From the moment he enrolled in the Golf School at Gothenburg as a 15-year old, Mathias Grönberg was destined to become a champion. So when he reached that exalted status by winning the Canon European Masters at Crans-sur-Sierre from an elite field that included world number one Greg Norman and US Open champion Corey Pavin, it was not just a major personal landmark for the 25-year old from Orebro. It was also a triumph for the Swedish development programme which is now producing a regular stream of high quality recruits to the benefit of the PGA European Tour and the wider world of professional golf.

Grönberg became the ninth Swede to win on the Tour, and the fourth, after Jarmo Sandelin, Robert Karlsson, and Jesper Parnevik during the 1995 season. But he is the first to 'graduate' with champion performances at every level from boys and youths to senior amateur and professional, and his two-stroke victory over Ryder Cup players Costantino Rocca and Barry Lane will have lasting significance for other European nations eager to emulate Sweden's golf success.

Grönberg had a handicap of five when as a teenager he was first given tuition under his national federation scheme administered by director Arne Andersson. It was not restricted to technical advice on his swing. Grönberg had access to a panel of experts that included physiotherapists, nutritionists, psychologists and advisers on playing schedules. 'We call our system 'smorgasbord' because it resembles a table of snacks and local dishes from which one can choose according to taste', explained Andersson. 'Everything the developing golfer needs is there and he can experiment to find what is best for him.'

Grönberg fed so well that he was down to scratch within two years and won the Swedish Boys' title in 1988. Two years later he won the British Youths' title at Southerness and was the individual winner when Sweden took the 1990 Eisenhower Trophy in New Zealand. Continuous backing from his federation made it a smooth transition to the professional ranks. He was soon cutting his teeth with distinction on the PGA European Challenge Tour, winning the Swedish Match-Play title in 1991 before moving on to the Volvo Tour in 1994.

After sampling more expert advice from the likes of Tommy Horton, Bob

183

commemorated by a bronze plaque. And Eduardo Romero, the Argentinian they call 'The Cat' because of his uncanny ability to pounce on top prizes, had returned hungry after a lean summer on the US Tour to defend his title.

When Romero was among eight joint leaders on five under par after the first round and Grönberg shot 70, prospects of a Swedish victory looked as bleak as the weather which had greeted the golfers by depositing a few feet of fresh snow on the surrounding peaks.

Grönberg, who began the week in 112th place in the Volvo Order of Merit, first hinted that he was 'on a high' when he followed up with a 65 in the second round when anyone not under par was eliminated. The departees included

Early departure for Greg Norman (left) as spectators poured in (below).

Torrance and Alan Fine at the annual Apollo Week at San Roque in Andalucia, he quickly made his mark by finishing runner-up to countryman Mats Lanner in the Madeira Open in his debut season. It was clearly only a matter of time before the sturdy Grönberg reached a peak and became a force to be reckoned with. Appropriately his hour arrived in the high country of the Alps.

Yet there was little indication when Norman arrived in his personal jet direct from a thundering World Series victory at Akron which had set US Tour and world money-winning records, and Pavin, the master strokeplayer who conquered the world's best at Shinnecock Hills, joined a cavalcade of ten Ryder Cup players at Europe's most spectacular venue. There was also three times champion Seve Ballesteros, whose miraculous vertical recovery through a tiny gap in the fir trees behind the swimming pool wall at the 18th two years earlier, had been freshly

Norman (73-72) and Ballesteros, whose scores of 74 and 76 were further indication of his slump in form.

Steven Richardson was however, on an upward graph taking the halfway lead after a 64 which contained nine birdies and only 25 putts. It gave him a two-shot advantage at 13 under par over Romero (66) with Spain's Ignacio Garrido one further back and Grönberg on 135 alongside Irishman Darren Clarke and France's Jean Van de Velde.

An extraordinary finish to the third round engendered thoughts of victory for Grönberg who had been taking regular

weekend breaks in the previous three months. In his last 13 tournaments he had survived only four cuts, and there were just two top ten placings on his 1995 record. Armed with a new driver, and an old putter he had not used since the start of the season, Grönberg took a double bogey at the short 13th when he three-putted from two feet. His response was to eagle the long 15th with a long iron approach to a yard, then add tap-in birdie threes at the 16th and 18th for a 66.

It was overshadowed by a rampaging 64 from Vardon Trophy contender Sam Torrance which rocketed the Scot from last place to the fringe of the top ten, but Grönberg had gone into the lead on a 15 under par 201 and was in no mood to fall off his perch. A carefully compiled outward 33 in company with Romero and Peter Mitchell gave him the cushion of a three shot lead for the finishing stretch. But Lane and Rocca were closing fast, and now Grönberg was voyaging in uncharted

waters with only his training at the golf school and his new caddie to sustain him.

Grönberg chose the scenic route, gazing at the mountains rather than the leader boards which showed the looming menace of his challengers. First there was 1993 champion Lane, who closed with a 64. Then Rocca caught Lane on a 16 under par 272 with his 66. It was crisis time for the Swede who had missed the 12th green with his pitch and was only one shot better when he stood on the 15th tee. However, he was not under immediate pressure, for Mitchell had already marked three sixes on his card and was fading to a 76, while Romero was also out of the running after failing to make par at the short

Michael Jonzon (above) in Alpine setting. Canon sharp-shooters Barry Lane and Costantino Rocca (below).

11th and 13th.

When Grönberg hit the 15th flagstick with his chip and birdied to reach 18 below, he had only to play the last three holes without mishap. That he accom-

plished without difficulty, staying cool and calm to collect a prize of more than £116,000. 'My first win has come earlier than I thought and naturally I was nervous', he said. 'But my strategy was to play my own game and not worry about others. That is why I preferred to look at the scenery rather than the scoreboards. I didn't want to have too much uncertainty on my mind.'

There will be much less in future now that Grönberg's place on the Tour is secure and he has the opportunity to follow in the footsteps of Joakim Haeggman and Per-Ulrik Johansson, the first two Swedes to win Ryder Cup honours.

Mike Britten   185

Crans-sur-Sierre, Switzerland, August 31-September 3, 1995 · Par 72 · Yardage 6745

Pos	Name	Country	Rnd 1	Rnd 2	Rnd 3	Rnd 4	Total	Prize Money £
1	Mathias GRÖNBERG	(Swe)	70	65	66	69	270	116660
2	Barry LANE	(Eng)	67	71	70	64	272	60795
	Costantino ROCCA	(It)	70	69	67	66	272	60795
4	Eduardo ROMERO	(Arg)	67	66	69	71	273	32320
	Joakim HAEGGMAN	(Swe)	71	66	66	70	273	32320
6	Darren CLARKE	(N.Ire)	67	68	70	69	274	21000
	Sandy LYLE	(Scot)	71	66	70	67	274	21000
	Steven RICHARDSON	(Eng)	67	64	71	72	274	21000
9	Sam TORRANCE	(Scot)	73	70	64	68	275	14805
	Mats LANNER	(Swe)	71	67	68	69	275	14805
11	Michael CAMPBELL	(NZ)	71	66	69	70	276	11725
	Vicente FERNANDEZ	(Arg)	68	69	71	68	276	11725
	Colin MONTGOMERIE	(Scot)	68	70	68	70	276	11725
	Michael JONZON	(Swe)	72	65	67	72	276	11725
15	Olle KARLSSON	(Swe)	70	71	69	67	277	10080
	Jamie SPENCE	(Eng)	71	70	70	66	277	10080
17	Oyvind ROJAHN	(Nor)	73	70	67	68	278	8382
	David J RUSSELL	(Eng)	74	67	70	67	278	8382
	Domingo HOSPITAL	(Sp)	67	69	70	72	278	8382
	Alexander CEJKA	(Ger)	73	69	70	66	278	8382
	Sven STRÜVER	(Ger)	69	70	68	71	278	8382
	Ignacio GARRIDO	(Sp)	68	66	70	74	278	8382
	Paul LAWRIE	(Scot)	70	71	68	69	278	8382
	Peter MITCHELL	(Eng)	67	69	66	76	278	8382
25	Stuart CAGE	(Eng)	68	75	70	66	279	6825
	Jay TOWNSEND	(USA)	69	72	69	69	279	6825
	José RIVERO	(Sp)	67	74	69	69	279	6825
	Dean ROBERTSON	(Scot)	68	70	71	70	279	6825
	Jean Louis GUEPY	(Fr)	69	71	70	69	279	6825
	Peter O'MALLEY	(Aus)	71	70	69	69	279	6825
31	Paolo QUIRICI	(Swi)	74	68	72	66	280	5827
	Corey PAVIN	(USA)	73	68	71	68	280	5827
	Mike HARWOOD	(Aus)	71	68	70	71	280	5827
	Roger CHAPMAN	(Eng)	73	67	72	68	280	5827
35	Paul AFFLECK	(Wal)	73	68	69	71	281	4830
	Andrew OLDCORN	(Eng)	71	71	69	70	281	4830
	Fabrice TARNAUD	(Fr)	73	69	66	73	281	4830
	Jean VAN DE VELDE	(Fr)	69	66	74	72	281	4830
	José Maria CAÑIZARES	(Sp)	73	69	71	68	281	4830
	Tony JOHNSTONE	(Zim)	72	69	71	69	281	4830
	Jeremy ROBINSON	(Eng)	74	69	69	69	281	4830
	Joakim GRONHAGEN	(Swe)	72	71	69	69	281	4830
	Christian CEVAER	(Fr)	69	74	68	70	281	4830
	Jon ROBSON	(Eng)	71	69	70	71	281	4830
45	José COCERES	(Arg)	71	72	68	71	282	3920
	Robert KARLSSON	(Swe)	74	68	74	66	282	3920
	Per-Ulrik JOHANSSON	(Swe)	71	70	70	71	282	3920
48	Peter FOWLER	(Aus)	70	71	68	74	283	3570
	Scott WATSON	(Eng)	72	70	70	71	283	3570
50	Philip TALBOT	(Eng)	69	67	74	74	284	2940
	Russell CLAYDON	(Eng)	73	69	70	72	284	2940
	Peter HEDBLOM	(Swe)	74	69	72	69	284	2940
	Miguel Angel MARTIN	(Sp)	68	68	73	75	284	2940
	Eamonn DARCY	(Ire)	71	69	72	72	284	2940
	Anders FORSBRAND	(Swe)	72	68	71	73	284	2940
	Klas ERIKSSON	(Swe)	70	70	71	73	284	2940
57	Richard BOXALL	(Eng)	72	71	71	71	285	2222
	Iain PYMAN	(Eng)	70	69	75	71	285	2222
	Andrew SHERBORNE	(Eng)	70	70	72	73	285	2222
	Mike MILLER	(Scot)	72	67	73	73	285	2222
61	Mark MOULAND	(Wal)	67	73	73	73	286	1574
	Gary ORR	(Scot)	72	70	67	77	286	1574
	Alberto BINAGHI	(It)	68	75	73	70	286	1574
	Wayne RILEY	(Aus)	71	67	73	75	286	1574
	Christy O'CONNOR JNR	(Ire)	73	68	71	74	286	1574
	Paul MOLONEY	(Aus)	71	70	76	69	286	1574
	Paul BROADHURST	(Eng)	72	70	72	72	286	1574
	Jim PAYNE	(Eng)	72	69	72	73	286	1574
69	Phil GOLDING	(Eng)	74	68	73	72	287	1042
	Ross DRUMMOND	(Scot)	70	73	74	70	287	1042
	Malcolm MACKENZIE	(Eng)	71	68	73	75	287	1042
72	Steen TINNING	(Den)	71	70	71	77	289	1038
73	Chris MOODY	(Eng)	70	73	73	74	290	1036
74	Derrick COOPER	(Eng)	71	72	74	74	291	1034
75	John BICKERTON	(Eng)	72	71	73	76	292	1031
	Manuel PIÑERO	(Sp)	73	67	77	75	292	1031
77	Thomas LEVET	(Fr)	73	70	71	80	294	1028

THE COURSE

Crans-sur-Sierre which has been a championship venue for over almost 60 years will shortly see considerable change. Seve Ballesteros has been retained to redesign the Alpine course, but promises that the uphill par five ninth with its severely sloping triple-tiered green will not be altered. Even in the rarified air its 618 yards provides a searching test for the longest hitters.

OUR CONFERENCE ROOM

TO RECEIVE A FREE BOOKLET OUTLINING CANON'S CARING, SHARING PHILOSOPHY, CONTACT: CANON EUROPA N.V., P.O. BOX 2262, 1180 EG AMSTELVEEN, THE NETHERLANDS.

IN SOME CONFERENCE ROOMS, YOU DON'T HAVE TO SUFFER.

BECAUSE CANON BELIEVES IN BREAKING DOWN BARRIERS OF

COMMUNICATION. BRINGING PEOPLE CLOSER TOGETHER.

BY PROVIDING PRODUCTIVE, FRIENDLY, FLEXIBLE PRODUCTS.

WHICH MEANS YOU SAVE TIME INSIDE THE OFFICE.

SO YOU CAN SPEND MORE TIME OUTSIDE, DOING WHAT YOU

REALLY WANT TO DO. SUCH AS CONCENTRATING ON THE

REAL CHALLENGE, ON THE GOLF COURSE. THE DRIVE FOR

EXCELLENCE. THE THRILL OF THE CONTEST. THE PLEASURE

OF ACHIEVEMENT. IT'S A PASSION WE ALL SHARE.

AFTER ALL, BUSINESS WORKS BETTER WHEN IT BRINGS

A LITTLE MORE LEISURE INTO YOUR LIFE.

SO TOGETHER, LET'S CARE.

Canon
PLEASURE TO WORK WITH

Montgomerie's double puts him on top

With his second victory in three weeks
Colin Montgomerie moved to the top
of the Volvo Order of Merit

Colin Montgomerie had had a damned hard day at the office. When the big Scot teed off for the final round of the Trophée Lancôme, he was three shots clear of his countryman Sam Torrance. In theory, it should have been a doddle. He was 12 under par, Torrance nine under and the best of the rest a mere five under. His lead over Torrance, the main threat to his chances of topping the Volvo Order of Merit for a third successive season, ought to have been ample given his astonishing form since missing the cut at the Open.

Following that St Andrews hiccup, Montgomerie had played 23 rounds in 79 under par, in the process retaining the Volvo German Open, losing a play-off for the US PGA Championship and coming second in the Volvo Scandinavian Masters.

He was beginning to look unbeatable. 'The expectations on me get greater every

time I go out,' he said after his opening, six under par 64. 'I'm favourite to win most weeks, especially when Nick Faldo's not playing.'

On the strength of his first three rounds at St Nom-la-Bretéche, it would be hard to argue with that billing. After 54 holes, Montgomerie had taken just 198 strokes, hardly missing a fairway or green. But converting leads into victories is something that he, for all his monumental consistency, has not quite mastered. Before the Lancôme, he had only won eight times on the PGA European Tour, a surprisingly slim statistic for such a colossus.

His problem all season had been his putter. In the US PGA, no-one came anywhere near to matching his mastery of Riviera, but until the last round the putts just would not drop.

But a tip from his caddie, Alastair McLean, turned out to be the touchstone to his improved form on the greens. 'He told me to relax my grip on the club to give me less tension in my hands'. And how he needed that relaxed grip on the last day as his grip on the title relaxed. 'Of all my rounds since the Open,

David Gilford's last round 63 thrust him into third place.

this has to be the worst for ball striking.' he said having scraped home by the narrowest possible margin over Torrance after playing a miraculous chip at the 18th and holing out for a tournament-winning par.

'I couldn't get my irons right at all. I was pulling most of them. I knew it would be hard. It's never easy, three shots ahead you can only go one place, that's back. I bogeyed the first and fourth and only led by one. I birdied the fifth, the sixth and the eighth, but I wasn't playing well and got tense having been ahead for most of the tournament. I bogeyed the ninth and 12th, again bad iron shots, but managed to scramble my way home. It was a hard day.'

Realistically, Torrance was his only threat. He briefly held the lead after the second round, following his opening 65 with a 67 while Montgomerie stuttered to a 69. And, unusually, the pair ended up playing alongside each other on all four days. 'You end up running out of things to say to each other,' said Montgomerie.

Trailing by two shots with just the 195-yard 18th to go, Torrance threw down one last gauntlet with a majestic five iron tee shot which finished six feet from the cup. Montgomerie's six iron hooked long and left but he then coaxed a superb chip three feet from the hole to turn the heat back on Torrance.

The 42-year old Scot rolled his putt in to be sure of second place on his own ahead of Ryder Cup teammate David Gilford whose closing 63 was only one shot outside the course record. But Montgomerie still had to sink his putt to clinch the £100,000 winner's cheque. A year or two ago he might have missed it but this time there was no mistake. 'Obviously I looked relieved when the

THE COURSE

A week of heavy rain, and thunder at times, had restored St Nom-la-Bretéche's customary green and pleasant appearance after an arid summer. A teasing wind swirled throughout the tournament round the tree-lined parkland layout, making scoring considerably harder than it had been in 1994. The greens were generally slick, but were not easy to read due to variations in pace caused by their excessive dampness. The par threes are the course's key holes as three of them (the seventh, 12th and 18th) are protected by water hazards – beautiful but potentially deadly.

putt went in – it was missable. It's nice to play well under the utmost pressure when it really matters. I did it at the Volvo German Open and Riviera. Important shots seem to be coming off now. When I was learning this game they weren't'.

The US Ryder Cup player Tom Lehman came fourth on 273 after briefly threatening the leading duo in the final round. Bernhard Langer was fifth (his best finish in two months), Australia's Wayne Riley tied for sixth with the fast-improving Swede Michael Jonzon, and Paul Broadhurst maintained his love affair with Paris (he won the Peugeot Open de

Sam Torrance (above) finds a watery grave. The Chateau at Nom la Bretéche (below).

France on the nearby National course three months earlier) by finishing eighth.

Among those sharing 26th place on 281, one over par, were France's Jean Louis Guepy and José Maria Olazábal. In the second round, Guepy followed his opening 77 with an eight under par 62 to equal Mats Lanner's six-year old course record.

But Olazábal had an unhappier tournament and later telephoned Europe's Ryder Cup captain Bernard Gallacher to withdraw from the team to meet the Americans at Oak Hill because of the foot injury which had dogged him all season.

Ironically, Ian Woosnam, who it was announced later, was to take Olazábal's place, finished a shot worse than the Spaniard on 282.

Paul Trow   191

St. Nom la Bretéche, Paris, September 7th-10th, 1995 Par 70 · Yards 6758

Pos	Name	Country	Rnd 1	Rnd 2	Rnd 3	Rnd 4	Total	Prize Money £
1	Colin MONTGOMERIE	(Scot)	64	69	65	71	269	100000
2	Sam TORRANCE	(Scot)	65	67	69	69	270	66660
3	David GILFORD	(Eng)	70	71	67	63	271	37560
4	Tom LEHMAN	(USA)	67	70	69	67	273	30000
5	Bernhard LANGER	(Ger)	70	69	69	66	274	25400
6	Michael JONZON	(Swe)	72	67	70	66	275	19500
	Wayne RILEY	(Aus)	68	69	68	70	275	19500
8	Paul BROADHURST	(Eng)	69	69	70	68	276	15000
9	Costantino ROCCA	(It)	70	70	68	69	277	13440
10	Steven RICHARDSON	(Eng)	70	68	68	72	278	10740
	David J RUSSELL	(Eng)	69	67	74	68	278	10740
	Mike CLAYTON	(Aus)	73	72	70	63	278	10740
	José COCERES	(Arg)	71	72	69	66	278	10740
14	Michael CAMPBELL	(NZ)	66	68	74	71	279	7866
	Oyvind ROJAHN	(Nor)	66	72	72	69	279	7866
	Paul MCGINLEY	(Ire)	71	70	67	71	279	7866
	Doug MARTIN	(USA)	71	73	68	67	279	7866
	Mathias GRÖNBERG	(Swe)	72	68	72	67	279	7866
	Peter HEDBLOM	(Swe)	72	70	70	67	279	7866
	Greg TURNER	(NZ)	73	72	69	65	279	7866
	Darren CLARKE	(N.Ire)	70	70	70	69	279	7866
	Seve BALLESTEROS	(Sp)	67	73	70	69	279	7866
23	Peter O'MALLEY	(Aus)	73	71	68	68	280	6480
	Vicente FERNANDEZ	(Arg)	67	70	70	73	280	6480
	David CARTER	(Eng)	69	71	70	70	280	6480
26	Christian CEVAER	(Fr)	73	72	69	67	281	5497
	Vijay SINGH	(Fij)	70	71	69	71	281	5497
	José Maria OLAZABAL	(Sp)	71	67	70	73	281	5497
	José RIVERO	(Sp)	73	71	70	67	281	5497
	Jean Louis GUEPY	(Fr)	77	62	70	72	281	5497
	Mark JAMES	(Eng)	73	73	67	68	281	5497
	Roger WESSELS	(SA)	72	71	71	67	281	5497
	Carl MASON	(Eng)	70	70	71	70	281	5497
34	Richard BOXALL	(Eng)	72	72	72	66	282	4500
	Gordon BRAND JNR.	(Scot)	71	67	72	72	282	4500
	Malcolm MACKENZIE	(Eng)	73	70	69	70	282	4500
	Alexander CEJKA	(Ger)	69	70	73	70	282	4500
	Ian WOOSNAM	(Wal)	69	72	72	69	282	4500
	Silvio GRAPPASONNI	(It)	74	70	70	68	282	4500
40	Robert KARLSSON	(Swe)	71	73	70	69	283	4080
41	Gary ORR	(Scot)	70	73	72	69	284	3780
	Mats LANNER	(Swe)	71	75	71	67	284	3780
	Olle KARLSSON	(Swe)	76	70	70	68	284	3780
	Eduardo ROMERO	(Arg)	71	75	71	67	284	3780
45	Paul AFFLECK	(Wal)	68	72	76	69	285	3240
	Jay TOWNSEND	(USA)	69	74	70	72	285	3240
	Marc FARRY	(Fr)	74	68	70	73	285	3240
	Thomas LEVET	(Fr)	73	70	71	71	285	3240
	Andrew COLTART	(Scot)	73	72	69	71	285	3240
50	Des SMYTH	(Ire)	73	73	70	70	286	2880
51	Peter BAKER	(Eng)	70	73	75	69	287	2460
	Miguel Angel JIMÉNEZ	(Sp)	71	73	71	72	287	2460
	Rodger DAVIS	(Aus)	71	71	71	74	287	2460
	Pedro LINHART	(Sp)	71	73	71	72	287	2460
	Niclas FASTH	(Swe)	73	70	72	72	287	2460
	Paul MOLONEY	(Aus)	74	71	73	69	287	2460
57	Ignacio GARRIDO	(Sp)	71	70	74	73	288	1980
	Jean VAN DE VELDE	(Fr)	70	71	73	74	288	1980
59	Iain PYMAN	(Eng)	69	66	80	74	289	1740
	Derrick COOPER	(Eng)	70	74	75	70	289	1740
	Paul EALES	(Eng)	71	73	73	72	289	1740
	Mark MOULAND	(Wal)	73	69	75	72	289	1740
	Jamie SPENCE	(Eng)	72	74	74	69	289	1740
64	Mike MCLEAN	(Eng)	70	70	75	75	290	1214
	Peter MITCHELL	(Eng)	74	72	71	73	290	1214
	Barry LANE	(Eng)	72	74	76	68	290	1214
	Mark LITTON	(Wal)	73	71	75	71	290	1214
68	Jarmo SANDELIN	(Swe)	71	75	75	70	291	895
	Stewart CINK	(USA)	74	71	73	73	291	895
	Raphael EYRAUD	(Fr)	75	69	74	73	291	(Am)
70	André BOSSERT	(Swi)	72	72	78	74	296	892
71	Lee WESTWOOD	(Eng)	74	70	74	79	297	890

SHOT OF THE WEEK

When Torrance flighted a majestic five iron to within six feet of the hole at the 195-yard 18th on the final day, Montgomerie suddenly found himself under pressure. After leading for most of the four days, he hooked his six iron into a horrible lie—hard, tight, damp and trampled down. A treacherous water hazard beckoned beyong a green sloping away from him. 'It was not my idea of fun,' he said. Montgomerie nonetheless made the shot look ridiculously easy by chipping it to three feet. 'I had already given Sam his putt in my mind so I knew I had to get down in two as my play-off record isn't very good (five defeats out of five). Then I hit my best shot of the week. I'd been working on my short game and it paid off.'

Why Irish eyes are smiling

Torrance back on top again

With his third victory of the season
Sam Torrance took over the leadership of the Volvo
Order of Merit and set up a cliff-hanger finish to the year

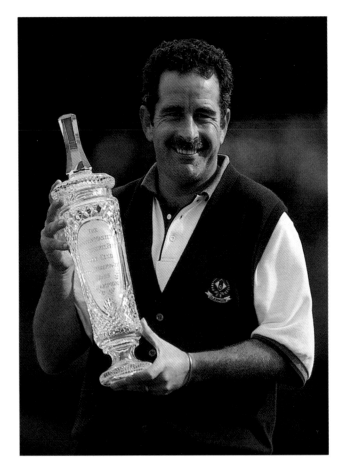

Anybody turning up for the Collingtree British Masters believing Sam Torrance and Colin Montgomerie might temporarily suspend title race hostilities to focus on the following week's Ryder Cup by Johnnie Walker matches was forgetting how desperately the two Scots wanted to finish European number one.

Montgomerie's Volvo German Open and Trophée Lancôme victories in the previous three weeks had swept him more than £63,000 ahead of his rival and Torrance was determined that by the time he climbed aboard Concorde to face the Americans he would once again be top-dog, and so it came to pass.

Nine members of Bernard Gallacher's team teed it up on the 6,768 yards Johnny Miller-designed layout, sited on the outskirts of Northampton an hour's drive from London.

It marked the debut of regular Tour competition on a PGA European Tour course within the British Isles, Collingtree Park being a joint venture between the PGA European Tour and the International Management Group through the property division.

With Sky Television stepping in with substantial sponsorship and the offer of five hours of live coverage each day, plus evening highlights, and BBC TV set to show extensive recorded coverage at the finish, the scene was set for messrs Torrance and Montgomerie to resume their battle royal. And it was first blood to Sam, an opening 67 leaving him one of five players a stroke behind co-leaders Sandy Lyle, Mats Hallberg and Jean-Louis Guepy and two strokes ahead of Montgomerie.

On a rainy second day that saw Ulsterman Darren Clarke fire a course record 62 with the help of six birdies, two eagles and only 27 putts, Montgomerie shot 69 again as Torrance posted a 66 to move 11 under par and into a one stroke halfway lead over Ryder Cup team-mate Mark James and Spain's Santiago Luna. As the wind picked up and the rain came down even heavier he calmly added a 68 to stretch that lead on day three to two strokes over New Zealander Michael Campbell and Spain's Domingo Hospital. Peter Mitchell was one behind them and, ominously, Montgomerie, after a 67, a single stroke further back.

It could and should have been better, for the big Scot, after helping himself to six birdies and an eagle, was set for a last day head-to-head with Torrance until he

came to Collingtree's tough 18th with water all the way along the left and in front of the green. 'I had 190 yards to go and went with a four iron but the ball travelled only 150 yards and finished in the lake, the fairway was very wet and my foot slipped and to say I was disappointed is an understatement,' he confessed after taking a penalty drop, pitching short, then chipping stiff for a bogey six.

Four Ryder Cup team members had missed the halfway cut. Defending champion Ian Woosnam, despite some late night reading of a new book on positive thinking entitled 'Neuro Linguistic

THE COURSE

The Championship course at Collingtree Park, Northampton, is sited just two miles from Junction 15 on the M1 motorway. It measures 6,768 yards and was designed by Johnny Miller, former Open and US Open Champion, built at a cost of more than £5 million to USGA specifications and opened in May, 1990. It has the benefit of sand-based greens, which presented no drainage problems in the prolonged rain of British Masters week. Greens and fairways are subtly shaped and water comes into play on no fewer than ten holes, most notably at the signature hole 18th, flanked the length of the fairway by a lake to the left with a spectacular island green.

Ryder Cup warm-up for Colin Montgomerie (above left), Howard Clark (above right) and Severiano Ballesteros (below).

**Michael Campbell (above) is under orders.
Sam Torrance and Mark James (below) see the funny side.**

Programming' and spending hours hard at work on his game with Bill Ferguson, the coach he shares with Montgomerie, and David Gilford, sniffling with a head cold, taking two too many with 145 totals, Per-Ulrick Johansson scoring 148 and Philip Walton 151 after a nine at the last.

With Seve Ballesteros slipping to a third round 74 following two encouraging 69s and Howard Clark doing likewise after a pair of opening 70s, it was left to Torrance (201), Montgomerie (205) and James (206) to carry the Ryder Cup banner into the final day.

It was to be Torrance who would emerge the champion in an event which started life way back in 1946 as the Dunlop Masters and whose roll of victors includes 12 major winners.

As Montgomerie took 40 to come home in the wind and rain for a 72 and 277 to tie seventh and James shot 72 for 278, rookie Campbell became the biggest threat to Sam's return to the top of the money list when he birdied the 12th and 13th to edge past the 42-year old Scot,

only to three-putt the 16th.

The pair went to the last deadlocked. Campbell hooked into the lake, took a drop in the rough and then hit a courageous three wood 257 yards on to the green to throw down the challenge. Torrance declared: 'It forced me to go for it and I hit a ripper out of my boots to make the green and two-putted for victory'.

Campbell's repeat of his Volvo PGA Championship second place was his seventh top ten finish of an impressive first full European season, but it was Sam's day and he confessed: 'I haven't been so happy since my children were born. My dad always told me I'd play my best golf in my 40s and he was right, this win is more special than anything else in this wonderful season.'

Gordon Richardson

COLLINGTREE PARK ETC, NORTHAMPTON, SEPTEMBER 14-17, 1995 • PAR 72 • YARDAGE 6768

Pos	Name	Country	Rnd 1	Rnd 2	Rnd 3	Rnd 4	Total	Prize Money £
1	Sam TORRANCE	(Scot)	67	66	68	69	270	108330
2	Michael CAMPBELL	(NZ)	70	67	66	68	271	72210
3	Miguel Angel JIMÉNEZ	(Sp)	73	65	68	67	273	40690
4	Vicente FERNANDEZ	(Arg)	70	68	67	69	274	32500
5	Iain PYMAN	(Eng)	69	67	71	69	276	25140
	Andrew OLDCORN	(Eng)	67	70	68	71	276	25140
7	Stephen AMES	(T&T)	68	67	71	71	277	15815
	Peter BAKER	(Eng)	70	69	67	71	277	15815
	Colin MONTGOMERIE	(Scot)	69	69	67	72	277	15815
	Peter HEDBLOM	(Swe)	70	69	66	72	277	15815
11	Pedro LINHART	(Sp)	69	69	74	66	278	10146
	José COCERES	(Arg)	70	69	72	67	278	10146
	Santiago LUNA	(Sp)	67	67	75	69	278	10146
	Greg TURNER	(NZ)	69	71	69	69	278	10146
	Des SMYTH	(Ire)	68	67	72	71	278	10146
	Mark JAMES	(Eng)	67	67	72	72	278	10146
	Peter MITCHELL	(Eng)	68	69	67	74	278	10146
18	Miguel Angel MARTIN	(Sp)	67	74	71	67	279	7962
	Roger CHAPMAN	(Eng)	68	72	70	69	279	7962
	Darren CLARKE	(N.Ire)	73	62	74	70	279	7962
	José RIVERO	(Sp)	70	67	71	71	279	7962
22	Paul MOLONEY	(Aus)	71	69	72	68	280	7020
	Retief GOOSEN	(SA)	70	69	73	68	280	7020
	Sven STRÜVER	(Ger)	72	71	69	68	280	7020
	Jonathan LOMAS	(Eng)	68	67	75	70	280	7020
	Steven RICHARDSON	(Eng)	69	71	67	73	280	7020
27	Joakim HAEGGMAN	(Swe)	70	73	71	67	281	6045
	Jean Louis GUEPY	(Fr)	66	76	70	69	281	6045
	Jamie SPENCE	(Eng)	70	72	70	69	281	6045
	Brian MARCHBANK	(Scot)	70	72	70	69	281	6045
	Ian PALMER	(SA)	74	69	66	72	281	6045
32	Mats HALLBERG	(Swe)	66	73	74	69	282	5330
	Andrew COLTART	(Scot)	69	74	69	70	282	5330
	Carl MASON	(Eng)	69	70	71	72	282	5330
35	John BICKERTON	(Eng)	72	69	72	70	283	4745
	Ross MCFARLANE	(Eng)	72	70	72	69	283	4745
	Christy O'CONNOR JNR	(Ire)	69	71	74	69	283	4745
	Mike CLAYTON	(Aus)	70	71	71	71	283	4745
	Robert KARLSSON	(Swe)	69	69	72	73	283	4745
	Sandy LYLE	(Scot)	66	71	71	75	283	4745
41	Jim PAYNE	(Eng)	69	68	75	72	284	3770
	Mike MCLEAN	(Eng)	69	73	71	71	284	3770
	Marc FARRY	(Fr)	72	69	72	71	284	3770
	Mats LANNER	(Swe)	70	73	71	70	284	3770
	Frank NOBILO	(NZ)	70	71	74	69	284	3770
	Ronan RAFFERTY	(N.Ire)	72	70	74	68	284	3770
	Ross DRUMMOND	(Scot)	73	70	68	73	284	3770
	Nic HENNING	(SA)	68	70	72	74	284	3770
	Olle KARLSSON	(Swe)	71	68	70	75	284	3770
50	Christian CEVAER	(Fr)	69	73	71	72	285	3055
	Derrick COOPER	(Eng)	72	70	69	74	285	3055
52	Seve BALLESTEROS	(Sp)	69	69	74	74	286	2795
	Tony JOHNSTONE	(Zim)	70	71	76	69	286	2795
54	Gary ORR	(Scot)	69	73	72	73	287	2237
	Paul MCGINLEY	(Ire)	72	70	72	73	287	2237
	Phillip PRICE	(Wal)	73	70	72	72	287	2237
	Wayne RILEY	(Aus)	71	70	75	71	287	2237
	David CARTER	(Eng)	71	69	76	71	287	2237
	Adam HUNTER	(Scot)	70	73	74	70	287	2237
	Peter TERAVAINEN	(USA)	73	70	76	68	287	2237
61	Anders SORENSEN	(Den)	71	70	71	76	288	1787
	Peter FOWLER	(Aus)	68	71	73	76	288	1787
	Barry LANE	(Eng)	71	72	71	74	288	1787
	Howard CLARK	(Eng)	70	70	74	74	288	1787
65	Rodger DAVIS	(Aus)	70	73	72	74	289	1625
66	Dean ROBERTSON	(Scot)	76	67	75	73	291	974
	Gordon BRAND JNR.	(Scot)	72	70	79	70	291	974
68	Peter O'MALLEY	(Aus)	68	70	77	77	292	969
	Rolf MUNTZ	(Hol)	75	68	73	76	292	969
	Keith WATERS	(Eng)	69	74	76	73	292	969
71	Mathias GRÖNBERG	(Swe)	69	70	83	72	294	965
72	Domingo HOSPITAL	(Sp)	69	67	67	DISQ		963

SHOT OF THE WEEK

Andy Oldcorn holed out for an eagle two with a nine iron at the 387-yard 11th on day three, Swede Mats Hallberg also holed his second shot at the 350-yard tenth on day four and the wooden shots to the 72nd green under the utmost pressure of Sam Torrance and Michael Campbell were majestic. But the shot of the week surely came at the last on day three from 26-year old Campbell, who led the Open Championship going into the final round at St Andrews. He struck a three iron 216 yards with a little draw from a perfect lie straight into the hole on the fly. The ball spun around inside the cup and then jumped back out, sucking back to finish ten feet short and Campbell calmly tapped in for his eagle three.

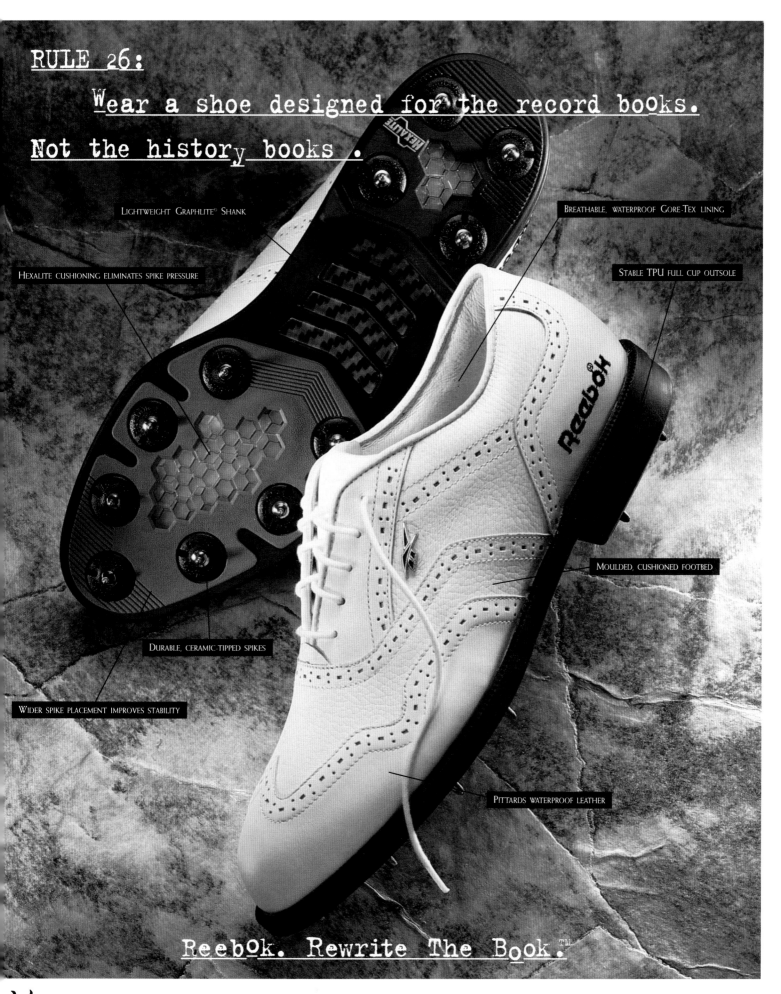

RULE 26:

Wear a shoe designed for the record books.
Not the history books.

LIGHTWEIGHT GRAPHLITE® SHANK

BREATHABLE, WATERPROOF GORE-TEX LINING

HEXALITE CUSHIONING ELIMINATES SPIKE PRESSURE

STABLE TPU FULL CUP OUTSOLE

MOULDED, CUSHIONED FOOTBED

DURABLE, CERAMIC-TIPPED SPIKES

WIDER SPIKE PLACEMENT IMPROVES STABILITY

PITTARDS WATERPROOF LEATHER

Reebok. Rewrite The Book.™

You don't make it into the record books by living in the past. You do it by outperforming everyone else right now. Take the Reebok® Attack, for example. No one else makes a shoe with the same stability, durability, and comfort features you need to compete today. And with our Pittards® waterproof leather upper and Gore-Tex® lining, you can compete any day, rain or shine. That's why we back the Attack with a two-year waterproof guarantee. Which leaves us with one final conclusion. Next to the Reebok Attack, all other shoes are history. For the Reebok stockist nearest you, call 01524 580100.

Reebok
GOLF

Europe triumphs in stunning finale

Bernard Gallacher's men overcame the odds

to record an unforgettable victory at Oak Hill

They said it was Mission Imposs-ible, going to Oak Hill, a US Open course, and bringing back the Ryder Cup without José Maria Olazábal, one of our major men.

They said Bernard Gallacher was an unlucky captain who could never win. Eight times as a player, twice as the skipper, and never on the winning side yet.

They said Seve was past it and too many of the others were out of form.

They said Europe were 3-1 outsiders with the bookmakers, it would be a massacre, we didn't have a chance.

Wrong, wrong, wrong, wrong, and wrong again.

And when Europe went into the singles trailing by two, they said it was all over, Europe had never won the singles in the States. In fact, they only won the singles anywhere once in a blue moon. 'History is for amateurs,' said Gallacher prophetically. 'Professionals only think of the future.'

In the end, it came down to Nick

Faldo and the rookie, Philip Walton. Could Nick win the last two holes from Curtis Strange, America's controversial wild card, and turn round a one hole deficit? Could Walton, three up with three to play, halve a hole and see off Jay Haas?

With three defeats out of four going into the final day it had not been Faldo's week. But beneath that rugged exterior, there beats the heart of a lion, and he has always thrived on adversity. Once again in the moment of crisis, Nick's nerve held firm, first with a par-saving putt at the

17th that squared the match, then 'with the most important up-and-down of my life' after driving into thick rough at the last – a 93-yard wedge shot to four feet that put Strange under the sort of pressure he could not handle. Provided Walton in the match behind did not crumble, this was it, a four-footer for the Ryder Cup, to give Europe its first victory since Muirfield Village in 1987. It had been a long time between drinks – pass the Johnnie Walker!

'Everything was shaking but the putter,' said Faldo. 'I knew how important the point was.' Cometh the hour, cometh the man. Now came the tears, from Faldo, from Seve, too, as the two great men, the two who had done more, far more, than anyone to make Europe a match, and sometimes more than a match, for the Americans in the previous decade, collapsed in a warm embrace.

It was not over yet though. Haas had holed out of a bunker at the 16th to huge American cheers and Walton had missed from four feet for the match on the 17th. 'There was a little bit of pressure on, okay,' explained the Irishman later.

Walton needed a little bit of help from Haas to get through the ordeal of the 18th and he got it. 'Playing 18, my legs were shaking,' said Walton. 'they were somebody else's legs.' Haas, thankfully, reduced the pressure substantially by driving poorly, laying up in two, then hitting a weak pitch that spun back off the green. When Haas' fourth shot sailed past the hole, all Walton had to do was get down

in two from 12 feet for a bogey and the half that would make it a boom night for Guinness shareholders in Dublin. Europe had won the singles 7½-4½, the match 14½-13½.

Suddenly the ball was at the hole-side and it was all over. Gallacher was leaping high in the air in his supreme moment of triumph, then rushing on to the green to hug a mightily relieved Walton. Against all the odds, Europe had regained the Ryder Cup by Johnnie Walker and we who had been there, privileged to see it, could tell our grandchildren about one of sport's truly great moments.

The champagne flowed, grown men wept floods of tears of unashamed joy, Even Gallacher cried. 'I didn't cry before when we lost,' he admitted. 'But I cried a little this time.'

Earlier, his confidence had barely

Overwhelming moment for Nick Faldo on the last day.

wavered, though Corey Pavin had done his damnedest to crush Europe's spirit by chipping in for the last hole birdie on the second day that deflated Faldo and Bernhard Langer and sent Europe into the final day with a seemingly impossible task, two behind instead of all square. 'We were down when Pavin chipped in but the team knew they were better than the Americans. I'd been telling them all week they were. In the singles, they just had to go out there and prove it. The team was angry. After his two defeats on the first day, Colin Montgomerie wasn't a very nice person to be with. That's the sort of person I want on my side. In some ways it was an advantage to be down,' said Gallacher.

It ended in tears, it began more in hope than confidence. The 12 good men and true that accompanied Gallacher to Rochester, 380 miles north of New York City and not too far from the Canadian border, knew they had it all to do. The

Joy for Bernhard Langer (left) and David Gilford and Severiano Ballesteros (right).

Americans were on home ground, they were the Cup holders and they had chosen Oak Hill, scene of Strange's 1989 US Open victory, because they knew Europeans had, with few exceptions, fared badly in US Opens. Worse for morale, the most winning combination in Ryder Cup history, Ballesteros and Olazábal was missing because of Olazábal's foot injury.

The men with the uphill task were Montgomerie, Faldo, Ballesteros, Langer, Costantino Rocca, Sam Torrance, David Gilford, Walton, Per-Ulrik Johansson, Mark James, Howard Clark and Ian Woosnam, who had been preferred over Jesper Parnevik when Olazábal was compelled to withdraw.

American captain Lanny Wadkins felt he could not risk John Daly, the reigning Open champion, on Oak Hill's tight fairways, and also had the luxury of omitting prolific winners Lee Janzen and Jim Gallagher Junior. His team was: Pavin, Fred Couples, Phil Mickelson, Tom Lehman, Davis Love III, Peter Jacobsen, Loren Roberts, Jeff Maggert, Haas, Strange, Ben Crenshaw and Brad Faxon. Couples and Strange were the wild cards for them, Faldo and Woosnam for Europe.

After the introduction of the teams to the full house on Thursday ('I've never been cheered before for shots I've hit on the practice range' said Crenshaw, amazed at the huge turnout to watch the Ryder Cup foreplay), the omens were good for Europe: we had won the battle of the national anthems 6-1 after they had struck up God Save The Queen, Deutschland Über Alles, the Italian, Spanish, Swedish equivalents, and Amhran Na Fhiann for Walton. All of a sudden, it didn't seem a fair fight!

From Oak Hill on Thursday to Soak Hill on Friday – torrential rain for the last ten holes of the morning foursomes (with all the squeegeeing and club-drying, Langer and Johansson took 4 hrs 40 mins to complete theirs) and for the early part of the afternoon four-balls. Faldo and Montgomerie were our bankers in the top match, against Pavin and Lehman. Quickly four down, they hit back to level after 13 when Faldo holed from 35 feet only to lose to Lehman's magnificent 205-yard five

203

iron from sopping wet semi-rough at the last after Faldo's pushed tee-shot and bunkered pitch had left the British pair with no chance of salvaging par.

But still Europe managed parity at 2-2 thanks to rock-solid Rocca and Torrance who won five holes in a row from the sixth and survived an American fightback to ease home by three and two over Couples and Haas.

They bagged Europe's first point of the week and after Love and Maggert had proved too strong for veterans James and Clark, the new team of Langer and debutant Johansson hung on in a dramatic finale, to account for the experienced Crenshaw and Strange on the home green, Langer sinking a crucial putt for par after the Europeans had frittered a three up lead with two double bogeys and a bogey on the rain-lashed back nine.

Gallacher's luck was right out. Forced to name his afternoon pairing at mid-day, he had naturally opted for Langer and Johansson, who at that time stood three up with six to play, seemingly heading for a comfortable victory. He could not foresee the struggle, the stress and the soaking his men were to suffer before they clinched their nerve-racked success: 'Otherwise I would have played Woosnam and Walton in the afternoon,' admitted the captain later. 'It was an error.' Langer and Johansson were pitched into battle too quickly and with only half an hour for a sandwich, a change of clothing and a 'rest', lost the first four holes on the way to a six and four hammering from Pavin and Mickelson.

The unlikely four-ball heroes were a new team, Ballesteros and Gilford, or, to be more precise, Gilford and Ballesteros, for the Englishman had to play Faxon and Jacobsen on his own for much of the match. 'I caddied for him,' said Ballesteros with a mischievous grin. It was not too far

Tom Lehman (above) charges home a putt. Corey Pavin (opposite) recovers.

from the truth, for Seve had told the retiring Gilford on the first tee: 'You are the best player out here' – a masterstroke of timing. Then he read all of Gilford's putts so brilliantly that the balding man from Crewe, seemingly couldn't miss, even when it came to a putt of 20 feet with ten feet of break on the 13th. The Americans had made it even harder for themselves when day-dreaming Jacobsen, not realising his partner had gone in the water at the seventh, picked up his marker thinking Faxon had made four. In fact, Faxon was

down in five and Jacobsen had a shortish putt to halve the hole. But it was a freak concession and it had the galleries buzzing. Skipper Wadkins said: 'I went up to Jacobsen on the next hole and asked him if he'd like a mathematician sent over to help them keep score.' But it wasn't funny for the likeable Jacobsen who was inconsolable until he had sunk the winning putt, in partnership with Roberts, to beat Woosman and Walton the following morning. No one is better than Seve in cashing in on a team in disarray, and home came the Europeans triumphantly four and three.

It was to be Europe's only afternoon joy. Torrance and Rocca, so formidable in foursomes, found the magic simply wasn't there as a four-ball, though rookies Maggert and Roberts were outstanding and four under par in their six and five dismissal.

Elsewhere, it was a second defeat in the day for poor Faldo and Montgomerie, this time by three and two against Couples and Love, the World Cup winners. Faldo was birdieless and grim-faced, but Gallacher was to give them one more chance, in the Saturday foursomes, and how their win there was needed as the score at the end of the first day was: USA 5, Europe 3.

From Soak Hill on Friday to Croak Hill on Saturday as that cold-eyed assassin Pavin plunged the knife into European hearts with a miraculous birdie three chip-in after Faldo's immaculate approach shot had looked likely to win the point and send Gallacher's men into the singles all square.

To European eyes, it was the imperfect end to a stunning match. Pavin, round

in 67, three under par, had 'done' us again… or so it seemed.

Despite Rocca's hole-in-one (five iron at the 167-yard sixth and only the third in Ryder Cup history) on the way, with Torrance, to their second landslide four-somes triumph, this time six and five over Love and Maggert, and a second great win for Gilford, this time with Langer as over-seer, the day was to end where it started – with Europe still two adrift.

Far better weather now for the morn-ing foursomes. Faldo and Montgomerie needed to play no more than solidly to dispose of the error-prone Haas and Strange by four and two, while, for once Langer, thanks to some brilliant Gilford iron play, got the measure of his deadly rival, Pavin, who suffered his only setback of the week, going down four and three with his first-day partner Lehman.

THE COURSE

Oak Hill, 6,902 yards, par 70. 'Just about the best course I've ever played,' said Sam Torrance. 'A great, traditional course. It's all there in front of you. You've just got to go out there and do it.' Wonderfully green, perfectly manicured. The 13th, 598-yards, a great amphitheatre – and then that ferocious finish, the 16th at 439 yards, the 17th at 458 and the 18th at 445. Any score under 70 a work of art. As good as it gets in golf course design. Originally by Donald Ross, remodelled by Trent Jones. A masterpiece.

It could so easily have been a foursomes whitewash as Woosnam and Walton had a handy lead for much of the way against Roberts and Jacobsen. When Roberts missed his first fairway of the day at the 18th, it still looked as if Europe would sneak a half, but the same player then produced one of the shots of the week, a 100-yard pitch to less than a yard, which a grateful Jacobsen duly converted.

Still, things were looking up. It was 6-6. Surely Europe would make a better fist of the fourballs, traditionally the strongest part of their armoury, second time around? Sadly, it was the same story as before, 3-1 to the home side, though Rocca's great Ryder Cup continued with his third victory, this time with Woosnam, by three and two over Love and the struggling Crenshaw.

Gallacher split up Faldo and Montgomerie, but neither of the new pairings caught fire, Torrance and Montgomerie losing four and two to Faxon and Couples, and Faldo's fine late play in partnership with Langer deserving, but not getting, the half against an inspired Pavin, with strong assist from Roberts. Pavin's birdie at the 445-yard uphill 18th after missing the fairway badly to the right will long be remembered. It looked like the hole that would decide the 31st Ryder Cup, but how wrong we all were.

And so to the last day. From Soak Hill to Croak Hill and now, according to the hard-hitting America media who took no prisoners when five of their stars came to the last hole and not one went away with a win, it was Choke Hill.

Only Couples, with a gutsy birdie at the 17th and a superb up-and-down at the last to deprive brave Woosnam, was

Severiano Ballesteros (opposite): still the crowd-puller. Costantino Rocca (above) celebrates his hole-in-one. Any vantage point will do (left).

absolved from blame, though there was little Jacobsen could do against Clark's cast-iron par that clinched a crucial one up early win for the charging Europeans.

Gallacher's policy was to pack his in-form players into the middle, hoping and praying to have it all wrapped up before the pressure mounted on his tail-end rookies Walton and Johansson. He was only one match out in his reckoning. We had already seen Europe's second ace of the week, from Clark against Jacobsen, a 192-yard six iron at the 11th. Now we needed more miracle shots from Europe – and we got them.

Ballesteros, sent out first against Lehman in the off-chance that leading the team on the last day might inspire him to his former greatness, holed out over a bunker at the second. Then James converted from the back bunker at the long fourth.

Suddenly, the impossible looked possible. The boards all round the course said as much. The rapturous noise swelling from the 5,000 Europeans who had loyally made the transatlantic trip told you who was winning. Europe, quoted 5-1 going into the singles, was making the British bookmakers look foolish. The over-40s were being fortified, with Clark, James (four and three over Maggert) and Torrance (two and one over Roberts) all coming through with the points.

Against the odds, Seve was through the turn in 36, having hit only one fairway, the sixth. Trouble was he was playing the fifth at the time! Still, it was only a matter of time in the top match, Lehman proving far too steady for the wayward Spaniard, who hit only three fairways all week. 'I have cleared out all the rough and the branches,' he said ruefully. 'The members aren't going to lose any more balls!'

Love always had Rocca's measure and despite Langer's fighting birdie replies whenever Pavin went two ahead, the bulldog American looked to have that match under control. Yet everywhere else, it was looking brilliant. We still needed Gilford to win, Faldo to win, Walton to win.

It was unbearable, unwatchable even, as Gilford, one up playing the last against Faxon, overclubbed the green, left his chip in the green's deep collar, then trundled his second chip ten feet past the hole. A

double bogey would hand it to the nervous Faxon, but Gilford's putting, his strong suit for the week, again held up under the most intense pressure. In went the putt, straight as a die, and a startled Faxon, missed from six feet.

The half-point needed to keep America's hands on the cup would have to come from elsewhere. But with the spotlight now switched to Strange, and the dogged Faldo snapping at his heels, the man who had conquered Oak Hill six years earlier was wilting. Bogey, bogey, bogey. Faldo needed no second bidding.

If he was the key player in the final

hour, they were all heroes. This was team golf at its best, and they played as a team. Everyone won at least one point, Gilford, Torrance and Rocca three.

Wadkins, shattered but gracious, said: 'The Europeans played awfully well. They did some things out of the ordinary. They made two holes-in-one and chipped in a lot. They played inspired golf. I've seen more chip-ins this week then you see in a tournament with 150 players. They deserved to win, but we'll be back for that trophy at Valderrama in 1997.'

In the moment of triumph, Gallacher didn't miss the human touch: 'We all know Seve has been struggling,' he said, 'and the whole team thought we should do something for him because he has been such an inspiration to European golf for so long. I was glad it was my turn to win – and the team's turn.'

It was a wonderful emotional note on which to bow out as captain. Thanks for the memories, Bernard – and thanks to 24 great players for putting the word 'chivalry' and 'sportsmanship' back into sport.

Jeremy Chapman

SHOT OF THE WEEK

So many – two aces from Rocca and Clark, a quite outstanding 100-yard wedge shot from Roberts that saw off Woosnam and Walton in the second-day foursomes, Lehman's 205-yard five iron on day one that accounted for Faldo and Montgomerie. But in the context of its timing and importance, you would have to bring it down to Faldo's 93-yard wedge to four feet in the decisive singles against Strange. No good, of course, if you miss the subsequent putt. But Faldo didn't!

Oak Hill was jumping for Bernard Gallacher (opposite) and the Europeans (above).
Woe for Curtis Strange and the Americans (below left), delight for Gallacher (below right).

OAK HILL COUNTRY CLUB, ROCHESTER, NEW YORK, USA, SEPTEMBER 22ND-24TH, 1995

• CAPTAINS: B GALLACHER (EUROPE), L WADKINS (USA) •

EUROPE		USA	
DAY ONE			
Foursomes: Morning			
N Faldo & C Montgomerie	0	C Pavin & T Lehman (1 hole)	1
S Torrance & C Rocca (3 & 2)	1	J Haas & F Couples	0
H Clark & M James	0	D Love III & J Maggert (4 & 3)	1
B Langer & P-U Johansson (1 hole)	1	B Crenshaw & C Strange	0
Fourballs: Afternoon			
D Gilford & S Ballesteros (4 & 3)	1	B Faxon & P Jacobsen	0
S Torrance & C Rocca	0	J Maggert & L Roberts (6 & 5)	1
N Faldo & C Montgomerie	0	F Couples & D Love III (3 & 2)	1
B Langer & P-U Johansson	0	C Pavin & P Mickelson (6 & 4)	1
DAY TWO			
Foursomes: Morning			
N Faldo & C Montgomerie (4 & 2)	1	C Strange & J Haas	0
S Torrance & C Rocca (6 & 5)	1	D Love III & J Maggert	0
I Woosnam & P Walton	0	L Roberts & P Jacobsen (1 hole)	1
B Langer & D Gilford (4 & 3)	1	C Pavin & T Lehman	0

EUROPE		USA	
Fourballs: Afternoon			
S Torrance & C Montgomerie	0	B Faxon & F Couples (4 & 2)	1
I Woosnam & C Rocca (3 & 2)	1	D Love III & B Crenshaw	0
S Ballesteros & D Gilford	0	J Haas & P Mickelson (3 & 2)	1
N Faldo & B Langer	0	C Pavin & L Roberts (1 hole)	1
DAY THREE			
Singles			
S Ballesteros	0	T Lehman (4 & 3)	1
H Clark (1 hole)	1	P Jacobsen	0
M James (4 & 3)	1	J Maggert	0
I Woosnam (halved)	½	F Couples (halved)	½
C Rocca	0	D Love III (3 & 2)	1
D Gilford (1 hole)	1	B Faxon	0
C Montgomerie (3 & 1)	1	B Crenshaw	0
N Faldo (1 hole)	1	C Strange	0
S Torrance (2 & 1)	1	L Roberts	0
B Langer	0	C Pavin (3 & 2)	1
P Walton (1 hole)	1	J Haas	0
P-U Johansson	0	P Mickelson (2 & 1)	1
EUROPE	**14½**	**USA**	**13½**

Champagne moment for the captain and supporters.

Savour that wonderfully warm glow as a Johnnie Walker Black Label goes down in ne

Langer swoops to victory

Bernhard Langer's stunning eagle putt
on the final hole set up play-off triumph

*B*ernhard Langer could have been excused for declining the challenge of the Smurfit European Open at the splendid K Club, an Arnold Palmer creation being presented to the Tour players for the first time. So, too, could nine of the other members who formed the European Union that destroyed the American Ryder Cup dream in so dramatic a fashion a few days earlier. Drained by the physical and mental demands of modern day Ryder Cup matches, they would have preferred more time to savour the enormity of their achievement and, no doubt, the tumultuous welcome they received when Concorde touched down at Dublin Airport.

But the show had to go on. The European Open, with its new sponsor and new venue, is one of the Tour's high profile titles and only Nick Faldo and Seve Ballesteros were missing from the dozen Oak Hill heroes. For the others it was

another week at work. Langer had been down the road before. Four years earlier he returned from Kiawah Island under very different circumstances but still displayed the great strength of character that is the hallmark of his professionalism. He eliminated the painful memory of the missed putt on the last green of the last

match on the last day by winning the Mercedes German Masters. This time he was riding on the back of a Ryder Cup victory, a highly emotive victory, and he admitted: 'The first few days in Ireland were a bit of a let down after the excitement of the Ryder Cup. I felt very bad on Tuesday but as the week went on my physical and mental strength improved. So did my game.'

In fact, it improved to the extent that his final rounds of 68, 68 constituted the best 36 hole aggregate of the tournament by two shots and left him in a tie with all-the-way leader Barry Lane at eight under par 280. But that statistic hides the real story of what Langer himself described as 'the most dramatic finish of my career.' One seldom sees the disciplined German let go of his emotions to such an extent that he does something akin, if not as graceful, to a high-flying ballet routine over his putter. Then again, one seldom sees a putt from 70 feet for eagle drop in the hole on the 72nd green.

212

Sam Torrance (left) lost his lead in the Volvo Order of Merit. Big boost for Fabrice Tarnaud (right).

Lane, a couple of two-balls behind, heard the roar and knew that he had to birdie one of the last three to win his first title in over eighteen months. The K Club does not offer many realistic birdie opportunities but on this day the par five 18th, despite the lake down the left of the fairway and around three parts of the green, was reachable with a drive and mid-iron.

Lane, from a good position on the fairway, pushed his second to the right, chipped ten feet past the hole and only narrowly missed the birdie putt. They played the 18th again in the first hole of sudden-death and halved it in birdies after Langer had sailed his second so close to the water that it stayed dry by only a couple of feet. Then it was down the tenth where the German's putter was once again the lethal weapon, ironic considering the agony he went through with several doses of the 'yips' earlier in his career. He holed from 20 feet for birdie which meant that he had covered his last three holes in four under par.

That was real drama considering he was seven shots behind first round leaders, Carl Mason and Lane who had 67, a shot ahead of American Jay Townsend, New Zealander Michael Campbell and Frenchman Fabrice Tarnaud. By the halfway stage Lane was the sole leader at six under par and two ahead of Stephen Ames, Mason, Sandy Lyle and Colin Montgomerie with Langer still six behind. The cut was four over par and it is a tribute to the resilience of the Ryder Cup players that nine of the ten survived.

Unfortunately, from a local standpoint

SHOT OF THE WEEK

Bernhard Langer's putt from 70 feet for eagle on the 72nd green was the most sensational stroke of the tournament. He hit the par five 18th with a drive and five iron and needed at least an eagle three to force a play-off. He had holed one from 60 feet on Friday but this was even more outrageous and it sent him prancing around the green. 'If you cannot get excited about a putt of 70 feet on the 72nd green of a major tournament, I don't know what you can get excited about' said Langer, who emphasised the importance of the stroke by saying it was the most dramatic finish of his career.

The K Club was the brain child of Dr Michael Smurfit, head of the multinational Jefferson Smurfit organisation, and in keeping with the grandeur of the Kildare Hotel and Country Club just 40 minutes from Dublin city centre, he employed the services of Arnold Palmer to produce a top quality championship course. The result was a tough par 72, 7,159-yard layout through parkland that is bordered by the River Liffey. Water, in fact, is a major feature of the course with only five holes where a lake or the river is not in play.

Philip Walton, the man who won the point that secured the Ryder Cup for Europe, was the absentee. He immediately drew sympathy from Montgomerie who said that it was most unfortunate for Philip that the tournament immediately after the Ryder Cup should have been in Ireland. 'After the reception at Dublin Airport it was obvious that he had little chance so close to home.' It is also worthy of mention that England's Roger Chapman improved on his first round by 11 shots with a course record 66 which earned him the £3,000 Johnnie Walker Tour Course Record Award.

Montgomerie himself admitted that if it was not for the private battle he was engaged in for the Volvo Order of Merit he would probably have taken three weeks off. He came into the event some £29,000 behind Sam Torrance and, after filling a share of third place, left it back on the top. 'I came to Ireland to make inroads into the £29,000 I was behind

Sam. I have done that and I am happy.'

Another man to leave the event very satisfied with his week was Fabrice Tarnaud. The young Frenchman, a graduate from the 1994 PGA European Tour Qualifying School, started the week in 133rd position on the Volvo Order of Merit but a share of sixth place and a cheque for £21,125 left him 106th and assured of his card for 1996.

Good news for the future of the tournament came during the event when it was announced that Smurfit and the PGA European Tour had entered a joint partnership in the European Golf Championship Ltd. Smurfit secured the option of staging the event at the K Club or in countries in Europe where they have business operations.

Colm Smith

Sandy Lyle on the 15th.

THE K CLUB, CO. KILDARE, SEPTEMBER 28TH - OCTOBER 1, 1995 • YARDAGE 7159 • PAR 72

Pos	Name	Country	Rnd 1	Rnd 2	Rnd 3	Rnd 4	Total	Prize Money £
1	Bernhard LANGER	(Ger)	74	70	68	68	280	108330
2	Barry LANE	(Eng)	67	71	71	71	280	72210
3	Jay TOWNSEND	(USA)	68	76	67	72	283	36595
	Colin MONTGOMERIE	(Scot)	71	69	73	70	283	36595
5	Costantino ROCCA	(It)	69	75	70	70	284	27530
6	Steen TINNING	(Den)	69	75	70	71	285	21125
	Fabrice TARNAUD	(Fr)	68	73	69	75	285	21125
8	Joakim HAEGGMAN	(Swe)	71	70	71	74	286	16250
9	Paul LAWRIE	(Scot)	69	72	73	73	287	12222
	Anders FORSBRAND	(Swe)	70	71	72	74	287	12222
	Carl MASON	(Eng)	67	73	71	76	287	12222
	Dean ROBERTSON	(Scot)	73	72	71	71	287	12222
	Tom LEHMAN	(USA)	70	72	73	72	287	12222
14	Peter TERAVAINEN	(USA)	73	75	70	70	288	9162
	Stephen AMES	(T&T)	69	71	77	71	288	9162
	Mark DAVIS	(Eng)	73	71	72	72	288	9162
	Mark JAMES	(Eng)	72	70	74	72	288	9162
	Santiago LUNA	(Sp)	71	72	73	72	288	9162
19	Per-Ulrik JOHANSSON	(Swe)	72	71	70	76	289	7821
	Miguel Angel MARTIN	(Sp)	73	73	70	73	289	7821
	Ian WOOSNAM	(Wal)	72	72	72	73	289	7821
22	Sandy LYLE	(Scot)	70	70	74	76	290	7410
23	Paul BROADHURST	(Eng)	70	72	75	74	291	7215
24	Fredrik LINDGREN	(Swe)	73	70	75	74	292	6532
	Russell CLAYDON	(Eng)	73	70	74	75	292	6532
	Sam TORRANCE	(Scot)	73	73	73	73	292	6532
	Lee WESTWOOD	(Eng)	71	77	73	71	292	6532
	Mats LANNER	(Swe)	75	73	67	77	292	6532
	John BICKERTON	(Eng)	79	69	73	71	292	6532
30	Sven STRUVER	(Ger)	71	71	77	74	293	5573
	Jimmy HEGGARTY	(N.Ire)	76	69	70	78	293	5573
	Iain PYMAN	(Eng)	73	70	74	76	293	5573
	Miguel Angel JIMENEZ	(Sp)	76	72	71	74	293	5573
34	Christian CEVAER	(Fr)	73	75	70	76	294	4745
	Klas ERIKSSON	(Swe)	70	72	79	73	294	4745
	Andrew COLTART	(Scot)	76	69	79	70	294	4745
	Anders GILLNER	(Swe)	76	70	70	78	294	4745
	Wayne RILEY	(Aus)	70	75	74	75	294	4745
	Oyvind ROJAHN	(Nor)	73	68	75	78	294	4745
	Jose Maria CANIZARES	(Sp)	74	73	67	80	294	4745
	Steven BOTTOMLEY	(Eng)	75	72	74	73	294	4745
42	Michael CAMPBELL	(NZ)	68	77	75	75	295	3900
	Roger CHAPMAN	(Eng)	77	66	74	78	295	3900
	Jean Louis GUEPY	(Fr)	74	72	72	77	295	3900
	Mats HALLBERG	(Swe)	72	75	69	79	295	3900
	Olle KARLSSON	(Swe)	74	72	73	76	295	3900
47	Howard CLARK	(Eng)	72	76	71	77	296	3380
	Michael JONZON	(Swe)	73	73	77	73	296	3380
	Pedro LINHART	(Sp)	74	71	74	77	296	3380
50	Mike CLAYTON	(Aus)	75	73	72	77	297	2860
	Christy O'CONNOR JNR	(Ire)	74	74	74	75	297	2860
	Ronan RAFFERTY	(N.Ire)	75	71	73	78	297	2860
	Phillip PRICE	(Wal)	71	73	77	76	297	2860
	David CARTER	(Eng)	72	72	75	78	297	2860
55	Steven RICHARDSON	(Eng)	73	72	76	77	298	2223
	Mathias GRONBERG	(Swe)	74	74	73	77	298	2223
	Derrick COOPER	(Eng)	74	72	72	80	298	2223
	David GILFORD	(Eng)	72	72	72	82	298	2223
	Paul WAY	(Eng)	72	74	72	80	298	2223
60	Raymond BURNS	(N.Ire)	72	69	74	84	299	1917
	Jonathan LOMAS	(Eng)	74	73	76	76	299	1917
62	Gordon J BRAND	(Eng)	71	72	77	80	300	1787
	Andrew MURRAY	(Eng)	72	73	76	79	300	1787
64	Stuart CAGE	(Eng)	72	74	76	79	301	1690
65	Paul CURRY	(Eng)	75	71	73	83	302	1625
66	Domingo HOSPITAL	(Sp)	75	71	72	85	303	973
	Peter HEDBLOM	(Swe)	72	76	73	82	303	973
	David J RUSSELL	(Eng)	76	72	76	79	303	973

Bernhard Langer
drives off in the
final round.

Achieving
the Objective

**The world's leading paper-based
packaging company**

Main Sponsor of
The Smurfit European Open
at
The Kildare Hotel & Country Club
The most prestigious Hotel and
Championship Golf Course in Ireland

Forsbrand ahead in birdie rampage

Birdies and eagles flew thick and fast in Germany and when the dust had settled Anders Forsbrand was on top

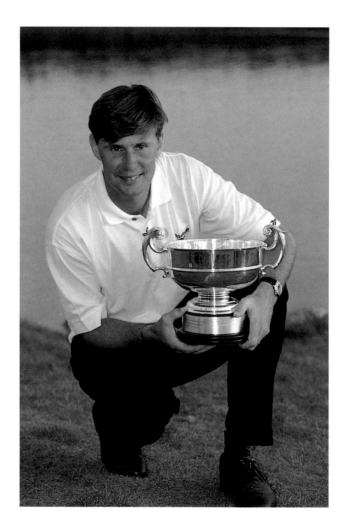

There were two big winners at Motzener See.

Anders Forsbrand warded off an inevitable bid from a tired, but determined, Bernhard Langer, to earn his sixth PGA European Tour title and collect his largest purse of £108,330.

The other champion was Motzener See itself.

When correspondents talk of a 'birdie blitz', it is, of course, hyperbole. This time when the press corps waxed lyrical, they were not exaggerating. The first two rounds alone produced nearly 1,000 birdies. In four rounds, 1,524 went up on the scoreboard, with 51 eagles and one albatross, courtesy of Peter Baker. It really did rain birdies.

Russell Claydon produced the greatest opening deluge, collecting 18 in the first two rounds. On day two he bagged 12, breaking Ernie Els' course record by two shots as he posted an 11 under par 61. He also equalled the PGA European Tour record for most birdies, held by Els and Fred Couples. This enabled Claydon to lead by a stroke after the second round from Forsbrand, who had shared top billing on Thursday with compatriots Per-Ulrik

Johansson, Klass Eriksson and Retief Goosen of South Africa. Their opening rounds of 64 put them one ahead of Paul Eales.

As if pre-empting there would be a birdie-shoot, an airline offered two round-the-world air tickets for the most collected during the week. It was always going to

be a close-run thing. Over the first two days the birdie-count averaged out at five a man.

'Is it really that easy?' asked one sports desk, when staggering feats were filed. At 6,480 yards and with its holes embroidered throughout with lakes, tightish greens and the occasional hidden flag,

Motzener See is by no means easy. But with perfectly manicured greens, benign conditions-and the remarkable golf played by Tour professionals, it 'seemed' easy.

Colin Montgomerie forecast on the eve of the event that there would be a glut of low scoring. Not from him, though. A recurring left wrist injury, one he had suf-

**Most birdies for
Per-Ulrik Johansson.**

As Claydon slipped badly in the third round with a 74, Forsbrand took over. Putting like a genius with a curiously-shaped 'Delta' putter designed for him by a retired furniture-maker, and trusting a remodelled swing designed for him by David Leadbetter in Orlando, he fashioned a five-stroke lead over Langer on Saturday. Forsbrand was also six ahead of Claydon and Johansson.

Coming off his play-off victory the week before, and two weeks after the mentally exhausting triumph at Oak Hill, the chances of Langer making up five shots should have been slim, taking into consideration Forsbrand's experience. That was, though, not taking into consideration Montzener See's vulnerability, nor Langer's indomitability.

Forsbrand came under threat first from Johansson, then Claydon, who

fered quietly for two months, forced him out of the Volvo Order of Merit title race temporarily, after a 76. Montgomerie had gained a late invitation to play. This was to try to stop money-list rivals Sam Torrance, who was less than a £1,000 behind him, and the in-form Langer, lying third and creeping up on them with only two events to go, from stealing a march. Under instructions to not hit a golf ball

for a week, Montgomerie thus left the scene, and left the door open for Torrance and Langer.

Torrance only had to make the halfway cut to go past Montgomerie and he duly did that, closing 68s for a 33rd place giving him a £3,830 cushion going into the Volvo Masters. However, Langer ensured that the Volvo Masters would be a three-way shoot-out.

THE COURSE

The professionals responded to its superb condition by producing the most spectacular golf of the season. Designer Kurt Rossknecht could justifiably be proud of the accolades bestowed upon the three-year old course, built at a former Soviet Army HQ. Similarly, greens superintendent Trevor Mitchell, whose St Andrews roots were evidenced by the occasional tough pot-bunker, saw fruition of a year's hard work. With the help of the PGA European Tour's greenkeeping consultant Richard Stillwell, there was no sign of any ill effects from a very dry summer.

caught him by the tenth. But down the closing stretch it was Langer who ran him closest. A chip-in birdie on the 11th out of the blue left Langer only a stroke behind and the German eyed the first prize which would have left him a mere £20,000 off the top of the Volvo Order of Merit.

On a day when for once Langer's

Bernhard Langer (left) and Russell Claydon (above) were both in the running for the title.

normally immaculate putting stroke was found wanting, a crucial miss from three feet to bogey the 15th, took the pressure off Forsbrand. Then when Forsbrand birdied the short 17th from only four feet, he had an unassailable three-shot lead as he clambered on to the final tee, knowing even the tricky lake-protected 18th could hold no fears.

For Claydon the consolation of a Johnnie Walker Tour Course Record Award and of clinching a Volvo Masters spot as he finished four behind in third place. For Johansson those round-the-world tickets. For Montzener See, a week when the records had to be rewritten.

Norman Dubell 221

MOTZENER SEE G & CC, BERLIN, OCTOBER 5 - 8, 1995, • YARDAGE 6848 • PAR 72

Pos	Name	Country	Rnd 1	Rnd 2	Rnd 3	Rnd 4	Total	Prize Money £
1	Anders FORSBRAND	(Swe)	64	64	67	69	264	108330
2	Bernhard LANGER	(Ger)	67	66	67	66	266	72210
3	Russell CLAYDON	(Eng)	66	61	74	67	268	40690
4	Per-Ulrik JOHANSSON	(Swe)	64	66	71	68	269	30015
	Jesper PARNEVIK	(Swe)	68	64	70	67	269	30015
6	Paul EALES	(Eng)	65	69	70	67	271	21125
	Joakim HAEGGMAN	(Swe)	67	67	68	69	271	21125
8	Heinz P THÜL	(Ger)	70	70	66	66	272	13380
	José COCERES	(Arg)	68	73	65	66	272	13380
	Richard BOXALL	(Eng)	71	66	67	68	272	13380
	Sven STRÜVER	(Ger)	69	71	65	67	272	13380
	Ignacio GARRIDO	(Sp)	70	66	67	69	272	13380
13	Tom LEHMAN	(USA)	67	67	70	69	273	10200
	Jarmo SANDELIN	(Swe)	67	67	70	69	273	10200
15	Silvio GRAPPASONNI	(It)	68	71	67	68	274	8217
	Greg TURNER	(NZ)	67	68	69	70	274	8217
	Peter TERAVAINEN	(USA)	69	69	69	67	274	8217
	Jim PAYNE	(Eng)	68	66	69	71	274	8217
	Sandy LYLE	(Scot)	67	72	66	69	274	8217
	Robert ALLENBY	(Aus)	71	67	71	65	274	8217
	Steven RICHARDSON	(Eng)	69	68	68	69	274	8217
	Jay TOWNSEND	(USA)	68	74	66	66	274	8217
	Robert KARLSSON	(Swe)	69	70	69	66	274	8217
24	Malcolm MACKENZIE	(Eng)	67	72	69	67	275	6532
	Peter MITCHELL	(Eng)	68	64	71	72	275	6532
	Miguel Angel JIMÉNEZ	(Sp)	66	67	74	68	275	6532
	Vijay SINGH	(Fij)	73	63	71	68	275	6532
	Retief GOOSEN	(SA)	64	69	70	72	275	6532
	Peter HEDBLOM	(Swe)	67	66	75	67	275	6532
30	Stephen AMES	(T&T)	69	70	67	70	276	5655
	José RIVERO	(Sp)	69	70	70	67	276	5655
	Fredrik LINDGREN	(Swe)	68	63	72	73	276	5655
33	Ronan RAFFERTY	(N.Ire)	71	70	71	65	277	4810
	Klas ERIKSSON	(Swe)	64	73	70	70	277	4810
	Erol SIMSEK	(Ger)	74	64	67	72	277	4810
	Miguel Angel MARTIN	(Sp)	68	72	69	68	277	4810
	Andrew COLTART	(Scot)	69	71	68	69	277	4810
	Andrew SHERBORNE	(Eng)	69	65	71	72	277	4810
	Ross MCFARLANE	(Eng)	73	64	71	69	277	4810
	Sam TORRANCE	(Scot)	71	70	68	68	277	4810
	Santiago LUNA	(Sp)	67	67	72	71	277	4810
42	André BOSSERT	(Swi)	69	67	72	70	278	4095
	Andrew MURRAY	(Eng)	71	70	70	67	278	4095
44	Ralf BERHORST	(Ger)	71	67	68	73	279	3900
45	Peter O'MALLEY	(Aus)	70	70	69	71	280	3575
	Peter BAKER	(Eng)	71	69	70	70	280	3575
	Mats LANNER	(Swe)	69	70	69	72	280	3575
	Brian MARCHBANK	(Scot)	69	68	69	74	280	3575
49	Paul WAY	(Eng)	71	70	72	68	281	3055
	Paul CURRY	(Eng)	70	69	70	72	281	3055
	Paul BROADHURST	(Eng)	71	70	71	69	281	3055
	Fabrice TARNAUD	(Fr)	75	64	72	70	281	3055
53	Vicente FERNANDEZ	(Arg)	71	68	69	74	282	2535
	Jamie SPENCE	(Eng)	70	71	69	72	282	2535
	Ross DRUMMOND	(Scot)	71	69	70	72	282	2535
	Gary ORR	(Scot)	75	67	70	70	282	2535
57	Michel BESANCENEY	(Fr)	73	69	72	69	283	2028
	Jean VAN DE VELDE	(Fr)	70	72	72	69	283	2028
	Michael CAMPBELL	(NZ)	74	67	70	72	283	2028
	Steen TINNING	(Den)	67	70	71	75	283	2028
	Wayne WESTNER	(SA)	71	70	70	72	283	2028
62	Eoghan O'CONNELL	(Ire)	70	68	69	77	284	1787
	Gavin LEVENSON	(SA)	67	73	69	75	284	1787
64	David J RUSSELL	(Eng)	67	69	78	72	286	1657
	Mark DAVIS	(Eng)	69	71	72	74	286	1657
66	Carl MASON	(Eng)	72	67	76	73	288	975

SHOT OF THE WEEK

Russell Claydon's eight iron to the short 12th in the first round, nearly earned him a £30,000 Mercedes. Agonisingly, his ball missed the cup by less than half-an-inch. Peter Baker only made the cut by producing the third albatross of the year, a stunning five wood approach in round two, over some 250 yards at the long second. However, it is in the heat of battle when really telling shots are hit. Like the seven iron, surely unintentionally, flirting dangerously with the lake to only four feet for birdie on his penultimate hole by Anders Forsbrand. It finally closed the door on Bernhard Langer.

BOSS

HUGO BOSS

Els is king of Wentworth

For the second year running

Ernie Els proved he has

no peer in match-play

October, it must be Wentworth and the Toyota World Match-Play Championship.

That simple piece of sporting logic has steadily developed in the nation's sporting psyche over the past three decades, ever since Neil Coles lost to the legendary Arnold Palmer in the first final in 1964. It is Europe's autumnal answer to America's spring starter at the Masters in Augusta, and it's a golfing date that Ernie Els seems set to pencil in to his diary for several years to come.

Els, South Africa's fast-rising international star, has yet to lose a match at Wentworth. On his debut in 1994 he took the Championship by storm, beating Colin Montgomerie in the final. This time, two days before his 26th birthday, he became the first player since Severiano Ballesteros in 1985 to successfully defend the coveted title.

His three and one final victory, over Australian Steve Elkington, not only earned him the £170,000 first prize (the richest purse in Europe this year) but also

moved him up to number two in the Sony World Rankings, his highest ever position. 'I'd like to be number one some day, but I don't think I am quite there yet,' said the modest Els. 'I would also love to win the World Match-Play five times like Gary Player and Seve, but there are some great players around and I am still learning. Right now this win has turned an ordinary year into a very good one.'

Wentworth has rarely looked more beautiful, in shades of russet, gold and green, bathed in the glow of an Indian summer. The course was still very wet from the September downpours, however, and playing every inch of its 6,975-yard length. Fog is the one drawback to fine autumn days in this part of the world and so it proved for the first round, with the clinging mist causing a two-hour delay.

The action, when it began, was fast and furious, with Montgomerie showing no signs of his recently injured left wrist as he went round in 66 (six under par) to lunch five up against America's rookie of the year David Duval. When he stood on the final tee just one up, however, Montgomerie, faced the possibility of an embarrassing exit, only to get the birdie four he needed to edge home by one hole.

There was no joy for Ryder Cup team-mate Sam Torrance, however.

Torrance who had been so keen to get an invitation, was never better than all square in his match with the doggedly determined Bernhard Langer. His broomhandle putter was inconsistent all day and Sam finally bowed out five and four.

Just three weeks before, Costantino Rocca declared he had 'lost a match but

made 12 friends' at the Ryder Cup. This time he won a match and secured many thousands of new admirers, as he smiled and strolled his way to an impressive four and three victory over Vijay Singh, who had been heavily backed with the book-makers. Meanwhile, Lee Janzen, still smarting over his controversial omission

Third place for Costantino Rocca.

from the US Ryder Cup team showed just why he thought he should have been picked by finishing six under par in dispatching the ailing Japanese Katsuyoshi Tomori seven and six.

Many observers expected that Janzen would give the seeded Els a hard battle in the second round, especially as the South African might be rusty after playing just once in four weeks. But Ernie was out of the blocks like Linford Christie, birdieing three of the first four holes and scorching round in 64 to lunch five up. In all, his smooth and rhythmical swing produced 13 birdies in 33 holes as the unfortunate Janzen was put to the sword four and three.

British interest disappeared as Colin Montgomerie, beaten in a one hole play-off for the US PGA crown by Steve Elkington, lost out to the Australian again. This time he was eight under par and heading for a 66 in the afternoon round when he was finally beaten two and one, after an absorbing match of fluctuating fortunes. The 17th and 18th in the morning round proved crucial. Elkington birdied them and Montgomerie could only get pars, and it was exactly the same in the eagerly awaited battle between Bernhard Langer and Nick Price, with Langer, winner on this course in the Volvo PGA Championship in May coming back to all square at lunch by winning those crucial holes. After winning the first

in the afternoon, Langer was never headed again, but with Price battling courageously it went all the way to the last hole before Langer could win by one hole.

The unfamiliar cries of 'Forza Italia' echoed around Wentworth's tree-lined fairways again, as new folk hero Costantino Rocca out gunned an out-of-sorts Ben Crenshaw. A kidney infection and missed flights had ruined Crenshaw's preparations but he showed great character in fighting back from eight down with 16 to play, to finally lose three and two.

With no Britons in the semi-finals for the first time in many a year, the home fans went into Europhile mode, but their hopes were tempered by the worry that all the efforts of the past few weeks, especially at Oak Hill, might prove decisive if the matches went the full distance.

And so it proved, with Langer, coming back from one down at lunch to be one up with three to play after a run of four birdies in five holes, but finding he had nothing left to give after Els claimed super birdies at the 34th and 35th. A sad three-putt at the last green finished the exhausted Langer.

It was a similar story in the other semi, where Elkington just edged out

THE COURSE

Prolonged rain had made the West Course play its full length and the greens were soft and holding, ideal conditions for low scoring. Because of this, the pin positions during the week became the main talking point among the players. PGA European Tour Tournament Director, Mike Stewart explained: 'We could not use the pin positions we used for the Volvo PGA Championship as the greens were very hard and there was a strong breeze. This week there was hardly any wind and the greens were soft and receptive so we decided to give the players more of a challenge.'

Rocca three and one in a see-saw encounter. The turning point came at the 30th hole (the 12th) where Elkington rolled in a killer putt for a winning eagle to match the one Rocca had claimed in the morning.

Bernhard Langer (above) ponders while Steve Elkington (right) despairs.

For the first time since 1979 there was no European in the final. Perhaps that added to the muted atmosphere, or maybe we had been so sated by the coruscating dramas of the Ryder Cup that anything else seemed tame by comparison.

Either way this will not go down as one of the Match-Play's more memorable finals. The play was solid and functional, rather than fiery and inspirational. Els was three up after 15 holes in the morning, but wild hooks off the tee at the next two holes saw that lead cut to one, only for a birdie at the 18th to restore a two-hole lead at lunch.

Els had seen Elkington roar past him with a closing round 64 in the US PGA, but this time he always had the Australian in his rear-view mirror, easing to four up after three holes in the afternoon. Elkington refused to go quietly, however, and cut the deficit to two holes at the eighth, but the next eight holes were halved until Els delivered the *coup de grace* with an imperious second shot at the long

35th for a birdie that sealed a three and one victory.

'Neither of us played at our best today', conceded Els, 'but I am just happy to have won for the second time. The only person with a better record is my cook this week, Sara Gaymer. She was also my cook last year when I won and

the year before she was cook for Corey Pavin when he won. I definitely want her on my team next year.'

In the match for third and fourth place Costantino Rocca earned £60,000 for defeating Bernhard Langer two and one.

John Whitbread   227

WENTWORTH CLUB (WEST COURSE), SURREY, OCTOBER 12-15, 1995 • YARDAGE 6,957 • PAR 72

First Round

		Prize money
Lee Janzen (USA) beat Katsuyoshi Tomori (Jap)	7 & 6	£30,000
Bernhard Langer (Ger) beat Sam Torrance (Scot)	5 & 4	£30,000
Colin Montgomerie (Scot) beat David Duval (USA)	2 holes	£30,000
Costantino Rocca (It) beat Vijay Singh (Fij)	4 & 3	£30,000

Second Round

		Prize money
Ernie Els (SA) beat Lee Janzen	4 & 3	£40,000
Bernhard Langer beat Nick Price (Zim)	1 hole	£40,000
Steve Elkington (Aus) beat Colin Montgomerie	2 & 1	£40,000
Costantino Rocca beat Ben Crenshaw (USA)	3 & 2	£40,000

Semi-Finals

Ernie Els beat Bernhard Langer	1 hole
Steve Elkington beat Costantino Rocca	3 & 1

Play-Off for Third & Fourth Places

		Prize money
Costantino Rocca		£60,000
beat Bernhard Langer	2 & 1	£50,000

Final

		Prize money
Ernie Els		£170,000
beat Steve Elkington	3 & 1	£90,000

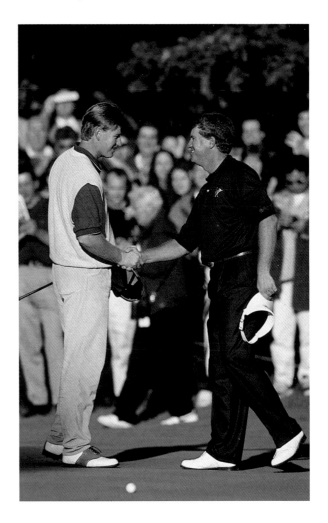

Final moment.

SHOT OF THE WEEK

Almost to the finish the top candidate for Shot of the Week was the superb four iron that Costantino Rocca flighted to 18 inches for a winning eagle at the 12th hole of his semi-final with Steve Elkington. It was topped, however, by the shot that clinched the championship for Ernie Els. Left with 250 yards to the green at the 35th (17th) he drilled a magnificent two iron that rolled over the hole to finish 15 feet from the flag and set up the decisive birdie.

So Grows Your Frustration With Your Three Iron.

You can't hit it. The one club in the bag that's rotten. So you're planting it at home. If you played with Apollo seamless steel shafts, you'd have that club back in the game. Other steel shafts have a hidden weld seam, but not Apollo. You don't have to worry about a weld bead that could distort the shaft dimensions and rob you of your consistency club to club, or a weld seam to weaken the performance. If you want all the consistency you can get, choose an alternative that lets you use everything you've got. **Pick the only seamless steel shaft.**

GOLF SHAFTS

ENGINEERED TO MAKE A DIFFERENCE

I APOLLO LTD., OLDBURY, WARLEY, WEST MIDLANDS B69 2DF. TELEPHONE: 021-544 7654. FAX: 021-544 4519. TELEX: 333356.

Scotland the bravest

Sam Torrance, Colin Montgomerie and Andrew Coltart

finally ended Scotland's long wait for victory

at the home of golf

They had waited a decade for this moment. And when it came on a grey, damp Sunday afternoon at St Andrews, the Scottish fans rose solidly to the occasion. As the wee, tartan army of Sam Torrance, Colin Montgomerie and Andrew Coltart stepped forward to receive the gleaming Alfred Dunhill Cup at last, the old town echoed to the cheering.

Twice before, in 1987 and 1992, the local heroes had made it to the final only for England to win the trophy and £300,000 worth of prize-money. But this

eleventh Alfred Dunhill Cup, each one of course, played on the most sacred turf in the game, was Scotland's at last and how the nation that gave golf to the world celebrated.

Just a month after he had wept over victory in the Ryder Cup in upstate New York, Torrance was back home and once again in tears. 'This is one of the proudest moments of my life,' he said eventually. 'To win here is unbelieveable. The feeling walking down the 18th fairway was incredible. I think that's what it must be like to win a major. It was truly a day to remember.'

It was Torrance who holed the victory putt, over Zimbabwe, his ball rolling in at the last for a 68 to Mark McNulty's 70. With young Coltart already home and metaphorically dry after a 67 to Tony Johnstone's 71, the match was over. Back out on the course Colin Montgomerie (74) was trundling to defeat by Nick Price

(68) but the grin that split the big man's face as he played the 18th denied any feeling of personal anti-climax on his part.

Quite right too, for this was a genuine team performance by Scotland's trio, each player winning four of his five individual matches over the four days of high-octane, high-class competition. Certainly the 16 teams qualifying for this glittering finale to an event that now reaches some 60,000,000 television viewers worldwide,

cannot complain that St Andrews failed to deliver her usual test.

The winds that hurtled in off the sea on the first day at least equalled the gale that blew throughout the last day of The Open in July. Having swung her horny old fist at the stars on the Thursday, the Old Course came up with a Friday afternoon filled with sunshine and lazy, hazy clouds. On Saturday she grew cold and distant while Sunday was the first, gen-

THE COURSE

The Old Course at St Andrews is a magnificent anachronism. At first sight it is a freak of nature but few players, amateur or professional, do not grow to love the place. On a calm day it is virtually defenceless but there are few calm days and many pot-hole bunkers waiting to extract a heavy price for not knowing this 400-year old links intimately.

Greg Norman aims for the clubhouse clock.

uine winter's day of this 1995 campaign.

By supper time on Thursday, the victors were Ireland and Sweden from Group One, Scotland and South Africa from Group Two, New Zealand and Zimbabwe in Group Three with Australia and Spain emerging victorious from

Group Four. Of these, it was Ireland who deserved the most serious round of applause after Darren Clarke, Ronan Rafferty and Philip Walton rubbed salt into America's gaping Ryder Cup wounds by defeating the USA 3-0. No wonder Lee Janzen, Peter Jacobsen and Ben Crenshaw appeared particularly glum over their neeps and tatties that evening. Janzen, particularly, had much to regret, having committed the cardinal sin of missing the widest fairway in golf at the 18th to balloon out-of-bounds and lose to Clarke.

By Friday evening the smile was still absent from Janzen's face but at least the pain had eased a bit for though he lost his match, the USA defeated Sweden to salvage pride and some small hope of making the semi-finals on Sunday.

The Group leaders were Ireland, Scotland, Zimbabwe and Australia. Each had two wins and therefore two points and the biggest talking point of this second day was the one stroke penalty suffered by Torrance when he dropped his ball marker on to his ball and moved it. He then threw the offending coin away in disgust.

No doubt either about the main focus

Jarmo Sandelin (below) plays the wall game at the 17th. Nick Price's caddie (below right) in balancing act.

for discussions on Saturday. With Ireland, Scotland and Zimbabwe duly completing their Group wins to head into the semis, it was down to Australia to complete the formality of winning just one of their three games against England. But skipper Greg Norman missed a putt of four feet at the last to lose to Mark James, Australia lost 3-0 to an English trio pointless until then and under the complex, but perfectly fair, rules of the Alfred Dunhill Cup, Spain progressed to Sunday instead.

There, Scotland narrowly beat Ireland 2-1, Coltart and Walton matching bogey for bogey only for the Scot to win by a stroke with a 75, while Zimbabwe, too, defeated Spain 2-1.

So the scene was set for Scotland's third appearance in a final with what was undoubtedly their strongest-ever team at St Andrews. 'Go on boys, do it for us,' roared someone in an unmistakable, almost incomprehensible, Glasgow accent, as Coltart yet again led the charge off the first tee.

And Scottish expectations were met by Scottish achievement. The pleasure it brought to a town drenched in golf was as clear to see as it was pleasing to behold to even an impartial observer. The hotel rooms are booked already for 1996.

Bill Elliott

SHOT OF THE WEEK

Andrew Coltart's hole-in-one during his match against Tony Johnstone in the final. The 24-year old struck his perfect six iron at the 178-yard eighth hole to establish a three stroke lead he never relinquished. It was a shot also that roared back down the links, inspiring the Scots to reach out for victory.

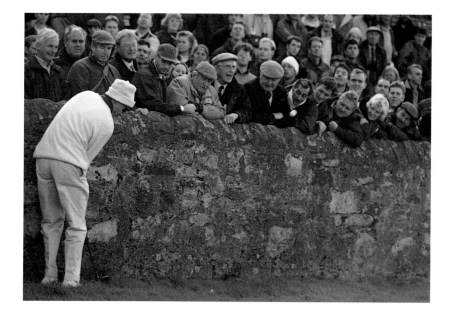

The Old Course, St Andrews, 19-22 October, 1995 • Yardage 6,933 • Par 72

Final

SCOTLAND	2	1	ZIMBABWE
Andrew Coltart	67	71	Tony Johnstone
Sam Torrance	68	70	Mark McNulty
Colin Montgomerie	74	68	Nick Price

Semi-Final

SCOTLAND	2	1	IRELAND
Andrew Coltart	75	76	Philip Walton
Colin Montgomerie	70	72	Darren Clarke
Sam Torrance	74	73	Ronan Rafferty

Semi-Final

ZIMBABWE	2	1	SPAIN
Tony Johnstone	71	70	Miguel Angel Jiménez
Nick Price	69	70	José Rivero
Mark McNulty	73	Disq	Ignacio Garrido

Group One

	Matches Played	Matches Won	Ind. Games Won
IRELAND	3	3	7
SWEDEN	3	1	5
CANADA	3	1	3
USA	3	1	3

Group Two

	Matches Played	Matches Won	Ind. Games Won
SCOTLAND	3	3	8
SOUTH AFRICA	3	2s6	
GERMANY	3	1	3
REP OF CHINA	3	0	1

Group Three

	Matches Played	Matches Won	Ind. Games Won
ZIMBABWE	3	3	8
WALES	3	2	5
NEW ZEALAND	3	1	2
JAPAN	3	0	3

Group Four

	Matches Played	Matches Won	Ind. Games Won
SPAIN	3	2	5
AUSTRALIA	3	2	4
ENGLAND	3	1	5
ARGENTINA	3	1	4

(Spain win on individual victories)

Group One

DAY 1

IRELAND beat USA 3-0
Darren Clarke (71) beat Lee Janzen (73)
Ronan Rafferty (70) beat Ben Crenshaw (71)
Philip Walton (72) beat Peter Jacobsen (73)

CANADA lost to SWEDEN 0-3
Dave Barr (77) lost to Jesper Parnevik (70)
Ray Stewart (73) lost to Jarmo Sandelin (72)
Rick Gibson (71) lost to Per-Ulrik Johansson (69)

DAY 2

CANADA lost to IRELAND 1-2
Rick Gibson (73) lost to Darren Clarke (69)
Ray Stewart (73) lost to Philip Walton (71)
Dave Barr (71) beat Ronan Rafferty (72)

USA beat SWEDEN 2-1
Peter Jacobsen (67) beat Jesper Parnevik (71)
Ben Crenshaw (67) beat Jarmo Sandelin (69)
Lee Janzen (72) lost to Per-Ulrik Johansson (72)
at 1st extra hole

DAY 3

USA lost to CANADA 1-2
Peter Jacobsen (71) lost to Ray Stewart (71)
at 1st extra hole
Lee Janzen (73) lost to Rick Gibson (72)
Ben Crenshaw (68) beat Dave Barr (72)

SWEDEN lost to IRELAND 1-2
Jarmo Sandelin (67) beat Darren Clarke (70)
Jesper Parnevik (72) lost to Philip Walton (72)
at 1st extra hole
Per-Ulrik Johansson (71) lost to Ronan Rafferty (68)

Group Two

DAY 1

SCOTLAND beat REPUBLIC OF CHINA 3-0
Andrew Coltart (66) beat Chen Liang-hsi (73)
Sam Torrance (75) beat Lu Wen-teh (81)
Colin Montgomerie (71) beat Chung Chun-hsing (80)

SOUTH AFRICA beat GERMANY 2-1
Retief Goosen (70) beat Heinz Peter Thül (72)
David Frost (74) lost to Sven Strüver (73)
Ernie Els (70) beat Alexander Cejka (72)

DAY 2

SOUTH AFRICA beat REPUBLIC OF CHINA 3-0
Retief Goosen (73) beat Chung Chun-hsing (77)
David Frost (68) beat Lu Wen-teh (75)
Ernie Els (70) beat Chen Liang-hsi (72)

SCOTLAND beat GERMANY 3-0
Andrew Coltart (68) beat Alexander Cejka (70)
Sam Torrance (71) beat Heinz Peter Thül (74)
Colin Montgomerie (72) beat Sven Strüver (73)

DAY 3

SCOTLAND beat SOUTH AFRICA 2-1
Andrew Coltart (75) lost to Ernie Els (70)
Sam Torrance (68) beat Retief Goosen (70)
Colin Montgomerie (69) beat David Frost (71)

GERMANY beat REPUBLIC OF CHINA 2-1
Sven Strüver (68) beat Chung Chun-hsing (75)
Heinz Peter Thül (77) beat Lu Wen-teh (78)
Alexander Cejka (70) lost to Chen Liang-hsi (68)

Group Three

DAY 1

NEW ZEALAND beat JAPAN 2-1
Michael Campbell (68) beat Hideki Kase (73)
Frank Nobilo (71) beat Tsukasa Watanabe (75)
Greg Turner (73) lost to Nobuo Serizawa (72)

ZIMBABWE beat WALES 3-0
Tony Johnstone (73) beat Mark Mouland (75)
Nick Price (67) beat Paul Affleck (70)
Mark McNulty (69) beat Ian Woosnam (74)

DAY 2

NEW ZEALAND lost to WALES 0-3
Michael Campbell (71) lost to Ian Woosnam (68)
Greg Turner (74) lost to Mark Mouland (71)
Frank Nobilo (70) lost to Paul Affleck (69)

ZIMBABWE beat JAPAN 2-1
Tony Johnstone (73) lost to Tsukasa Watanabe (71)
Mark McNulty (66) beat Hideki Kase (73)
Nick Price (68) beat Nobuo Serizawa (71)

DAY 3

WALES beat JAPAN 2-1
Ian Woosnam (72) beat Hideki Kase (73)
Mark Mouland (71) lost to Tsukasa Watanabe (70)
Paul Affleck (69) beat Nobuo Serizawa (71)

ZIMBABWE beat NEW ZEALAND 3-0
Tony Johnstone (73) beat Greg Turner (74)
Nick Price (68) beat Frank Nobilo (71)
Mark McNulty (70) beat Michael Campbell (72)

Group Four

DAY 1

AUSTRALIA beat ARGENTINA 2-1
Greg Norman (75) lost to José Coceres (72)
Steve Elkington (72) beat Eduardo Romero (74)
Craig Parry (70) beat Vicente Fernandez (71)

ENGLAND lost to SPAIN 1-2
Barry Lane (74) beat José Rivero (75)
Mark James (77) lost to Miguel Angel Jiménez (73)
Howard Clark (76) lost to Ignacio Garrido (75)

DAY 2

ENGLAND lost to ARGENTINA 1-2
Barry Lane (76) lost to Vicente Fernandez (68)
Mark James (74) lost to José Coceres (73)
Howard Clark (69) beat Eduardo Romero (72)

AUSTRALIA beat SPAIN 2-1
Greg Norman (67) beat Miguel Angel Jiménez (68)
Steve Elkington (72) lost to José Rivero (70)
Craig Parry (67) beat Ignacio Garrido (70)

DAY 3

ARGENTINA lost to SPAIN 1-2
Vicente Fernandez (68) beat Miguel Angel Jiménez (74)
Eduardo Romero (72) lost to José Rivero (70)
José Coceres (73) lost to Ignacio Garrido (71)

AUSTRALIA lost to ENGLAND 0-3
Steve Elkington (73) lost to Barry Lane (72)
Greg Norman (69) lost to Mark James (68)
Craig Parry (70) lost to Howard Clark (69)

Prize Money

	Team £	Player £	Total £
Winners			
SCOTLAND	300,000	100,000	300,000
Runners-Up			
ZIMBABWE	150,000	50,000	150,000
Losing Semi-Finalists			
IRELAND	95,000	31,666	
SPAIN	95,000	31,666	190,000

	Team £	Player £	Total £
Group 1			
IRELAND			
SWEDEN	45,000	15,000	
CANADA (8)*	25,500	8,500	
USA (1)*	19,500	6,500	90,000
Group 2			
SCOTLAND (4)*			
S.AFRICA (5)*	45,000	15,000	
GERMANY	25,500	8,500	
REP OF CHINA	19,500	6,500	90,000

	Team £	Player £	Total £
Group 3			
ZIMBABWE (3)*			
WALES	45,000	15,000	
N.ZEALAND (6)*	25,500	8,500	
JAPAN	19,500	6,500	90,000
Group 4			
SPAIN			
AUSTRALIA (2)*	45,000	15,000	
ENGLAND (7)*	25,500	8,500	
ARGENTINA	19,500	6,500	90,000

* Number in parentheses indicates seeds

Photograph shows Alfred Dunhill Londinium water-resistant steel and precious yellow metal watch with sapphire glass – essential for the gentleman plotting a voyage. Once underway, however, another timepiece may also come in handy.

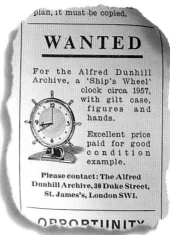

plan, it must be copied.

WANTED

For the Alfred Dunhill Archive, a 'Ship's Wheel' clock circa 1957, with gilt case, figures and hands.

Excellent price paid for good condition example.

Please contact: The Alfred Dunhill Archive, 30 Duke Street, St. James's, London SW1.

OPPORTUNITY

The Times, London.
16th October 1993.

dunhill

Sought after since 1893.

30, Duke Street, St. James's, London SW1.
Alfred Dunhill, sponsors of the Alfred Dunhill Cup, Alfred Dunhill Masters, Alfred Dunhill P.G.A. Championship and Alfred Dunhill Challenge.

Cejka's late burst steals the show

With five birdies in the last eight holes Alexander Cejka won the Volvo Masters as the outcome of the Volvo Order of Merit was finally decided

Few people paid much attention to Alexander Cejka when he arrived at Valderrama for his first Volvo Masters. But for him, being there was enough.

Never having finished in Europe's top 100, all the 24-year old had hoped for going into 1995 was 'a few good finishes'. Yet here he was with two titles under his belt – the same as Colin Montgomerie, no less – and a place in the Spanish sun. His mission had more than been accomplished.

Even if you weren't German it was Bernhard Langer on whom your interest centred. He was the defending Masters champion, the course record holder and, like Montgomerie, had a chance to overtake Sam Torrance and win the Volvo Order of Merit. Cejka was a member of the supporting cast.

The drama he found himself taking part in had been a compelling one all season and now the stage was perfectly set for the final act. Would Torrance, after 25 years of trying, finally become Europe's number one? Would Montgomerie, less than £4,000 behind, top the table for the third year in a row? Or would Langer,

236

£60,000 adrift, achieve the first or second place he needed and snatch the prize away from the two Scots?

Valderrama invariably brings the cream rising to the top and the tussle to be leading money-winner was rightly fought out on the leaderboard. Montgomerie maintained all week that his priority was to try to win the tournament. On a course he loves – in the previous three years he had finished second, first and fourth – he saw no reason to lower his sights. And when he opened with rounds of 71, 72 and 69 he was only one behind Sweden's Anders Forsbrand, the man who had set the pace from day one.

Alongside him, among others, was a certain Alexander Cejka.

Langer was just one stroke further back, but Torrance was a further four behind and knew he needed one of the rounds of his life to have a chance of achieving his lifelong ambition. He produced it. On a day when no-one else was

to break 70 the 42-year old overcame an opening bogey to reach the turn in 32, dropped a shot at the 213-yard 12th, but at the 432-yard last followed a massive drive with a wedge to four feet and holed it for a 68. 'It was one of the hardest putts I've had in a long time,' said Torrance, fully aware that if he had missed he could kiss goodbye to his dream. 'I'll let you know later if it's best round I've ever played.' He led in the clubhouse on 285, one over par, but seeing Montgomerie on the same mark with eight to play he added: 'I have a feeling he will do it.'

As for the championship itself, Ian Woosnam, without a win all year, had taken over at the top at two under from a faltering Forsbrand. Cejka, out in 29 in the second round, had taken 38 on the front nine this time and was four behind. But never mind. Being there was enough.

Langer moved to one over as well with a birdie on the long 11th, only to

Ian Woosnam (above)
and David Gilford (right) both
challenged for the title.

take four on the short 12th like Torrance. It was effectively the end of his challenge – now it was purely a question of whether Montgomerie could get the birdie and seven pars he needed.

Michael Jonzon (above) was bushed. Sam Torrance's brave finish came up just short (opposite).

On most courses that would seem a routine task for a golfer ranked sixth in the world. On Valderrama, Europe's sternest test, it was a real challenge. But Montgomerie rose to it.

At the 12th, yes the hole which had cost Torrance and Langer dear, he hit a pearl of a five iron to within ten feet of the flag and sank the putt for a two. Four

THE COURSE

Consistently voted the leading course in continental Europe, Valderrama has hosted the Volvo Masters since its inception in 1988 and will, in 1997, stage the first Ryder Cup by Johnnie Walker match outside of Britain. Remodelled by designer Robert Trent Jones at the request of club president Jaime Patiño, playing the course can be compared to tiptoeing your way through a minefield – an exquisitely beautiful minefield. A moment's lack of concentration can destroy a card. Bernhard Langer's course record 62 in 1994 is one of the wonders of the world. Any professional breaking the par of 71 should feel proud of their achievement, as should any amateur who plays to his handicap.

**Jesper Parnevik amid Valderrama's
verdant beauty.**

of the required pars followed, then another, to his great relief, at the long 17th. The re-designed hole – humps on the fairway, strip of rough across it, firm green and shaved bank leading down to the lake – had been causing nightmares all week, but Montgomerie, not without a moment's anxiety (see 'Shot of the Week'), survived it. By now, though, his hopes of winning the Championship as well as the Volvo Order of Merit had been thwarted. Not by Woosnam, who had double-bogeyed the 14th and bogeyed the 16th, but by Cejka.

Cejka, in a breath-taking finishing spurt, birdied the 11th, 13th, 14th 15th (after a glorious three iron to five feet) and 18th for a 70 and two under par total of 282. All of a sudden this refreshing new face had claimed one of the most prestigious titles on the PGA European Tour.

As the magnitude of Cejka's achievement began to register, Montgomerie still had some work to do. The 18th, despite the fact that Torrance and Cejka had birdied it, was far from a pushover, but he was safely on in two. From 25 feet he left his first putt three feet short. Hole it and he was top again, miss it and Torrance was king. He holed it.

'I have to offer my commiserations to Sam,' said Montgomerie. 'He's had the best season he's ever had, he led us to the Dunhill Cup last week and he had a great Ryder Cup. To shoot the best score of the last day, to finish third and still not win the Order of Merit has got to be hard for him to take.' 'C'est la vie,' said Torrance, disappointment written all over his face. 'Unbelievable,' said Cejka.

With his three victories he had climbed from 102nd in 1994 to sixth. With his stunning consistency, Montgomerie had maintained his remarkable rankings record of never going downwards. Alexander the Great, Montgomerie the Magnificent.

Mark Garrod   243

Valderrama, Sotogrande, Spain, October 26-29, 1995 · Yardage 6819 · Par 71

Pos	Name	Country	Rnd 1	Rnd 2	Rnd 3	Rnd 4	Total	Prize Money £
1	Alexander CEJKA	(Ger)	74	66	72	70	282	125000
2	Colin MONTGOMERIE	(Scot)	71	72	69	72	284	83400
3	David GILFORD	(Eng)	74	68	71	72	285	42225
	Sam TORRANCE	(Scot)	73	71	73	68	285	42225
5	José RIVERO	(Sp)	75	68	70	73	286	23680
	Per-Ulrik JOHANSSON	(Swe)	75	71	66	74	286	23680
	Bernhard LANGER	(Ger)	74	68	71	73	286	23680
	Ian WOOSNAM	(Wal)	70	71	71	74	286	23680
	Anders FORSBRAND	(Swe)	68	70	73	75	286	23680
10	Howard CLARK	(Eng)	73	70	73	71	287	14900
	Paul EALES	(Eng)	71	71	74	71	287	14900
12	Peter BAKER	(Eng)	77	70	70	71	288	12375
	Frank NOBILO	(NZ)	76	70	69	73	288	12375
	Costantino ROCCA	(It)	74	70	71	73	288	12375
	Jesper PARNEVIK	(Swe)	74	70	70	74	288	12375
16	Tony JOHNSTONE	(Zim)	77	71	71	70	289	10550
	Mark JAMES	(Eng)	74	73	68	74	289	10550
	Miguel Angel JIMÉNEZ	(Sp)	71	73	71	74	289	10550
19	Andrew COLTART	(Scot)	75	72	71	72	290	9525
	Santiago LUNA	(Sp)	73	74	71	72	290	9525
	Sandy LYLE	(Scot)	72	71	72	75	290	9525
	Jean Louis GUEPY	(Fr)	72	72	71	75	290	9525
23	José COCERES	(Arg)	69	72	78	72	291	8900
24	Greg TURNER	(NZ)	78	72	70	73	293	8275
	Peter O'MALLEY	(Aus)	75	70	75	73	293	8275
	Mats LANNER	(Swe)	74	74	72	73	293	8275
	Jamie SPENCE	(Eng)	73	76	72	72	293	8275
28	Michael CAMPBELL	(NZ)	78	73	72	71	294	7210
	Andrew OLDCORN	(Eng)	76	73	73	72	294	7210
	Peter MITCHELL	(Eng)	75	73	72	74	294	7210
	Sven STRÜVER	(Ger)	73	70	70	81	294	7210
	Barry LANE	(Eng)	70	74	73	77	294	7210
33	Wayne RILEY	(Aus)	78	72	73	72	295	6500
	Darren CLARKE	(N.Ire)	77	76	71	71	295	6500
	Ignacio GARRIDO	(Sp)	74	73	70	78	295	6500
36	Derrick COOPER	(Eng)	79	72	71	74	296	6200
37	Joakim HAEGGMAN	(Swe)	77	72	77	71	297	6050
38	Peter HEDBLOM	(Swe)	73	70	75	80	298	5900
39	Russell CLAYDON	(Eng)	78	75	72	74	299	5600
	Paul BROADHURST	(Eng)	77	76	72	74	299	5600
	Michael JONZON	(Swe)	75	69	77	78	299	5600
42	Mathias GRÖNBERG	(Swe)	75	76	73	77	301	5225
	Roger CHAPMAN	(Eng)	72	74	71	84	301	5225
44	Jay TOWNSEND	(USA)	80	72	75	75	302	4925
	Stuart CAGE	(Eng)	77	80	73	72	302	4925
46	Jarmo SANDELIN	(Swe)	76	77	73	77	303	4550
	Philip WALTON	(Ire)	76	77	72	78	303	4550
	Olle KARLSSON	(Swe)	76	76	71	80	303	4550
49	Robert KARLSSON	(Swe)	75	77	76	76	304	4250
50	Peter TERAVAINEN	(USA)	78	74	76	78	306	4100
51	Paul WAY	(Eng)	82	73	76	77	308	3950
52	Mike HARWOOD	(Aus)	82	73	73	81	309	3800
53T	Robert ALLENBY	(Aus)	77	74	77	RETD		3575
	Ronan RAFFERTY	(N.Ire)	DISQ					3575

SHOT OF THE WEEK

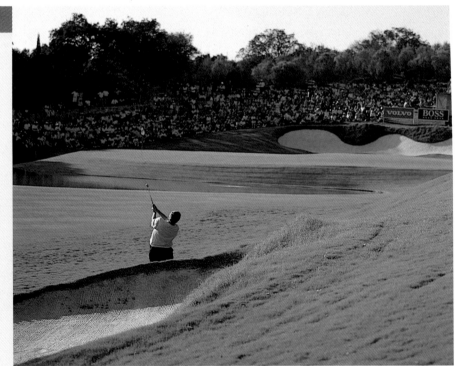

Colin Montgomerie did not know it as he contemplated his third shot at the 511-yard 17th, but already on that final day of the final tournament ten players had walked off the green with sevens, three with eights and one with a nine. What he did know was that he needed a par five to stay on course for the Volvo Order of Merit title. The flag was only a wedge away, but the ball was two feet above his feet in fluffy rough, not lying very well and in front of him was water. It was literally make-or-lake time – and he made it – just. 'I had 82 yards to the front and it went 82 yards,' he said. 'I was almost on the steel of the shaft with my grip and I was just praying it went far enough.' There may have been more spectacular strokes during the week – Andrew Coltart's third round hole-in-one, his second in seven days, at the 212-yard 12th, Alexander Cejka's tournament-winning three iron to five feet on the 225-yard 15th, but Montgomerie's pitch had wider implications. Rarely has a par five tasted so sweet.

OF COURSE WE CARE ABOUT THE ENVIRONMENT.

THIS PLANET IS OUR MAJOR MARKET.

VOLVO ECC.
ENVIRONMENTAL
CONCEPT CAR.

VOLVO

Lane books final ticket

Barry Lane emerged victorious from
the European Regional Final with a
superb performance at The Oxfordshire

PGA European Tour debut for The Oxfordshire.

*T*he inaugural $3.65 million Andersen Consulting World Championship of Golf which was conceived to pit the top players from the five main world tours against each other in head-to-head combat, got off to a flying start so far as Barry Lane was concerned.

Lane, whose experience of match-play is, like most touring professionals, minimal, collected some notable scalps en route to qualifying for the world semi-finals and finals as Europe's representative.

The first round of the European region was staged at La Moraleja in Madrid in May and eight of Europe's finest locked horns for a place in the semi-finals. Bernhard Langer, Severiano Ballesteros, Sam Torrance and Jesper Parnevik were the top seeds but it was Lane who caused the first upset when he defeated Torrance by two and one. The rest of the matches went with the seedings with Langer beating Sandy Lyle three and two, Ballesteros beating Miguel Angel Jimenez three and two and Parnevik closing out David Gilford two and one.

So it was off to The Oxfordshire, the Rees Jones designed layout nestling beneath the Chiltern Hills which only opened in 1993 and had already drawn high praise from many quarters. Played the day after the Open Championship in sweltering July heat, the semi-final pairings looked designed to produce a dream final between Langer and Ballesteros but somewhere along the line someone had forgotten to show Lane the script.

Lane, who had finished 20th at St Andrews, the highest placed of the four, pitched in with seven birdies against Langer, one of which was obtained with a stroke of epic proportions at a crucial

point. Two up with two to play, Lane came to The Oxfordshire's par five 17th and struck a conservative two iron from the tee which left him 240 yards from the green with water intervening. Langer meanwhile had driven further but then could only watch in despair as Lane struck a magnificent three wood over the attendant hazard to within 20 feet of the hole. Langer's attempt found the water and his part in the dream was ended.

Ballesteros and Parnevik had a close tussle but Ballesteros gained the advantage with a one iron to two feet at the par four 16th to go two up and he ran out the winner by three and one.

With a guaranteed $300,000 going to the winner, $150,000 to the loser there was all to play for, not to mention considerable pride. This is a quality that Ballesteros has in abundance but Lane disregarded his opponent's formidable match-play reputation. Four birdies in the space of five holes from the third put the Englishman six up and although Ballesteros fought back, Lane took the honours by four and three to qualify for the World Final with $1 million going to the eventual winner.

Naturally he was delighted: 'I know I can beat anyone when I play well, but it's still very special to beat two great players like Bernhard and Seve in the same day.'

The Rest of the World Regional semi-final and final were also staged at The Oxfordshire on the same day and this saw South Africa's David Frost defeat Australia's Robert Allenby to join Lane, Japan's Massy Kuramoto and America's Mark McCumber in the World Final at Grayhawk Golf Club, Scottsdale, Arizona.

David Frost (right) and Barry Lane (below) graduated with honours from The Oxfordshire.

The format of the Championship will change slightly in 1996. Instead of the regional championship being staged over several months at multiple venues, each regional championship will be contested over a single course on two consecutive days. Eight players, seven from the Sony Ranking and one invitee, will play in four matches on the first day and the semi-final and final will take place on the second day. The European regional championship will take place in May, prior to the Volvo PGA Championship, at a venue near London. The World Championship semi-finals and final will move forward and take place in January 1997 in Scottsdale.

Chris Plumridge

Nobilo's explosive finish clinches the title

Frank Nobilo burst through in the last round
to provide a consolation present for his daughter

Frank Nobilo's smash-and-grab Sarazen World Open victory on the Legends course at Chateau Elan, Atlanta, was worth £4,102 a hole – and that is good news for five-year old daughter, Bianca.

Four back nine birdies in five holes for a 68 and eight under par 208 – the event was reduced to 54 holes by bad weather – edged him a stroke clear of Spain's Miguel Jiménez, who bogeyed two of the last four for a 73, and Zimbabwe's Mark McNulty, who fired a day's best 67.

It netted the New Zealander a princely £221,518 and he declared: 'It will secure the future for my daughter by my previous marriage. When I called her before the last round she was in tears in London after burning her finger waving her first Guy Fawkes sparkler. I started thinking about the money with a couple of holes to go. Invested wisely it will set her up nicely.'

Nobilo, at 35, insists: 'I'm getting old and I'm very happy to stay on the PGA European Tour. I'd like to be recognised as having my base in Europe rather than

as an Australian Tour player.'

Nobilo, four behind Jiménez after two rounds and still four adrift after the 31-year old Spaniard birdied the 11th, grabbed twos at the 12th and 15th, where Jiménez three-putted, and more birdies at the 14th from 15 feet and 16th from five feet, then saved par from ten feet at 17.

Three putts at the last allowed Jiménez to draw level again but the man from Malaga bogeyed the 17th.

A £102,848 prize signed off a dismal

summer on a high note for McNulty and helped ease the pain for the doubly unlucky Jiménez. He crashed to a last day 77 at Chateau Elan last year after starting round four only two strokes off the lead.

'At 17, I didn't know Frank had three-putted the last and went for the pin instead of trying to play safe... it's as disappointed as I have ever felt in golf,' he said.

While Nobilo was totting up four twos in his three rounds, his rivals came to grief at the short holes. Open Champion John Daly hitting into the lake to double-bogey the 15th for a 73 and 211 after turning only one behind Jiménez.

Ryder Cup heroes Philip Walton, who hit two in the water there for a quadruple-bogey seven, and Sam Torrance, who matched Daly's five, also suffered.

It was the end of an unhappy week for Sam, who suffered a flare-up of a painful thigh strain, twice collapsing in pain on Saturday.

He said: 'It's like someone stabbing

249

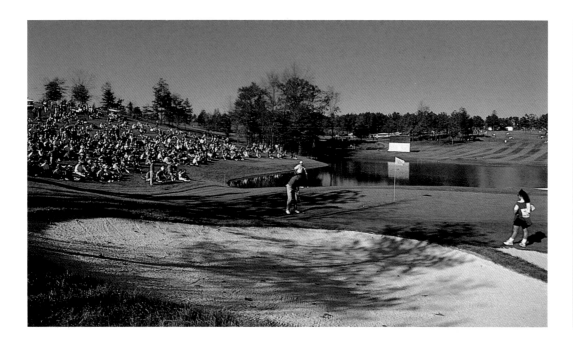

Ernie Els (above) and John Daly (right) were prominent.

you with a knife. I've had the trouble near the groin on my left leg for most of the year and despite treatment it's got worse this week.

'My leg just buckled under me as I was phoning my wife at the hotel and then it happened again on one tee in round two and I collapsed at John Daly's feet. He must have thought I was having a heart attack. It's worrying because I don't know what it is. I hope it's not a ligament or something that could pull away from the bone and cripple me for a month.'

Two decisions taken by Chief Referee, Wade Cagle, a veteran US Tour official, crucially influenced the stop-go course of the Championship.

Play was halted abruptly before even the first half of the field had completed their opening rounds when the Mobile Weather Team Incorporated, who were called into action after spectators were struck by lightning at the US Open and USPGA Championships in 1991, pinpointed approaching storms.

Within half an hour Cagle had announced abandonment for the day and no restart until 11am next day.

After torrential rain and flooding, the delay left 42 players still on the course by nightfall on day two. When

the first round was finally completed on Saturday morning it had taken 49 hours and 57 minutes.

A cold front passing through the area was the culprit and round two temperatures plummeted from the muggy mid 60s into the wind-chilled low 30s.

Yet another overnight suspension was on the cards as darkness fell on Saturday but all but one of the groups made it to the finishing post.

Fuzzy Zoeller, facing back surgery before Christmas, had sprung alongside Craig Stadler and Daly at six under par with a 71 after expunging a double-bogey five at the 15th (his sixth) by downing an eagle putt at the fifth (his 14th).

Jiménez jumped two strokes ahead with three birdies in the last six holes for a 69. His lead might have been bigger for he three-putted the last from 20 feet for a par five in his anxiety to avoid a dawn patrol finish next morning.

'More haste, less speed', goes the saying but stepping on the gas did no harm to Daly, defending champion Ernie Els, and Torrance. They played the last nine of the second round in one hour ten minutes and

waltzed round in three hours 59 minutes on Saturday. 'Five and a half hours for 27 holes can't be bad – and we dropped only one stroke between the three of us,' said Sam. Declared Daly: 'That's the way you're supposed to play. Just walk up and hit it – no sense in all that walking around.'

Daly's 68 was the day's best, Torrance, despite those stabbing pains in his thigh, posted a faultless 69.

Jiménez had to be content with sharing the lead on 67 after that marathon first round with Zoeller and Chris Williams, who was born in Liverpool but moved to South Africa with his parents at the age of four. The Zimbabwe Open champion, who had two and a half holes to complete when bad light stopped play on Saturday, sadly slipped to a 75.

Stadler was one behind on 68 with Daniel Chopra, a Swedish-born 21-year old with a father from New Delhi, who grew up in India and is trying for his card on both the European and US Tours after winning this year's Taiwan Open and finishing second in the Asian Order of Merit.

Unfortunately, he slipped back with a closing 81 for a seven-over-par 223, but must have gazed enviously in Nobilo's direction, hoping he can make similar progress.

Gordon Richardson

THE LEGENDS AT CHATEAU ELAN, ATLANTA, USA, NOVEMBER 2-5, 1995 • YARDAGE 6955 • PAR 72

Pos	Name	Country	Rnd 1	Rnd 2	Rnd 3	Total	Prize Money $
1	Frank NOBILO	(NZ)	70	70	68	208	350,000
2	Mark MCNULTY	(Zim)	72	70	67	209	162,500
	Miguel Angel JIMÉNEZ	(Sp)	67	69	73	209	162,500
4	Mark CALCAVECCHIA	(USA)	71	70	69	210	67,000
	Anders FORSBRAND	(Swe)	69	72	69	210	67,000
	Eduardo ROMERO	(Sp)	69	71	70	210	67,000
	Emlyn AUBREY	(USA)	70	70	70	210	67,000
8	John DALY	(USA)	70	68	73	211	52,000
	Craig STADLER	(USA)	68	70	73	211	52,000
10	Retief GOOSEN	(SA)	70	72	70	212	41,600
	Lucas PARSONS	(Aus)	70	72	70	212	41,600
	Ernie ELS	(SA)	71	70	71	212	41,600
13	Brad FAXON	(USA)	73	71	69	213	32,300
	Fuzzy ZOELLER	(USA)	67	71	75	213	32,300
15	Paul CURRY	(Eng)	73	71	70	214	25,650
	Lee JANZEN	(USA)	73	70	71	214	25,650
	Per-Ulrik JOHANSSON	(Swe)	72	71	71	214	25,650
	Sam TORRANCE	(Scot)	71	69	74	214	25,650
19	Neil KERRY	(Aus)	73	71	71	215	20,900
20	Tod HAMILTON	(USA)	71	72	73	216	18,050
	Paul MOLONEY	(Aus)	74	70	72	216	18,050
	Andrew OLDCORN	(Eng)	71	75	70	216	18,050
23	Christian POST	(Den)	70	74	73	217	12,910
	Eric CARLBERG	(Swe)	73	71	73	217	12,910
	Chris PERRY	(USA)	72	72	73	217	12,910
	Brandt JOBE	(USA)	69	74	74	217	12,910
	Mark DAVIS	(Eng)	72	73	72	217	12,910
	Chris WILLIAMS	(Eng)	67	75	75	217	12,910
	Mike CUNNING	(USA)	75	71	71	217	12,910
	Mark O'MEARA	(USA)	73	68	76	217	12,910
	James LEE	(Wal)	72	75	70	217	12,910
32	Mark JAMES	(Eng)	76	68	74	218	9,310
	Joakim HAEGGMAN	(Swe)	73	72	73	218	9,310
	Raymond BURNS	(N.Ire)	70	75	73	218	9,310
	Raul FRETES	(Par)	72	73	73	218	9,310
	Robert ALLENBY	(Aus)	76	70	72	218	9,310
	Steve ALKER	(NZ)	74	73	71	218	9,310
38	Paul BROADHURST	(Eng)	72	72	75	219	7,552
	Carl MASON	(Eng)	72	74	73	219	7,552
	David FROST	(SA)	73	74	72	219	7,552
	Anssi KANKONNEN	(Fin)	77	70	72	219	7,552
42	Philip WALTON	(Ire)	70	72	78	220	6,935
	Jeff WAGNER	(Aus)	76	71	73	220	6,935
44	Ronan RAFFERTY	(N.Ire)	72	73	76	221	6,650
45	Fred FUNK	(USA)	73	71	79	223	6,080
	Daniel CHOPRA	(Swe)	68	74	81	223	6,080
	Jesus AMAYA	(Col)	75	71	77	223	6,080
	José CANTERO	(Arg)	76	71	76	223	6,080
	Ryan HOWISON	(USA)	73	74	76	223	6,080
50	Kyi HLA HAN	(Bur)	71	76	77	224	5,500
51	Stuart HENDLEY	(USA)	73	71	81	225	5,500
	Jeff LEONARD	(USA)	74	73	78	225	5,500
	Gary MARKS	(Eng)	75	72	78	225	5,500
54	Abdul HAMEED	(Pak)	74	72	83	229	5,500
55	Mark ROE	(Eng)	75	72	W/D		5,500

The Squire holds court.

Foursomes format hits the target

The introduction of foursomes alongside the

individual events in the Canon Shoot-Out

series was an unqualified success

*I*t was Severiano Ballesteros who first had the idea. Instead of ten players competing individually in the Canon Shoot-Outs that are now such an entertaining pre-tournament feature of so many of the Tour events, Ballesteros suggested that a foursomes format might be just as attractive.

Seve has been a vital participant in the Ryder Cup in which he and his Spanish compatriot José Maria Olazábal have both performed with so much style and success. The foursomes format he felt would also give potential Ryder Cup partnerships a chance to play together. In short, it would not only be an attractive format for spectators, it would be useful for the team captain as he sought to work out pairings.

Canon readily agreed and in 1995 six of the ten Shoot-Outs held between February and August in places as far apart as Johannesburg and Kilkenny, Malmo and Madrid, were played with the foursomes format with Ryder Cup rookie

Per-Ulrik Johansson involved in two winning partnerships.

At the highly praised Jack Nicklaus-designed Mount Juliet course, Johansson teamed up with New Zealander Michael Campbell to win the Shoot-Out staged before the Murphy's Irish Open. They were a strong partnership. Just a few

weeks earlier the two of them had finished joint second at Wentworth behind Bernhard Langer in the Volvo PGA Championship. For the seven holes they needed to play the blond Swede and the Maori were three under par, winning the final hole with a birdie against the all-Irish partnership of Christy O'Connor Junior and Philip Walton.

Later at the Volvo Scandinavian Masters, Johansson was in action again, this time with fellow Swede Jesper Parnevik who went on to win the main title that week and make history as the first Swede to win a Tour event in Sweden. It was, some thought, an inspired partnership that might be repeated in the Ryder Cup at Oak Hill but it was not to be. Parnevik, now a member of the US Tour, did not play often enough in Europe to make the Cup team automatically and missed out on a captain's selection. Johansson made it.

Still, at Barseback in Malmo they were in devastating form. Their victims that week when record crowds came to watch the golf every day were fellow Swedes Jarmo Sandelin and Robert Karlsson, Ian Woosnam and Colin Montgomerie, Frank Nobilo and Michael Campbell and

American John Daly, the newly crowned Open champion whose partner for the day was England's Barry Lane. Daly had played the week before in Holland when he partnered the eventual winner of the Heineken title, Scott Hoch in the Shoot-Out but that powerful all-American partnership was beaten in the end by England's talented Paul Eales and Ireland's Philip Walton.

Earlier in the year other foursomes style Shoot-Outs had been played in Paris, Madrid and at Wentworth. At Golf de Saint Cloud in Paris the winners were Miguel Angel Jiménez and José Rivero, surprisingly over the favourites and eventual tournament winners Ballesteros and Olazábal. Yet earlier the Jiménez-Rivero partnership had been quickly sidelined at the Shoot-Out which preceded the Peugeot Open de España at Club de Campo in Madrid where the winners were

Final Shoot-out winner Per-Ulrik Johansson (above). Golf's most formidable foursome, Seve Ballesteros and José Maria Olazábal (left).

the Swedish-Australian partnership of Joakim Haeggman and Robert Allenby, the current Australian number one and Australian Heineken Open champion.

The foursomes format was also used for the Champions Challenge Shoot-Out which is staged round Wentworth's famous West course prior to the Volvo PGA Championship in late May. Peter Senior, on a rare visit to Britain and Vijay Singh, who had earlier won the Phoenix Open on the US Tour and went on later to win the Buick Classic at Westchester, teamed up to win £8,000 each for their respective charities – Rainbow House, the children's hospice and the PGA European Tour's Benevolent Trust. They and a tried and trusted Ryder Cup partnership, Colin Montgomerie and Nick Faldo, were only separated by a closing hole shoot-out

from the front bunker at the last. Montgomerie's recovery to ten feet won the day.

All the other Shoot-Outs were of the traditional variety with Tony Johnstone of Zimbabwe winning at the Wanderers Club in Johannesburg, Sandy Lyle taking the honours at the Forest of Arden before the Murphy's English Open and Bernhard Langer winning the Volvo German Open Shoot-Out at Schloss Nippenburg, a course he helped design in Stuttgart.

For the final Shoot-Out of the year, the players went 5,000 feet up in the Swiss Alps to Crans-sur-Sierre where a year earlier inclement weather has caused such disruption that the event was cancelled and replayed at Valderrama later. Happily, this time there was no such problems with Johansson picking up the £16,000 first prize by beating Italy's Costantino Rocca with a birdie at the last hole.

Johansson had begun the Shoot-Out

indifferently with a drive into the rough at the first. He took six there at a hole where he would be expecting to make a birdie four but he survived an early bunker shoot-out with Paul Eales and never made another mistake against a quality field that also included Severiano Ballesteros, Miguel Angel Jiménez, Tony Johnstone, Sandy Lyle, Colin Montgomerie, Greg Norman, Corey Pavin, the reigning US Open champion and Eduardo Romero, the 1994 Canon European Masters winner.

Over the season 55 players took part in the Shoot-Outs including reigning major champions Pavin and Daly. Ten current European Ryder Cup players took part, only Howard Clark and Mark James

Bernhard Langer took the honours at Schloss Nippenburg (left). John Daly drew the crowds in Sweden (below).

were not involved. Nine Englishmen, five Americans and five Swedes, four Spaniards, South Africans, Irish and Scots, three New Zealanders, Australian and Germans took part in the ten Shoot-Outs

along with two Welshmen, two Zimbabweans, Italians and French and one Dutchman, Argentinian and Fijian.

In all, representatives from 17 different countries took part and maybe 1995 winner Johansson summed up best what the players think about the fun events that have now become part and parcel of the Tour scene. 'I enjoy these Canon Shoot-Outs. They are not only competitive but also good fun, especially for the spectator.' And so say all of us.

Renton Laidlaw

Canon Shot of the Year

Nick Faldo, 18th hole, Oak Hill, The Ryder Cup

Canon

When Nick Faldo arrived at the 18th hole at Oak Hill in his single against Curtis Strange he knew the outcome of the Ryder Cup was still in the balance. He had just squared his match on the previous hole while behind him Philip Walton was two up with two to play against Jay Haas. Nothing less than a win by Faldo would do if Europe was to regain the Ryder Cup.

Faldo's drive found the left-hand rough, Strange finished on the right of the fairway. Unable to reach the green, Faldo chopped his ball out down the fairway leaving himself 93 yards from the flag. Strange's second shot finished on the bank in front of the green.

Knowing he had to get down in two to have any chance of winning the hole, Faldo took his wedge and struck a magnificent shot which soared onto the green and stopped four feet from the hole. It was a stroke which fully deserved to be rated 'Canon Shot of the Year' in the circumstances which prevailed.

Strange was unable to get down in two and with the pressure still bearing down on him, Faldo holed his putt before being engulfed by his team-mates. 'The best scrambling par of my life,' said Faldo.

Minutes later, Walton closed out Haas on the last green and the Ryder Cup was safely back in European hands.

255

Rising to the challenge

The PGA European Challenge Tour
continued to provide an ideal
training ground for the future

Michael Campbell, Jarmo Sandelin, Stuart Cage and Neal Briggs further demonstrated the aptitude and resilience of golfers emerging from the PGA European Challenge Tour when they produced significant performances on the 1995 Volvo Tour.

Sandelin's immediate elevation to the champions' register on a Tour that produced Europe's 1995 Ryder Cup winning team strengthened the existing belief that the Challenge Tour provides an outstanding learning ground for those who crave success at the highest level. What is more no fewer than eight of the ten golfers who advanced from the 1994 Challenge Tour successfully secured their playing privileges for the 1996 PGA European Tour by finishing in the top 126 money winners.

These included Campbell, who not only finished runner-up in both the Volvo PGA Championship and Collingtree British Masters but also third in the Open Championship. Meanwhile both Cage and Briggs also came within a whisker of winning by finishing runners-up in the Murphy's Irish Open and Peugeot Open de France respectively.

Now the eighth season of the PGA European Challenge Tour will again offer a wealth of tournament experience for

Michael Campbell pointed the way for future Challenge Tour players.

champions in the making. They will all be inspired not only by the progress of the 1994 graduates, but also by the formidable advancement made by Costantino Rocca and Paul Eales.

Rocca has provided ample evidence of the rewards that exist for those who lay a sturdy foundation by virtue of his outstanding accomplishments since finishing third on the Challenge Tour Order of Merit in 1989 when he won three times. In 1993 he became the first Italian winner on the Tour since Massimo Mannelli in 1980. A few months later he became the first Italian member of Europe's team for the Ryder Cup by Johnnie Walker, and he emphasised the value of experience at major championship level – he was beaten only in a play-off for the Open Championship – by contributing three points to Europe's Ryder Cup victory at Oak Hill last September.

Meanwhile Eales, a former Lancashire County player, was third on the Challenge Tour Order of Merit in 1992, and became a winner on the Volvo Tour in 1994 when he captured the Open de Extremadura.

Thus all who started out on the 1995 PGA European Challenge Tour at the Keyna Open in March had good reason to acknowledge that for them, eight months of honing their skills in such a competitive arena would provide the ultimate examination to proving their readiness to play weekly alongside world-class golfers.

Such was the intensity of competition that not until the UAP Grand Finale in Portugal on the beautiful Quinta do Peru course were the ten graduates from the 1995 Challenge Tour confirmed. Indeed Francisco Valera, the former British Boys' champion from Sitges in Spain, snatched a dramatic victory which hoisted him from 28th to 8th place in the Order of Merit, and opened the door for the Spaniard to play alongside compatriots like Seve Ballesteros and José Maria Olazábal. 'Playing on the Tour is all I have ever thought about, and now the dream has come true,' Valera said. 'The way I qualified through the Challenge Tour was very exciting.'

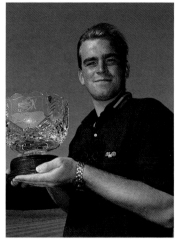

(Top, left to right) Eric Giraud,
Thomas Bjorn and Simon Hurley.
(Above) Tim Planchin, Francisco Valera
and Joakim Rask took top billing
in the UAP Grand Finale.

The story of the 1995 Challenge Tour began with James Lee's win at the Kenya Open, but it was in June at the Himmerland Open in his native Denmark that Thomas Bjorn first served notice of his intention to challenge for the number one position in the Order of Merit. His success in a play-off took him to the top, although Eric Giraud, by gaining his second win of the year in the Championnat de France Pro, regained first place the following week and remained there until Bjorn won again in the Interlaken Open.

Thereafter there was no holding Bjorn. The 24-year old, big-hitting Dane won the Esbjerb Danish Closed, and then came from three stokes behind with two holes to play to complete a memorable triumph in the Coca-Cola Open at East Sussex National in England. With that win Bjorn was assured of a place on the 1996 PGA European Tour, but he is also fully aware of the benefits that 1995 delivered. 'The Challenge Tour is a great opportunity for young players, and it helps them to improve so much,' he said. 'It's a good step to take, better than going straight into the PGA European Tour. If the Challenge Tour keeps improving it's going to be great for the younger players of the future. We would then have two strong Tours.'

Bjorn went into the UAP Grand Finale as the curtain came down on the 37-tournament programme, with an unassailable lead ahead of Spain's Diego Borrego and Giraud. Sadly, Giraud was unable to compete following a scuba-diving accident in Tunisia. In the event Tim Planchin, another French golfer, birdied the closing hole at Quinta do Peru to take second place in the Order of Merit behind Bjorn. 'In all the years I have been playing golf, it has always been my dream to play at least one full season on the PGA European Tour,' said Planchin.

The need for the Challenge Tour became apparent with the introduction of the All-Exempt Tour followed by a 'boom' in golf on the Continent. The PGA European Tour tournaments can only cater for 144 professionals which means that for those who do not hold a high enough category it is a week off. Thus the Challenge Tour has grown along with the PGA European Tour, offering the incentive of the leading ten players being granted Category 11(b) membership.

For Simon Hurley the philosophy of opportunity and incentive adopted and operated by the PGA European Tour has rewarded his patience and perseverance. His win in the Memorial Oliver Barras event in Crans-sur-Sierre in June helped him to fifth place in the Order of Merit. 'I've been trying for ten years to get onto the European Tour,' he said. 'And I've been to the Qualifying School nine times. I'm very happy.'

More than 60 Challenge Tour players have now progressed to the PGA European Tour. Alain de Soultrait, Challenge Tour Director, said: 'The success of Challenge Tour players on the PGA European Tour continues to provide inspiration for all players, but neither they nor we can be complacent. We must in 1996 continue to develop opportunities, improve facilities and maintain the high standards of competitive play. We have made great strides, but there is still much work to be done.'

Mitchell Platts

Barnes to the fore

In his first season Brian Barnes finished on top of the Order of Merit on the growing Seniors Tour

*I*f the success of the PGA European Seniors Tour partly leans on an annual top-up of new personalities, it certainly received a potent injection in 1995.

Most of it arrived in the hefty shape of Brian Barnes, the self-confessed former European Tour extrovert and now freshly dedicated to chasing a potentially lucrative seniors career. The former Ryder Cup star adhered to a dramatic script of Hollywood proportions in winning the Senior British Open at Royal Portrush on his European debut. That he achieved it with a monster eagle putt at the third play-off hole against American seniors giant Bob Murphy, defied even a Spielberg imagination.

Unhappily, a serious thrombosis problem in his right leg prevented Barnes from completing more than one additional tournament, the Collingtree Park Seniors at Northampton. But second place prize money there plus his £58,330 Portrush cheque was sufficient to keep him on top of the Order of Merit – a posi-

tion he officially maintained subsequently by limping painfully through 14 holes of the London Masters to fulfil the three-tournament qualification.

It left John Morgan requiring the £9,710 top prize in the final event, the Zurich Pro-Am Lexus Trophy, to overtake Barnes and keep the Order of Merit title he won so convincingly the previous year. The consistently efficient West Kirby professional had collected the Forte PGA title for the second successive year and had

occupied top four positions in four other events. However, his game lacked the edge it required to win in Switzerland and he had to settle for a share of third and reflect on another rewarding year's golf.

The growing Tour had reached another milestone with more than £1 million prize-money on offer for the first time from its eleven events. It included a handsome £350,000 in the Senior British Open which had moved from Royal Lytham to Royal Portrush. Indeed, it had such illustrious visiting participants as Arnold Palmer, Gary Player, Bob Charles and the vociferous Murphy eulogising over the championship's improving status and magnificent venue.

The season had opened in the vastly different environment of Kenya where Brian Huggett won the Windsor Senior Masters with a thrilling last hole birdie to pip Spain's Antonio Garrido.

Huggett continued to parade all the skill and competitive edge that has earned him 30 tournament wins worldwide.

259

Never out of the top ten in eight starts last year, the 59-year old Welshman was at his best in a classic last-day, head-to-head duel with his 61-year old former Ryder Cup colleague, Neil Coles, in the Shell Scottish Senior Open at Royal Aberdeen. The pair hurled 13 birdies at each other before Huggett clinched his second victory with a final 66 and tournament record ten-under-par 200.

Coles had to settle for second place a week after winning the Collingtree Seniors by four shots from Barnes with a closing 68 which included a five-birdie

the Lawerence Batley three weeks later at Fixby. And he treated us to a grandstand finale with a winning eagle putt from 25 feet. The closing birdie of playing partner Tommy Horton was only good enough to

earn second place. And the Channel Islander had to wait for his first Tour win of the year until the De Vere Hotels Seniors Classic at Belton Woods. Here he edged out the unfortunate Garrido by a stroke for his seventh seniors win in four years.

Garrido must have wondered whether he had upset somebody in higher places after a season of near misses including three runners-up cheques. None was more devastating than the PGA Forte at Sunningdale where he tied with Morgan on 208. The ex-Ryder Cup man and former World Cup partner of Seve Ballesteros, then faltered in the play-off, twice finding sand on the way with a double-bogey six. Morgan had the luxury of keeping his title with a bogey five.

The only man to beat par at beautiful Slaley Hall was Nottingham's Brian Waites whose one under par 215 was good enough to win the Northern Electric Seniors. It was Waites' second win since suffering multiple car crash injuries four years earlier and, as he put it: 'A very spe-

cial bonus'.

Ireland's charismatic big-hitter Liam Higgins finally secured the success his exciting brand of golf deserves when he retained the Lexus Trophy in Zurich.

Using a £15 driver he picked up in a Cork supermarket he powered to a five-shot win over Randall Vines, an Australian seniors rookie who made the top 25 in the merit table and looks a real threat for next season.

John Bland turned 50 just two days before pocketing the £13,350 winning cheque on his senior debut in the London Masters at the new London Golf Club.

first nine of 31 that required only 13 putts.

The European flavour of the Tour was strengthened with a couple of Italian successes. Renalto Campagnoli led from start to finish in the International German Seniors at Idstein, Frankfurt. Alberto Croce shared second place with Tommy Horton, but picked up the top cheque at

Liam Higgins (above) triumphed in Zurich while Arnold Palmer (left) and Gary Player (right) drew the crowds at Royal Portrush.

'This has been a great tournament,' he said. 'You can rest assured I shall be back for the main senior events next season. I have always thoroughly enjoyed playing European golf.'

A sentiment no doubt echoed by most of the seniors in 1995.

Bryan Potter

TIME
Covers the Olympics

TIME's history with the Olympic Games spans more than 70 years: one year after the magazine started publishing, the 1924 Paris Games graced its first Olympic cover. TIME will be there again in 1996, as an official worldwide sponsor, bringing our readers all the excitement, the color, and the spectacle of the Atlanta Centennial Olympic Games.

Atlanta 1996

TM, © 1992 ACOG

Official Worldwide Publishing Sponsor

Golfer of the Month Awards 1995

The winners of the Johnnie Walker Golfer
of the Month Award receive a trophy designed
by Tiffany & Co. of London and earn £1,000
for the PGA European Tour Benevolent Trust
and £1,000 for the Golf Foundation

Colin Montgomerie, (right)
with Angel Gallardo,
August and October.

Michael Campbell,
(below left) January;
Jarmo Sandelin,
(below centre) , February;
Paul Broadhurst,
(below right) June.

Nick Faldo,
(left) March;
Philip Walton,
(right) April.

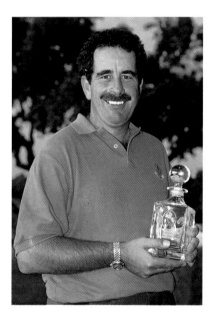

Bernard Gallacher, (below) September.

Sam Torrance, (above left) July; Bernhard Langer, (above right) May.

There is also a Johnnie Walker
Golfer of the Year Award.
The winner in 1994 was Ernie Els (left).

263

Volvo Order of Merit 1995

				£
1	Colin MONTGOMERIE	(Scot)	(20) *	835051
2	Sam TORRANCE	(Scot)	(26)	755706
3	Bernhard LANGER	(Ger)	(15)	655854
4	Costantino ROCCA	(It)	(24)	516320
5	Michael CAMPBELL	(NZ)	(21)	400977
6	Alexander CEJKA	(Ger)	(23)	308114
7	Mark JAMES	(Eng)	(26)	297377
8	Barry LANE	(Eng)	(24)	284406
9	Anders FORSBRAND	(Swe)	(20)	281726
10	Peter O'MALLEY	(Aus)	(21)	260726.
11	Wayne RILEY	(Aus)	(27)	256932
12	Howard CLARK	(Eng)	(21)	242068
13	Philip WALTON	(Ire)	(24)	234106
14	Darren CLARKE	(N.Ire)	(27)	226175
15	David GILFORD	(Eng)	(23)	220048
16	José RIVERO	(Sp)	(21)	209238
17	Jesper PARNEVIK	(Swe)	(8)	207254
18	Paul BROADHURST	(Eng)	(30)	200542
19	Per-Ulrik JOHANSSON	(Swe)	(21)	188859
20	Frank NOBILO	(NZ)	(18)	185831
21	Jarmo SANDELIN	(Swe)	(31)	173856
22	Mathias GRÖNBERG	(Swe)	(30)	172713
23	Miguel Angel JIMÉNEZ	(Sp)	(23)	171471
24	Greg TURNER	(NZ)	(22)	161419
25	Peter BAKER	(Eng)	(29)	159661
26	Peter TERAVAINEN	(USA)	(29)	159597
27	Ronan RAFFERTY	(N.Ire)	(23)	153145
28	Andrew COLTART	(Scot)	(27)	150884
29	Ignacio GARRIDO	(Sp)	(27)	150338
30	Jamie SPENCE	(Eng)	(28)	148812
31	Sandy LYLE	(Scot)	(18)	146169
32	Sven STRÜVER	(Ger)	(25)	145756
33	Seve BALLESTEROS	(Sp)	(11)	145285
34	Peter MITCHELL	(Eng)	(30)	144499
35	Andrew OLDCORN	(Eng)	(23)	142479
36	Michael JONZON	(Swe)	(22)	139159
37	Santiago LUNA	(Sp)	(26)	138714
38	Derrick COOPER	(Eng)	(27)	137742
39	Russell CLAYDON	(Eng)	(27)	133649
40	Joakim HAEGGMAN	(Swe)	(24)	133541
41	Robert KARLSSON	(Swe)	(28)	131849
42	Stuart CAGE	(Eng)	(30)	130792
43	Jay TOWNSEND	(USA)	(25)	129720
44	Paul EALES	(Eng)	(26)	127619
45	Peter HEDBLOM	(Swe)	(27)	125261
46	José COCERES	(Arg)	(23)	125115
47	Robert ALLENBY	(Aus)	(14)	123580
48	Mats LANNER	(Swe)	(26)	121987
49	Roger CHAPMAN	(Eng)	(25)	119488
50	Jean Louis GUEPY	(Fr)	(24)	117534

Colin Montgomerie

51	Olle KARLSSON	(Swe)	(26)	114198
52	Paul MCGINLEY	(Ire)	(27)	107807
53	Dean ROBERTSON	(Scot)	(25)	106972
54	Vijay SINGH	(Fij)	(8)	103982
55	Eamonn DARCY	(Ire)	(22)	103441
56	Niclas FASTH	(Swe)	(24)	101272
57	Andrew SHERBORNE	(Eng)	(29)	99667
58	Richard BOXALL	(Eng)	(29)	98752
59	Gary ORR	(Scot)	(29)	97883
60	Roger WESSELS	(SA)	(14)	97756
61	Nick FALDO	(Eng)	(3)	93188
62	Pedro LINHART	(Sp)	(25)	91949
63	Adam HUNTER	(Scot)	(28)	91542
64	Steven BOTTOMLEY	(Eng)	(29)	90375
65	Ian WOOSNAM	(Wal)	(16)	90107
66	Peter SENIOR	(Aus)	(6)	89863
67	Silvio GRAPPASONNI	(It)	(22)	89051
68	Ross MCFARLANE	(Eng)	(28)	88646
69	Steven RICHARDSON	(Eng)	(29)	88251
70	Paul MOLONEY	(Aus)	(23)	87409
71	Vicente FERNANDEZ	(Arg)	(21)	86827
72	Christian CEVAER	(Fr)	(27)	86307
73	Paul AFFLECK	(Wal)	(24)	82839
74	Neal BRIGGS	(Eng)	(28)	82335
75	Lee WESTWOOD	(Eng)	(30)	80434
76	Jean VAN DE VELDE	(Fr)	(25)	80037
77	Stephen AMES	(T&T)	(22)	79869
78	Carl MASON	(Eng)	(24)	77643
79	Mike CLAYTON	(Aus)	(22)	77167
80	Mark MOULAND	(Wal)	(28)	74932
81	Mark DAVIS	(Eng)	(27)	74472
82	Des SMYTH	(Ire)	(25)	74235

83	André BOSSERT	(Swi)	(24)	74198
84	Pierre FULKE	(Swe)	(21)	72210
85	Wayne WESTNER	(SA)	(16)	72023
86	Fredrik LINDGREN	(Swe)	(21)	71625
87	Martin GATES	(Eng)	(23)	70442
88	Gordon BRAND JNR.	(Scot)	(25)	70138
89	Domingo HOSPITAL	(Sp)	(24)	69851
90	Oyvind ROJAHN	(Nor)	(26)	69574
91	Eduardo ROMERO	(Arg)	(8)	67677
92	David CARTER	(Eng)	(30)	66463
93	Steen TINNING	(Den)	(27)	65176
94	Retief GOOSEN	(SA)	(22)	62743
95	Terry PRICE	(Aus)	(12)	62507
96	Tony JOHNSTONE	(Zim)	(21)	61154
97	Malcolm MACKENZIE	(Eng)	(26)	60474
98	Thomas LEVET	(Fr)	(29)	58017
99	Raymond BURNS	(N.Ire)	(27)	56962
100	Fabrice TARNAUD	(Fr)	(23)	56293
101	Jonathan LOMAS	(Eng)	(26)	56062
102	Mike MCLEAN	(Eng)	(30)	55651
103	Iain PYMAN	(Eng)	(28)	55369
104	Marc FARRY	(Fr)	(22)	54747
105	Jon ROBSON	(Eng)	(26)	53772
106	Paul CURRY	(Eng)	(21)	53710
107	Paul LAWRIE	(Scot)	(23)	53561
108	Paul WAY	(Eng)	(27)	50168
109	Mark LITTON	(Wal)	(26)	49547
110	Phillip PRICE	(Wal)	(22)	49466
111	Ross DRUMMOND	(Scot)	(27)	49158
112	Mats HALLBERG	(Swe)	(25)	48601
113	Gary EMERSON	(Eng)	(19)	48560
114	John BICKERTON	(Eng)	(28)	47380
115	Miguel Angel MARTIN	(Sp)	(26)	46552
116	Michel BESANCENEY	(Fr)	(32)	46463
117	Emanuele CANONICA	(It)	(19)	46042
118	Stephen MCALLISTER	(Scot)	(26)	44519
119	Paolo QUIRICI	(Swi)	(22)	43574
120	José Maria CAÑIZARES	(Sp)	(18)	43291
121	David WILLIAMS	(Eng)	(26)	42868
122	Phil GOLDING	(Eng)	(24)	42193
123	Klas ERIKSSON	(Swe)	(25)	41858
124	David J RUSSELL	(Eng)	(27)	39507
125	Mike HARWOOD	(Aus)	(24)	39268
126	Mark ROE	(Eng)	(19)	39104
127	Mark MCNULTY	(Zim)	(4)	38240
128	Rolf MUNTZ	(Hol)	(18)	38142
129	Rodger DAVIS	(Aus)	(18)	37982
130	Ian PALMER	(SA)	(26)	36147
131	Anders SORENSEN	(Den)	(24)	34334
132	Jim PAYNE	(Eng)	(19)	33344

153	Nic HENNING	(SA)	(6)	19123
154	Craig CASSELLS	(Eng)	(26)	18564
155	Juan QUIROS	(Sp)	(18)	16994
156	David FEHERTY	(N.Ire)	(7)	16570
157	Paul MAYO	(Wal)	(21)	15871
158	Manuel PIÑERO	(Sp)	(17)	15708
159	Jeremy ROBINSON	(Eng)	(28)	15610
160	Jeff HAWKES	(SA)	(11)	14592
161	Keith WATERS	(Eng)	(16)	13862
162	Vanslow PHILLIPS	(Eng)	(3)	13640
163	Antoine LEBOUC	(Fr)	(18)	12881
164	Mike MILLER	(Scot)	(27)	12523
165	John BLAND	(SA)	(14)	12492
166	Daniel WESTERMARK	(Swe)	(26)	12449
167	Fredrik ANDERSSON	(Swe)	(17)	11953
168	Martyn ROBERTS	(Wal)	(17)	11229
169	Warren BENNETT	(Eng)	(4)	11093
170	Brian DAVIS	(Eng)	(2)	10733

Sam Torrance

133	Joakim GRONHAGEN	(Swe)	(20)	33005
134	Scott WATSON	(Eng)	(28)	30784
135	Gavin LEVENSON	(SA)	(27)	29753
136	Eoghan O'CONNELL	(Ire)	(28)	29662
137	Heinz P THÜL	(Ger)	(12)	29266
138	John HAWKSWORTH	(Eng)	(23)	27850
139	Liam WHITE	(Eng)	(24)	27600
140	Stephen DODD	(Wal)	(19)	27131
141	Philip TALBOT	(Eng)	(18)	27065
142	John MCHENRY	(Ire)	(14)	25018
143	John MELLOR	(Eng)	(23)	24583
144	Gary EVANS	(Eng)	(10)	24409
145	Brian MARCHBANK	(Scot)	(14)	23839
146	Anders GILLNER	(Swe)	(19)	23686
147	Peter FOWLER	(Aus)	(24)	21480
148	Andrew MURRAY	(Eng)	(18)	21412
149	Christy O'CONNOR JNR	(Ire)	(20)	20751
150	Michael ARCHER	(Eng)	(24)	20548
151	Alberto BINAGHI	(It)	(28)	20544
152	Paul R SIMPSON	(Eng)	(22)	20227

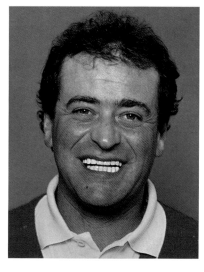

Costantino Rocca

* Figures in parentheses indicate number of tournaments played

Bernhard Langer

171	José Manuel CARRILES	(Sp)	(15)	10633
172	David R JONES	(Eng)	(10)	10499
173	Ricky WILLISON	(Eng)	(9)	10460
174	Juan PIÑERO	(Sp)	(9)	9206
175	Fredrik JACOBSON	(Swe)	(16)	9192
176	Ove SELLBERG	(Swe)	(14)	9118
177	Mark NICHOLS	(Eng)	(14)	8945
178	David RAY	(Eng)	(18)	8501
179	Per HAUGSRUD	(Nor)	(11)	8271
180	Ruben ALVAREZ	(Arg)	(16)	8160
181	Gordon J BRAND	(Eng)	(23)	7936
182	Andrew CLAPP	(Eng)	(6)	7885
183	Ian SPENCER	(Eng)	(13)	7583
184	Trevor DODDS	(Nam)	(2)	7386
185	Thomas GÖGELE	(Ger)	(3)	7121
186	Carlos LARRAIN	(Ven)	(13)	6914
187	David CURRY	(Eng)	(18)	6716
188	Diego BORREGO	(Sp)	(6)	6705
189	George RYALL	(Eng)	(15)	6012
190	Bill LONGMUIR	(Scot)	(3)	5878

1995 STATISTICS LEADERS

STROKE AVERAGE							BIRDIE LEADERS			DRIVING ACCURACY		%	GREENS IN REGULATION		%
1	Colin MONTGOMERIE	69.70	26	Vicente FERNANDEZ	71.74		1	Sam TORRANCE	388	1	John BLAND	90.87	1	John BLAND	78.57
2	Bernhard LANGER	69.93	27	Frank NOBILO	71.75		2	Darren CLARKE	359	2	Bernhard LANGER	85.71	2	Paul LAWRIE	76.61
3	Sam TORRANCE	70.28	28	José COCERES	71.77		3	Jarmo SANDELIN	354	3	Martyn ROBERTS	84.62	3	David WILLIAMS	73.61
4	Costantino ROCCA	70.46	29	Robert ALLENBY	71.82		4	Peter MITCHELL	353	4	Peter O'MALLEY	83.05	4	Mark JAMES	73.25
5	Mark JAMES	70.84	30	Joakim HAEGGMAN	71.83		5	Costantino ROCCA	350	5	Ross MCFARLANE	82.01	5	José RIVERO	72.47
6	Michael CAMPBELL	70.99	31	Wayne RILEY	71.84		6	Paul BROADHURST	348	6	Pedro LINHART	81.18	6	David CARTER	72.22
7	José RIVERO	71.16	32	Derrick COOPER	71.89		7	Mark JAMES	343	7	André BOSSERT	80.10	7	Andrew COLTART	71.97
8	Greg TURNER	71.28		Wayne WESTNER	71.89		8	Barry LANE	338	8	Mike MCLEAN	79.73	8	Peter O'MALLEY	71.84
9	Darren CLARKE	71.30	34	Paul BROADHURST	71.92		9	Wayne RILEY	329	9	Paul AFFLECK	79.65	9	André BOSSERT	71.45
10	Barry LANE	71.38		Paul MCGINLEY	71.92		10	Russell CLAYDON	325	10	David WILLIAMS	79.36	10	Mark LITTON	71.26
	Roger WESSELS	71.38		Per-Ulrik JOHANSSON	71.92										
12	Howard CLARK	71.39	37	Andrew COLTART	71.93		EAGLE LEADERS			PUTTS PER GREENS IN REGULATION		Av	SAND SAVES		%
	Anders FORSBRAND	71.39		Paul AFFLECK	71.93		1	Gary ORR	16	1	Alexander CEJKA	1.691	1	Mark NICHOLS	51.52
14	Sandy LYLE	71.42	39	Des SMYTH	71.94			Darren CLARKE	16	2	Wayne RILEY	1.720	2	Andrew COLTART	51.16
15	Ian WOOSNAM	71.50	40	Roger CHAPMAN	71.97			Peter MITCHELL	16	3	Bernhard LANGER	1.722	3	Colin MONTGOMERIE	50.00
16	David GILFORD	71.51		Peter HEDBLOM	71.97		4	Steven RICHARDSON	14	4	Robert ALLENBY	1.726	4	Alexander CEJKA	49.07
	Miguel Angel JIMÉNEZ	71.51	42	Ignacio GARRIDO	71.98		5	Sven STRÜVER	13	5	Michael CAMPBELL	1.727	5	Per-Ulrik JOHANSSON	48.64
18	Peter MITCHELL	71.54	43	Malcolm MACKENZIE	72.00			Peter BAKER	13	6	Sam TORRANCE	1.731	6	Jermey ROBINSON	48.33
	Alexander CEJKA	71.54	44	Jay TOWNSEND	72.01			Michael CAMPBELL	13	7	Wayen WESTNER	1.736	7	Phillip PRICE	48.08
20	Sven STRÜVER	71.56	45	Olle KARLSSON	72.02		8	Roger CHAPMAN	12	8	Anders FORSBRAND	1.737	8	Rolf MUNTZ	47.84
21	Ronan RAFFERTY	71.59	46	Richard BOXALL	72.03			Barry LANE	12	9	Sandy LYLE	1.738	9	Derrick COOPER	47.81
22	Peter O'MALLEY	71.64	47	Fredrik LINDGREN	72.05			Wayne RILEY	12	10	Jean VAN DE VELDE	1.744	10	Frank NOBILO	46.67
23	Silvio GRAPPASONNI	71.67	48	Heinz P THÜL	72.06			Costantino ROCCA	12						
24	Eamonn DARCY	71.71		Santiago LUNA	72.06			Ignacio GARRIDO	12						
25	Peter BAKER	71.72	50	Michael JONZON	72.07			Jay TOWNSEND	11						

The PGA European Tour

(A COMPANY LIMITED BY GUARANTEE)

BOARD OF DIRECTORS
N C Coles, MBE – Group Chairman
A Gallardo – (Tour, Enterprises, Properties)
B Gallacher (Tour, Enterprises, Properties)
T A Horton (Properties)
D Jones (Tour)
M G King (Enterprises, Properties)
B Langer (Enterprises)
C Moody (Tour)
J E O'Leary (Tour, Enterprises, Properties)
G W Ralph (Tour)
D Talbot (Tour)
P M P Townsend (Enterprises, Properties)
K R Waters (Tour)

EXECUTIVE DIRECTOR
K D Schofield

DEPUTY EXECUTIVE DIRECTOR
G C O'Grady

GENERAL COUNSEL
M D Friend

GROUP COMPANY SECRETARY
M Bray

PGA EUROPEAN TOUR TOURNAMENT COMMITTEE
M James – Chairman
K Waters – Vice Chairman
A Binaghi
R Chapman
I Gervas
D Jones
B Langer
M Lanner
C Mason
C Moody
R Rafferty
G W Ralph
D J Russell
O Sellberg
S Torrance

PGA EUROPEAN SENIORS TOUR
A Stubbs – Managing Director

DIRECTOR OF TOUR OPERATIONS AND CHIEF REFEREE
J N Paramor

SENIOR TOURNAMENT DIRECTORS
A N McFee (Director of Tour Qualifying
School Programme)
M R Stewart

TOURNAMENT DIRECTORS
D Garland
D Probyn

CHALLENGE TOUR DIRECTOR
A de Soultrait

Royal approval for the Ryder Cup.

TOURNAMENT ADMINISTRATORS
M Eriksson
M Haarer
K Williams
G Hunt (Referee)
M Vidaor
J M Zamora

PGA EUROPEAN TOUR ENTERPRISES LTD
G C O'Grady – Managing Director
S Kelly – Marketing Director
I Barker – Account Director
G Oosterhuis – Corporate Sponsorship
Director
P Adams – Event Promotions Manager
J Birkmyre – General Manager
European & English Opens
N Plunkett Dillon – Event Staging Manager

RYDER CUP VENTURE
R G Hills – Ryder Cup Director

PGA EUROPEAN TOUR PROPERTIES LTD
E Kitson – General Manager

PGA EUROPEAN TOUR (SOUTH)
A Gallardo – President

COMMUNICATIONS DIVISION
M Platts – Director of Communications
and Public Relations
M Wilson – Consultant
to Executive Director

GROUP FINANCE CONTROLLER
C Allamand

GROUP FINANCIAL PLANNER
J Orr

GROUP ACCOUNTS EXECUTIVE
C Dyce

CORPORATE RELATIONS CONSULTANT
H Wickham

The Contributors

Mike Britten
Moroccan Open
Turespaña Open de Baleares
Deutsche Bank Open ~ TPC of Europe
Canon European Masters

Colin Callander *(Golf Monthly)*
Apollo Week
The Scottish Open

Matthew Chancellor *(Golf Weekly)*
DHL Jersey Open

Jeremy Chapman *(The Sporting Life)*
The Ryder Cup by Johnnie Walker

Norman Dabell *(The Observer)*
Mercedes German Masters

Richard Dodd *(The Yorkshire Post)*
Murphy's English Open
Heineken Dutch Open
Chemapol Trophy Czech Open

Bill Elliott
Alfred Dunhill Cup

Andrew Farrell *(Golf Weekly)*
Turespaña Open de Andalucia
Conte of Florence Italian Open

Mark Garrod *(Press Association)*
Johnnie Walker Classic
Peugeot Open de France
Volvo German Open
Volvo Masters

Dermot Gilleece *(The Irish Times)*
Murphy's Irish Open

Tim Glover *(The Independent)*
Benson and Hedges International Open

David Hamilton *(Golf Weekly)*
Lexington SA PGA
Portuguese Open

Jeff Kelly *(Andalucia Golf)*
Peugeot Open de España

Renton Laidlaw *(The Evening Standard)*
Air France Cannes Open
Volvo Scandinavian Masters
The Canon Shoot-Out

Derek Lawrenson *(The Observer)*
Volvo Order of Merit Winner
Madeira Island Open

Michael McDonnell *(The Daily Mail)*
The Year in Retrospect

John Oakley
Hohe Brücke Open

Mitchell Platts *(PGA European Tour)*
PGA European Challenge Tour

Chris Plumridge *(The Sunday Telegraph)*
Volvo PGA Championship
124th Open Championship
Andersen Consulting
World Championship of Golf

Bryan Potter
PGA European Seniors Tour

Gordon Richardson
Open Catalonia Turespaña Series
Collingtree British Masters
Sarazen World Open Championship

Colm Smith *(Independent Newspapers)*
Smurfit European Open

Paul Trow *(Golf Weekly)*
Trophée Lancôme

Mel Webb *(The Times)*
Turespaña Open de Canarias
Turespaña Open Mediterrania ~
The Land of Valencia
Tournoi Perrier de Paris
BMW International Open

John Whitbread
(Surrey Herald Newspapers)
Toyota World Match-Play Championship

Michael Williams *(The Daily Telegraph)*
Dubai Desert Classic

The Photographers

Simon Bruty /Allsport
200, 201, 203 (left), 206 (below)

David Cannon /Allsport
8, 9 (upper middle and bottom), 10,
12, 18, 19, 20-21, 21, 22 (top row), 23,
24, 25, 26, 27, 28, 85 (left), 94, 95, 97,
98, 99, 100 (lower) 100-101, 102 (top),
134 (bottom), 138, 139, 140, 141, 144,
145, 151 (top), 174, 182, 183, 184 (left
and centre), 185, 186, 196 (below left),
202, 204, 206 (top), 207 (centre), 208
(bottom), 209, 210, 226 (bottom), 228
(bottom), 231, 233, 234, 236, 237, 238,
238-239, 240, 241 (bottom), 242-243,
252, 258, 262

John Cuban /Allsport USA
6, 14, 152, 154, 208 (top), 256 (below)

Graham Chadwick /Allsport
7, 46, 47, 48, 49, 54, 55, 56, 57, 58, 59,
76, 77, 78, 79, 80, 81, 106, 107, 108

(top), 109, 110, 128, 129, 130 (top),
131, 170, 171, 172, 173, 264

Phil Cole /Allsport
9 (lower middle), 30, 31, 32, 33, 68, 69,
70, 71, 118, 119, 120, 121, 122, 123, 124,
125 (top), 160, 161, 162, 163, 164, 188,
189, 190, 191, 192, 218, 219, 220, 221,
222, 249, 250 (bottom)

Michael Cooper /Allsport
22 (bottom), 213, 215, 226 (top)

John Gichigi
34, 35, 36, 37, 112, 113, 114, 115, 116,
117, 196 (top left), 197

Mike Hewitt /Allsport
247

Rusty Jarrett /Allsport USA
248, 249, 250, 251, 255

Tim Matthews /Allsport
102 (lower), 103 (bottom), 194, 196
(right above and below), 227 (right),
256 (top)

Clive Mason /Allsport
42, 43, 44, 45

Stephen Munday /Allsport
1, 9 (top), 13, 38, 39, 40, 41, 64, 65, 66,
67, 72, 73, 74, 75, 82, 83, 84, 85 (right),
86 (left), 88, 89, 90, 91, 92, 93, 96-97,
100(top), 102 (top) 104, 105 (lower),
125 (bottom), 132, 132-133, 134 (top),
135, 136, 137, 142, 146, 147 (top), 148,
148-149, 151 (bottom), 155, 156, 157,
158, 184 (right), 203 (right), 205, 224,
225, 227 (left), 228 (top), 230, 231, 233
(top), 241 (top), 244, 246, 248, 259,
260, 261, 263

Gary M Prior /Allsport
130 (bottom), 253 (top)

Andrew Redington /Allsport
5, 86 (right), 105 (upper), 108
(bottom), 166, 167, 168, 169, 176,
176-177, 178, 179, 180, 250 (top), 254

Dave Rogers /Allsport
195, 198

Anton Want /Allsport
147(bottom), 150,

Ian Hodgson
111

JC Holbart /UAP
253 (centre)

Phil Inglis
16, 17, 50, 51, 52, 53, 60, 61, 62, 63,
207 (top), 212, 214 (top),
215 (bottom), 216, 255

Nick Walker
214 (bottom)

267